The Mucukunda Murals

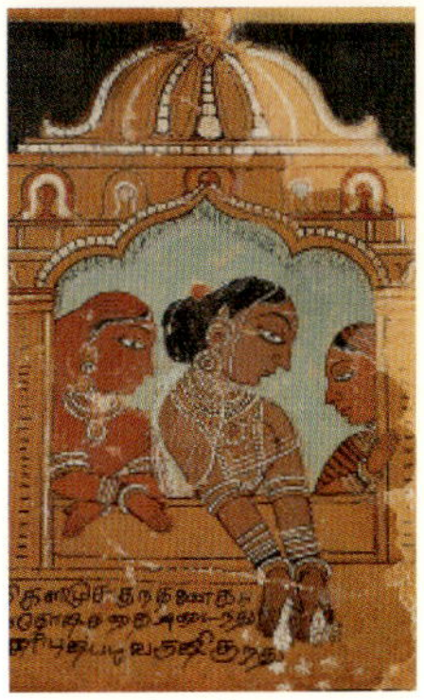

in the
Tyāgarājasvāmi
Temple, Tiruvārūr

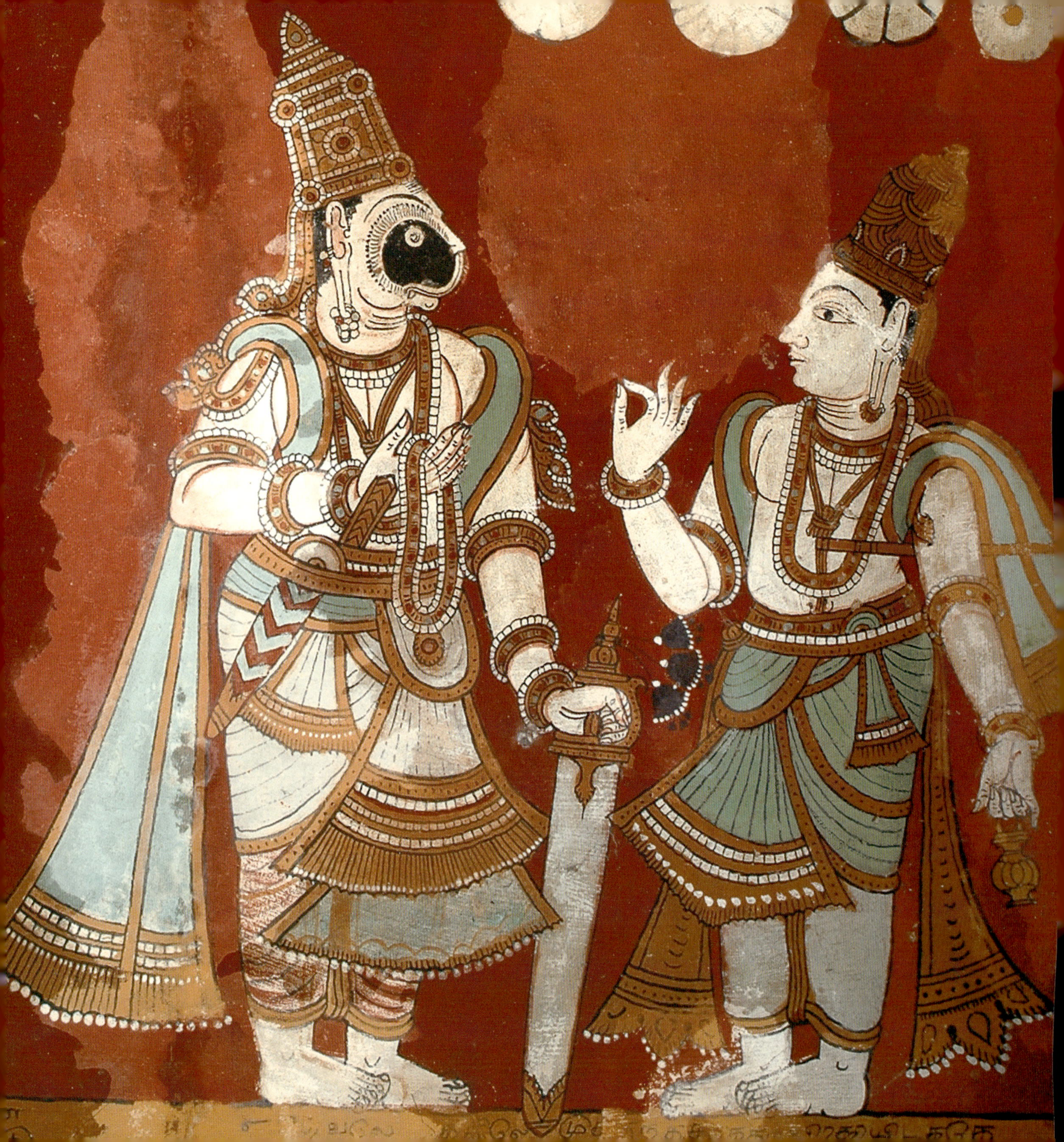

V. K. Rajamani and David Shulman

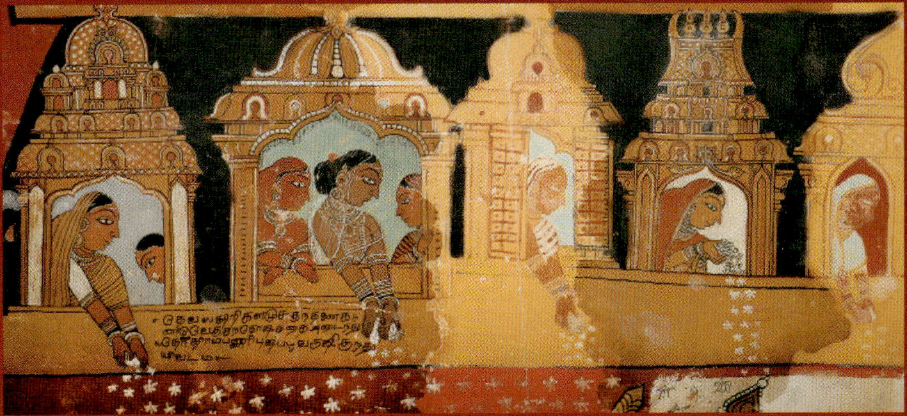

The Mucukunda Murals

in the Tyāgarājasvāmi Temple, Tiruvārūr

ISBN : 978-81-904443-2-3

First Published 2011

Prakriti Foundation

Prakriti Foundation
No. 1, C Block, 9th Floor
Gemini Parsn Apartments,
Anna Salai, Chennai - 600 006
Email: prakritifoundation@gmail.com
Website: www.prakritifoundation.com

Printed at
Lustra Print Process Pvt. Ltd.
B-249, Naraina Industrial Area, Phase-1,
New Delhi - 110028

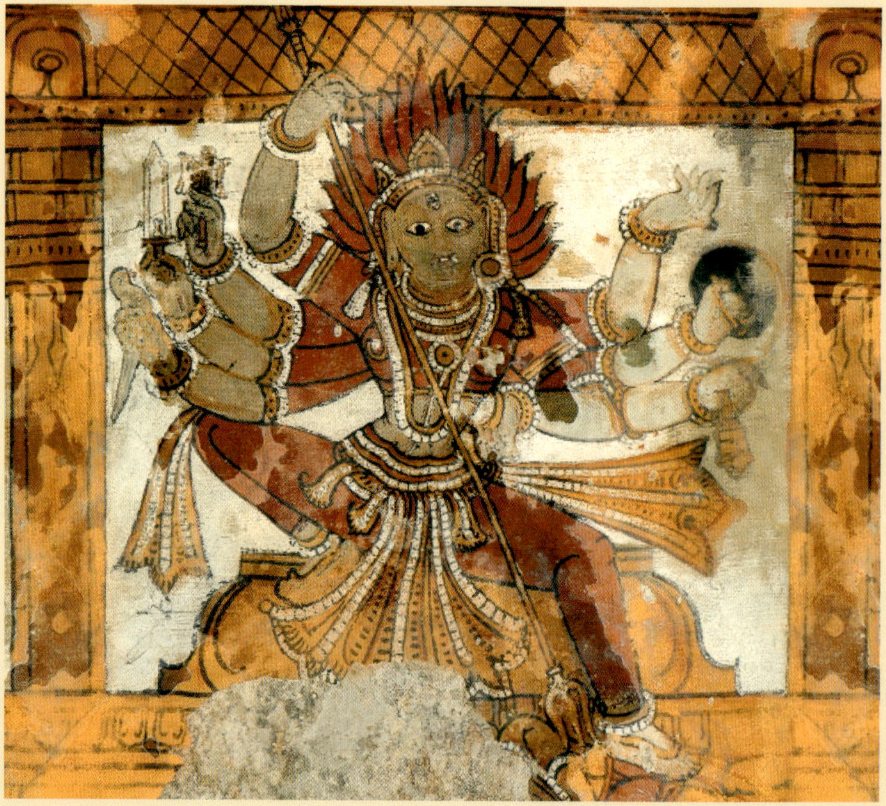

Contents

Publisher's Note

Until twelve years ago, I did not know of the existence of the Tyagarajaswamy Temple of Tiruvarur. By the happenstance of a dear friend, I came to visit this temple and felt an immediate connection with it. Miracles ensued and dreams were fulfilled. About ten years ago one of the priests requested me to do something about the paintings on the roof of the Devasariya Mandapam, since the authorities were going to whitewash them. It took me eight years to convince the authorities that these were among the finest frescoes of their time.

Irresponsible digging up of the terrace on the pretext of water-proofing it and then abandoning work on the roof over ten years ago had caused leakage, fungus and irreparable damage. Something needed to be done. Neither the Trustees nor the government took any action for over eight years. Then, suddenly, divine providence intervened. A senior government official related to a factory manager I had mentored was in a position to approve the project. Costs over eight years had gone up nearly five times. We started on a lengthy procedural adventure with the powers that be. Prakriti Foundation found support for the project from only two caring and sincere friends – S. Aravind, a college mate from the eighties and now a successful Silicon Valley czar, and Ramani Sivasothy, a Srilankan Tamil devotee of Tiruvarur who lived in London and cared so deeply about the paintings that on her own she got

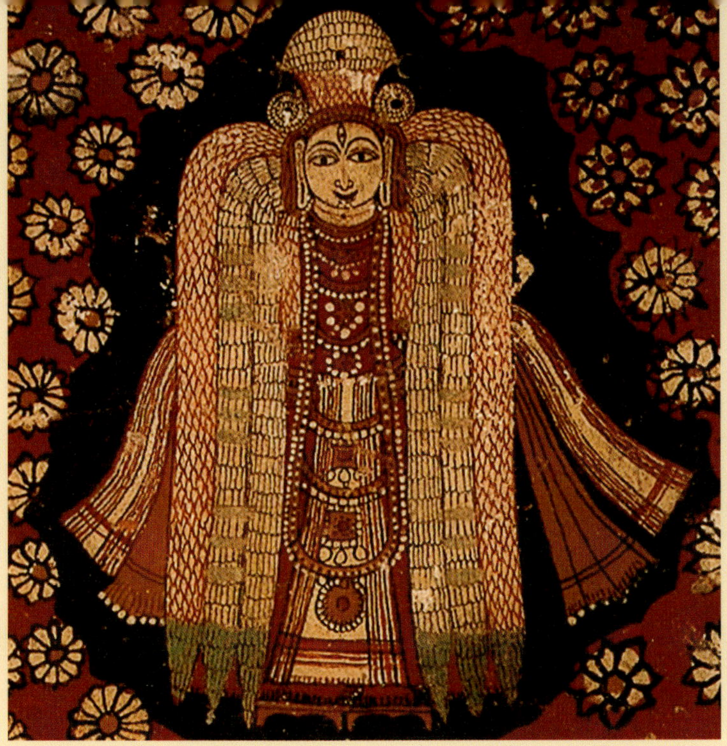

a photographer to document them before they were ruined further. My deepest thanks and gratitude to them for support on what has been a lonely journey.

What do I get out of this? Why should I be bothered? I am a Gujarati Jain. Why do I need to expend so much physical, emotional and financial energy on this? These questions have no logical response beyond the emotional connection I have felt for the last twelve years and continue to feel with Sri Tyagarajaswamy. He has nestled deep in the crevices of my spiritual sanctuary.

Two long years and many difficulties later the entire ICKPAC team led by Madhurani and her deeply sincere associates have completed cleaning, restoring and reviving the magic of the story of Mucukunda and the prehistory of the temple of Tiruvarur (as recorded in its Sthala Purana).

Faith has tested all of us severely, as we faced opposition at every level. For further private initiatives of this kind, I urge people to be committed for the long run, have faith and not give up. Miracles continue to happen and – as this book and the mandapam frescoes have proved – the Divine is here amongst us.

I want to also put on record how much I value the generous contribution of Prof. David Shulman. We are also deeply grateful to Shri V.K. Rajamani who shot these pictures in difficult circumstances, including severe health problems. Both of them were to publish this book on their own to showcase to the world the dire situation of these murals. Once again the divine intervened and they approached us at Prakriti Foundation to publish this work simultaneously with the Mandapam restoration.

At Prakriti Foundation we present this book as an offering in the sacred scheme of the universe of Sri Tyagarajaswamy and feel honoured and privileged to do so in the company of such generous people. We hope that this effort will inspire others to take up similar restoration, conservation, repair and revival projects within the heritage that we call India.

Ranvir R. Shah
Founder Trustee, Prakriti Foundation

Preface

Among its many treasures, the great Valmīkanātha/Tyāgarājasvāmi temple in Tiruvārūr, some 40 kilometres due east of Tañjāvūr, contains a set of mid-seventeenth-century ceiling paintings depicting the story of Mucukunda Cakravarti, the monkey-faced Chola king who is said to have brought the image of the god Tyāgarāja to earth. The paintings, in the late Nāyaka or early Marāṭha-period style, probably from the decade of the 1660's or 1670's, are among the finest to have survived from late-medieval South India. They cover four and a half long, serial rows on the ceiling of the Tevâciraya Maṇḍapa located in the third *prākāra* of the temple. This *maṇḍapa* is itself a site of unique cultural importance, for it is here that the ninth-century poet Cuntaramūrtti Nāyaṉār had a vision of all the assembled sixty-three nāyaṉmār, the Tamil saints of Śiva, at the start of his pivotal career as the first major systematizer of Tamil Śaiva hagiography.

This book seeks to document as many of the paintings as possible in the hope of preserving a record for posterity. The paintings, like the *maṇḍapa* as a whole, were, until recently, in a state of extreme dilapidation. Decades of neglect have taken their toll. Damage from fire, water leakage, dust, mould, the predations of birds and insects, and other factors is severe. When we last saw these paintings, in January 1988, they were in a much better state. On our visit to Tiruvārūr in March 2006, we were shocked to see that whole panels are now irreparably lost. Many of the seventeenth-century inscriptions accompanying the painting are no longer legible. We are happy to note that these paintings have now been cleaned and preserved by the professional INTACH team headed by K.P. Madhu Rani.

We wish to thank Tiru S. Gurumurthy of Coimbatore, who accompanied us to Tiruvarur and provided a veritable mine of precious knowledge about the temple and its deities. Maya Tevet Dayan and Miriam Cohen were invaluable assistants in mapping the panels, racing against time as afternoon turned to night. We are proud to publish Maya's essay on the Tiruvarur paintings in this volume. Tiru M. Chandramoorthy, accomplished archaeologist and epigraphist, helped with the early stages of deciphering the inscriptions accompanying the painted panels; we thank him sincerely for his willingness to work with us. Dr. R. Nagaswamy also helped check our readings. We are particularly grateful to Tiru Pichandi I.A.S Avargal, Special Commissioner, and the Hindu Religious and Charitable Endowments Board, Government of Tamil Nadu, for permission to photograph and publish these great paintings. Cidambararao Ganesan photographed the newly discovered panels (pages 72-73 and 82-83) and documented the entire sequence anew. Ranvir Shah and Prakriti Foundation made this publication possible; we thank them along with Logesvaran Devan and Vinay Jain, the superb designer of the book.

David Shulman and V.K. Rajamani

Introduction

Introducing Tyāgarāja

1 The monumental Śiva temple in Tiruvarur, in the heart of the Kaveri Delta, is usually known today as the Tyāgarāja-svāmi Koyil after the form of Śiva, together with his wife Umā and their son Skanda-Murukaṉ, which is situated immediately to the south of the foundational shrine of Valmīkanātha, Lord of the Anthill. Unlike Valmīkanātha, Tyāgarāja is a mobile image; twice a year he leaves his home inside the innermost domain of the temple to take up temporary residence in the Tevâciraya Maṇḍapa in the outer *prākāra*. During the Paṅkuṉi Uttaram festival in early spring, his festival image, Candraśekhara, goes still further outside to ride a series of vehicles through the streets adjacent to the temple; and the god also rides his great chariot (*āḻitter*) during the Vasantotsava or Spring Festival, in May. Thus Tyāgarāja shows us, at the most primary level of his activity, a god in movement through space, a dancing, breathing image imbued with a certain kind of active awareness; a god who reaches out to his servants and is in turn nurtured, enhanced, and further energized by them.

At the same time, this god is in large measure hidden from external view, wrapped in veils of varying opacity, absorbed within his own recesses. A cryptic or esoteric dimension is integral to his being. His dance is a tantalizing riddle that easily lends itself to elaborate exegesis, most of it rather late and oblique. This atmosphere of secret meanings and hidden layers of existence contributes to a pervasive sense of the deity's continuously deepening beauty. Tyāgarāja is a beautiful god, before all else. We may have reason to ask ourselves what a word like "beauty" really means in this case.

There are other permanent features of his personality, his modes and moods, his preferred ritual states, his diurnal and annual rhythms. Such rhythms define him, insofar as so manifold a deity can be defined. Perhaps we should put aside this word, and with it the hope of offering a definitive history, for the evolution of the Tyāgarāja system, as I would like to call it, is an enigmatic business at best. There is, however, a story to be told, one that resonates with but is by no means identical to the story the temple tells of this god's origins. We will study this latter story in its main versions, literary as well as pictorial. But no single narrative can exhaust the permutations: this deity is a grammarian, a linguist whose body is made up of mantric syllables, but whose mantra is *ajapā*, "unuttered"; he has a particular fondness for the *cĕnkaḻunīr* flowers, now rare in Tiruvarur; he is intimately linked, in annual ritual, to an outcaste community, one of whose members leads his procession; he has generated a family for himself and

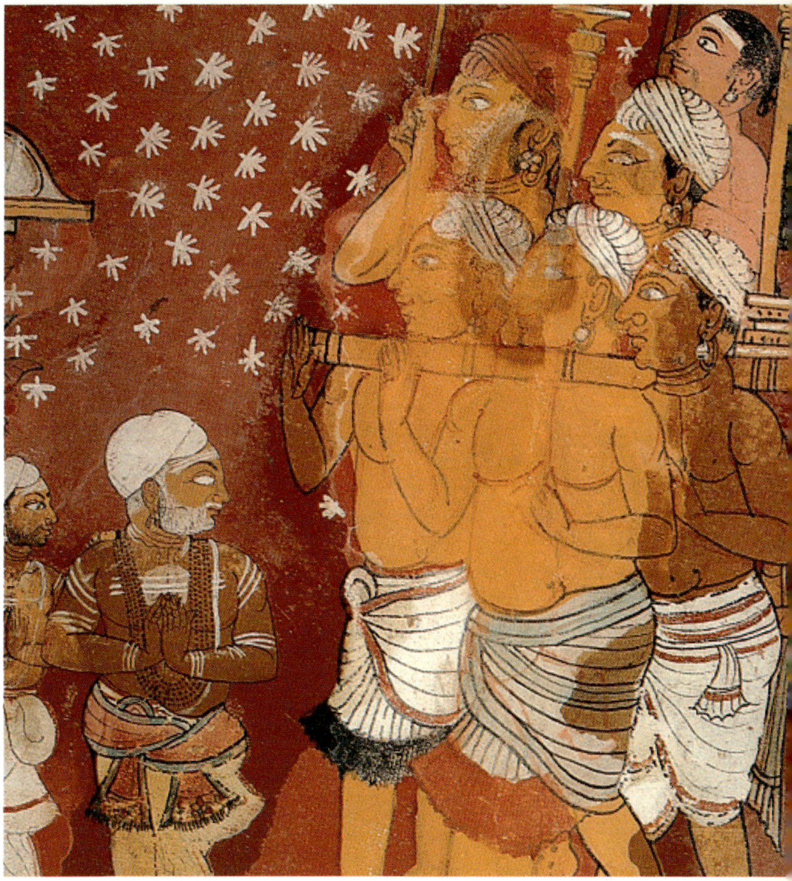

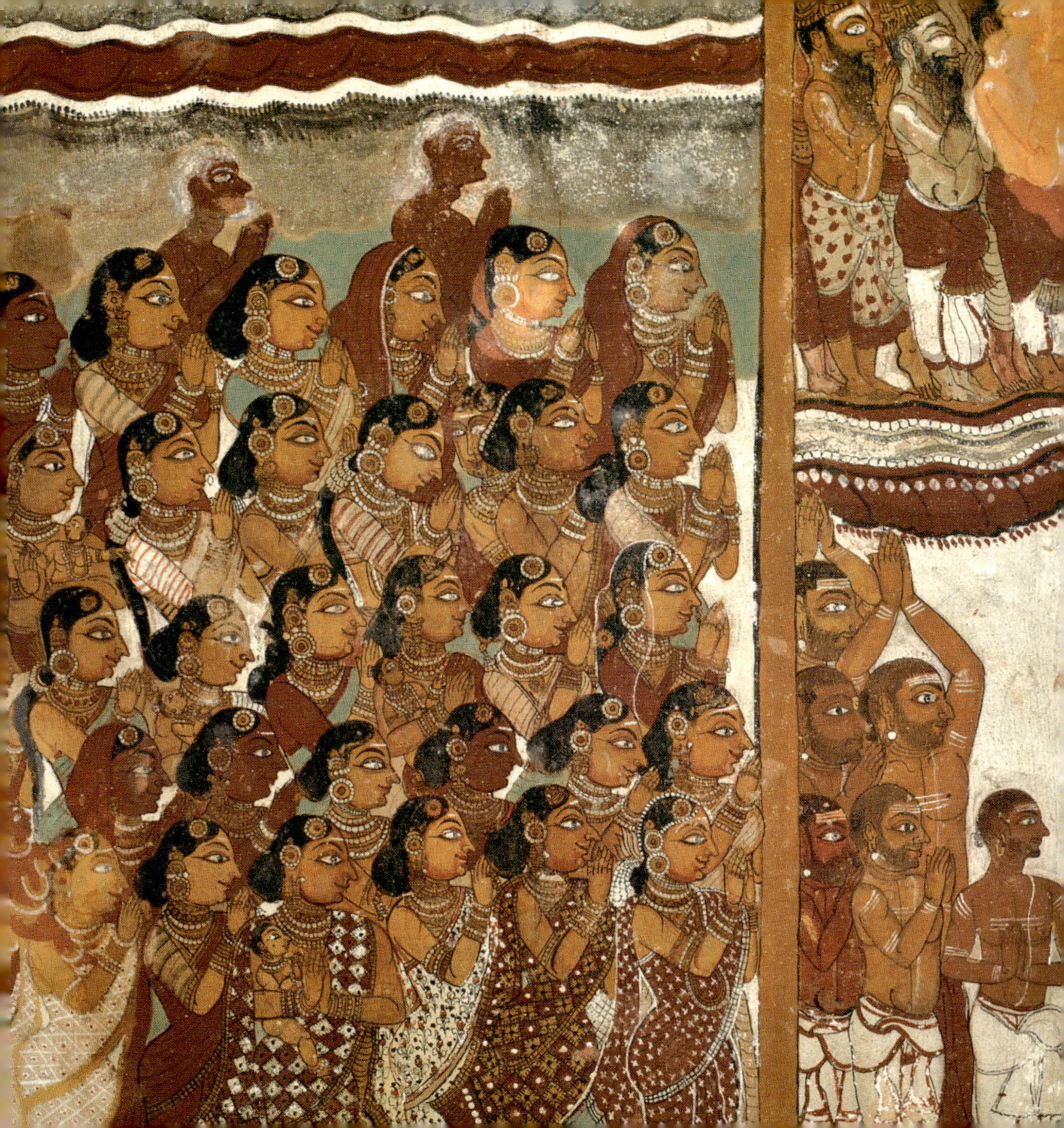

can apparently generate one for others. He exists in relation to his wife who takes up her position to his left and to their son, Skanda-Murukaṉ, who sits below these two parents. He is most emphatically not alone. Springtime, the moment of life's renewal, is his characteristic season.

In another sense, too, he is not alone: he inhabits a space next to the Anthill Lord, who has his own ancient story; and he lives, by his own choice and need, in the city of Kamalâmbāḷ, the unmarried goddess engaged in *tapas* who is, in some sense, coterminous with the city of Tiruvarur and embedded in this city's heart. Her vast tank, the Kamalâlayam, orients town and temple. This Kamalâmbāḷ occupies a separate space to the northwest of the temple, in the third *prākāra*; and she, too, is intimately linked to *mantra* and syllables (the *akṣara-pīṭha*, the seat of the phonemes, is immediately behind her shrine). Another form of the lonely goddess, the fierce Raudra Durgā, lives inside the enclosure. Tyāgarāja's consort, Nilotpalâmbāḷ,[1] sits in the second *prākāra*; and Valmīkanātha has his bride, Soma-kulâmbikā or Piriyāviṭaiyammai, "she who never goes away," next to his *garbhagṛha*. More generally, as the plethora of female deities attests, Tiruvarur is a *Śakti-pīṭha*, a power-site pregnant with female creativity. As we shall see, this fact is cited by Tyāgarāja himself as the rationale for his presence in the city.

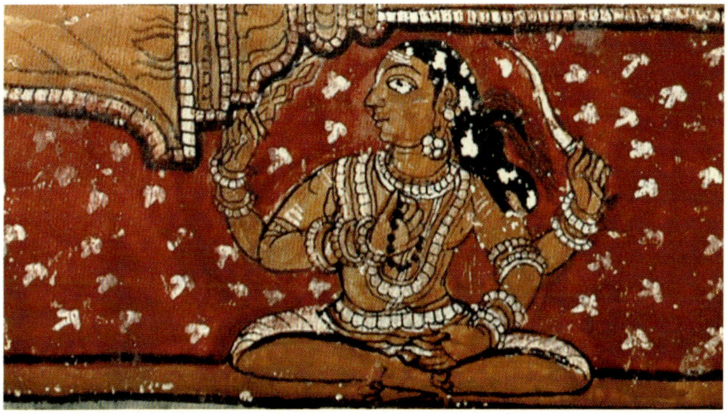

Rhythmic movement, a dance, a breath, an inaudible mantra, a mantric body, a certain restlessness that finds release in movement, a partly hidden self, opaque to others and to the self, an engaged openness to diverse feminine divinities, a creativity linked to these forms: to all of these initial features, easily articulated but not so easily combined, we need to add one more, perhaps the most conspicuous in the painted murals. Tyāgarāja is a royal god, at home in the world of politics and war; his decision to take up residence at Tiruvarur situates him firmly within the domain of a highly specific metaphysical politics. Indeed, as his very name indicates, Tyāgarāja is a king—of giving, or giving up, renouncing, releasing, endowing, offering (all this is *tyāga*). Some say he gave up the world, or the cosmos, in order to be at home in Tiruvarur. In this he was aided by a human king with a monkey's face named Mucukunda, whom the Cholas claimed as one of their

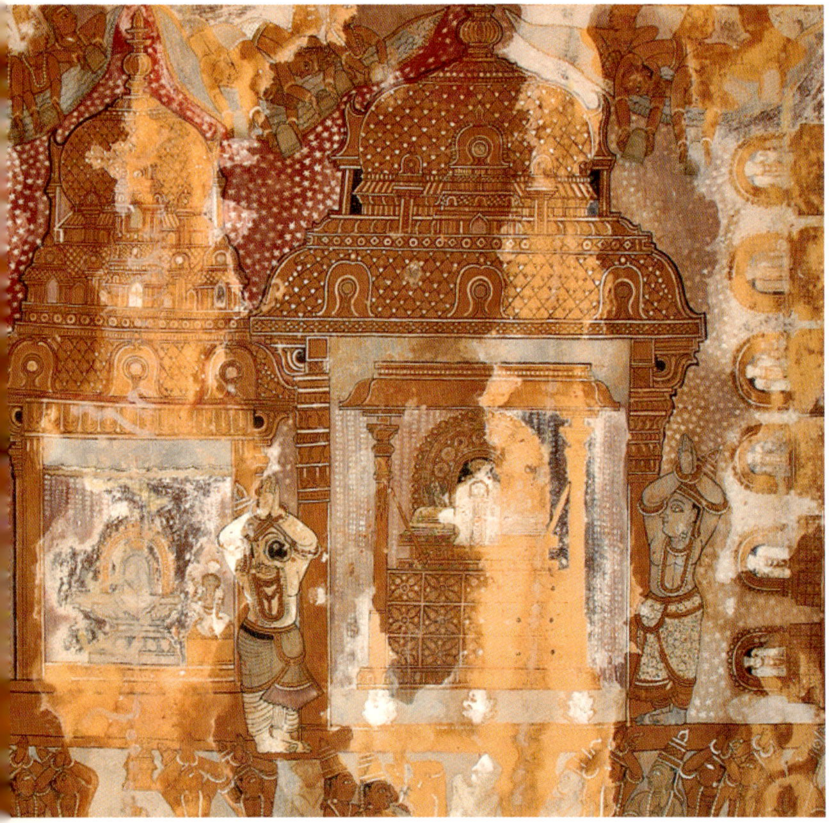

ancestors. So Tyāgarāja looks to the Cholas, who built the temple as we now know it, even as he embodies the vision of the Nāyaka kings of Tanjavur who made the Vasantotsava their major statement of regal identity and state power.

Vītiviṭaṅkaṉ

2 Who is this god, and how long has he been in Tiruvarur? According to the tradition recorded in the Tiruvarur *purāṇas*, the *Kantapurāṇam*, and many Tamil poetic works on the temple, it was the Chola king Mucukunda who brought Tyāgarāja to this site. This story, illustrated in the ceiling murals, will be the main focus of our essay. A Chola stratum is definitely fundamental to the evolution of the Tyāgarāja cult. But we can go a little farther back with the help of Tamil canonical sources, which know this god by the puzzling name Vītiviṭaṅkaṉ. The title Tyāgarāja itself appears only in works from the sixteenth-century onwards, if we put aside, for now, an isolated mention in a work known as *Īṭṭiyĕḻupatu*, popularly ascribed to the Chola-period poet Ŏṭṭakkūttar. The controversial dating of this latter text is still unresolved.

Śiva at Tiruvarur is Vītiviṭaṅkaṉ according to two verses in Appar's *Tevāram* 5.7.7-8 (mid-first millennium):

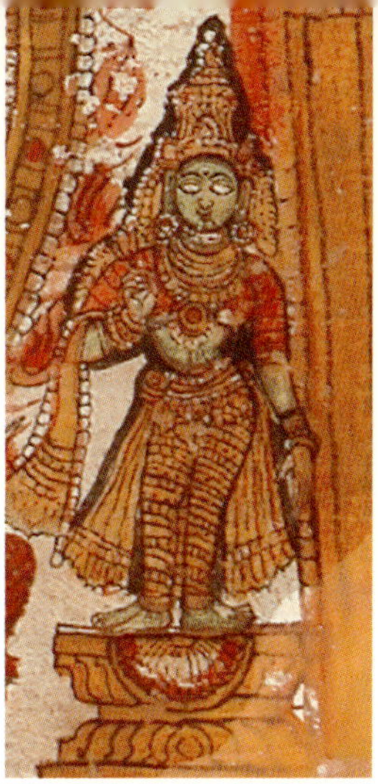

taṇṭav āḷiyait takkaṉ ṟaṉ veḷviyaic
cĕṇṭat' āṭiya vīti viṭaṅkaṉai?/ tevar akaṇṭaṉai
kaṇṭu kaṇṭ' ivaḷ kātalitt' aṉpatāyk
kŏṇṭiy āyiṉa vā ' ĕṉ ṟaṉ kotaiye

iva' ṇamaip pala pecat tŏṭaṅkiṉāḷ
avaṇam aṉṟ' ĕṉil ārūr araṉ ĕṉṉum
pavaṉi vīti viṭaṅkaṉaik kaṇṭ' ivaḷ
tavaṉiy āyiṉa vāṟ' ĕṉ ṟaṉ ṟaiyale

This girl of mine
is out of control:
she keeps looking and longing
for Vītiviṭaṅkaṉ, the one who destroyed
Dakṣa's sacrifice and all his power.

She starts to tell me something,
many things,
but if I say to her, "No, not like that"
she sees Vītiviṭaṅkaṉ, god of Arur,
in procession,
and goes wild.

The two verses belong to a short *akam*-inset, in the Caṅkam style: the 12-verse *patikam* as a whole appears to describe Śiva's procession through the streets of Arur; verses 6 to 8 suddenly move into a new mode, with a love-sick heroine whose unrestrained behavior is reported by her rather alarmed wet-nurse (*cĕvili*). Possibly, if the later processional template is adumbrated here, this heroine is one of the women thronging the streets of the city as the god passes by.[2] However, as A. Kandiah has shown,[3] such set-piece adaptations of the ancient *akam* conventions are not uncommon in the *Tevāram*. In any case, verse 8 makes it clear that Vītiviṭaṅkaṉ is moving through the streets of Tiruvarur (*pavaṉi vīti viṭaṅkaṉ*). There is no reason to doubt that this name applies to the god in his movable, festive form and thus, in all likelihood, distinct from Vanmīkanātaṉ/Valmīkanātha, Śiva as deity of the *mūlasthānam* at Tiruvarur, rooted in place in the anthill which is said by our texts to be the oldest cultic site in this temple.

The atmosphere of the two verses is feverish (the heroine is *tavaṉi*, a woman in a heated, love-stricken state), as suits a situation of passionate longing for the ultimately unreachable lover. Another term deserves attention: the young lady is *kŏṇṭi*, or has become *kŏṇṭi*, usually glossed as *paṭṭi* or *picci*, uncontrolled, wild, naughty. (An older instance – *Naṟṟiṇai* 174 – uses the word to mean "prostitute, concubine.")[4] Today "Kŏṇṭi" is the name of Tyāgarāja's consort, placed beside him on the *Somāskanda* image. It is likely that the *Tevāram* verse gave birth to this epithet, although we cannot rule out the possibility that the verse reflects an already existing name for the goddess at Tiruvarur, a playful, passionate concubine or wife.

But what about *his* name? All sorts of fanciful speculations have been put forward. The first element, *vīti*, is clear enough, from Skt. *vīthi*; it means "street", the proper location for a processional image. *Viṭaṅka* is, however, unclear. A standard gloss, which turns up in the dictionaries, derives it from *vi* + *ṭaṅka*, literally "unchiselled", as if the image were a purely natural one, not a stone or metal artifact. This reading is entirely unconvincing.[5] The simplest derivation is from a well-known Tamil word, *viṭaṅku*, "beauty." *Viṭaṅkaṉ* would thus mean "the handsome male", like such popular divine titles as Sundara/ Sundareśvara, Cŏkkanātaṉ, Aḻakar, and others. There is no doubt that the Tyāgarāja image is perceived as astonishingly beautiful. It also seems clear that *viṭaṅkaṉ* can, indeed, mean a "handsome male" in medieval Tamil.[6] It is also clearly the case that *viṭaṅkar* serves to indicate movable metal images of Śiva in Chola inscriptions, which speak of Tañjai-viṭaṅkar, Dakṣiṇa-meru-viṭaṅkar, Tillai-viṭaṅkar, Āṭal-viṭaṅkar, and also our Vīti-viṭaṅkar.[7] And this same Vītiviṭaṅkar of Tiruvarur is one, central figure in an important series of seven *viṭaṅka-sthalas*, bound together by this title and by a common body of ritual and mythic tradition: the others, all within the Kaveri Delta, are Tirunallaru, Tirunakaikkaronam, Karayil, Kolili, Tirumaraikkatu/ Vedaranyam, and Tiruvaymur.[8] We will have more to say about these seven *viṭanka* shrines and their relation to the Mucukunda frame-story.

So far so good; the epigraphic evidence seems to support the derivation from Tamil *viṭanku*. A *viṭankar*, nearly always the final element in a compositum, is probably a particularly ravishing image, usually a mobile festival *mūrti*. Yet there is reason to believe that the specific title Vītiviṭaṅkaṉ, at Tiruvarur, has its own semantic force, and that it is linked to a powerful notion of space and the way space is inhabited, perceived, or created. The evidence for this comes from classical texts in Telugu: the fifteenth-century *Krīḍâbhirāmamu*, Śrīnātha's slightly earlier *Bhīma-khaṇḍamu*, and Allasāni Pĕddana's early sixteenth-century *Manu-caritramu*. These sources show beyond doubt that the term had a much wider currency than its local usage at Tiruvarur. Look, first, at the latest of these three works, the *Manu-caritramu*. In 1.45, a *ṣaṣṭhyanta* verse paying homage to the poem's patron, Kṛṣṇa-deva-rāya, the later is described as *kha-viṭaṅka-naṭad-yaśo'bdhi-kallolunakun*, "a dancing wave in the ocean of fame that reaches to the very edge (or end) of space." Kṛṣṇa-deva-rāya is famous right up to the end of the cosmos, the final limit of the imaginable universe; *viṭanka* must mean just this, the edge of space, if space can have an edge. In that case, as M. C. Kanakaiah has suggested, Śiva at Tiruvarur would be "one who goes to the very end of the street(s)," the farthest spatial point. The god in his procession maps out space to its limit.[9]

Very close to this usage is Śrīnātha's description of a disembodied voice that fills the sky: *vinipiñcĕn aśarīra-bhārati nabho-vīthī-viṭaṅkambunan*," "an utterance was heard to the outer limit of space (or sky)."[10] Somewhat more opaque are two references in the parodic *Krīḍâbhirāmamu*, where the two protagonists, on a day-long tour of the city of Warangal, "leave this place and cross the crossroads" (*bāhya-kaṭaka-vīthi-viṭaṅkambun' atikramiñci*, 111); and there are "women, young and old, [who] have set pots full of water on the crossroads (*vīthi-viṭaṅkambu*, 146)."[11] The intention seems to be an open, public space (in 111, an area outside the walled city). Phil Wagoner has suggested, following a gloss in the *Sūryarāyândhranighaṇṭuvu* (*s.v.*) as *kapota-pālika*, that *vīthi-viṭaṅka* refers to the "ubiquitous reflex-curved eave" of medieval Deccani architecture and then, metonymically, to a street edged with such eaved colonnades.[12] In this case, given the other two examples, the eave would again mark the outer limit or edge (of a building); by extension, *vīthi-viṭaṅka* would imply a space seen from its furthest boundary. We cannot do much better than this with the available textual materials.

But already we can say something more about Vītiviṭaṅkaṉ at Tiruvarur. He has adapted to his ritual situation in the temple a term that connects him to the idea of space as such, and especially the notion of reaching the end of space, opening space to its end or limit. His processional trajectory marks the livable universe of the temple-town. Sometimes *viṭaṅka* is glossed as a "bird's nest". Again, there is a link to the eaves, so we might suspect that Tyāgarāja-Vītiviṭaṅkaṉ "nests" in the street, or at the farthest limit of the street. He has access to much wider expanses, as we know from the story of his arrival at Tiruvarur from heaven. If he has chosen to come to this temple, and the texts leave no room for doubt that it is his own ardent choice, then in doing so he has traced the boundary of his home, as he retraces it each year in his chariot-festival in the spring. Moreover, this space, fully inhabited and beautifully appointed by the god, allows him a particular form of rhythmic, dancing movement. Indeed, this space, *vīthi-viṭaṅka*, the final edge of the street, is itself alive with a definite rhythm, defined at Tiruvarur as a silent dance. The rhythm of Tyāgarāja's dance is the regular, continuous flow of space itself, space that is generated or created by a conscious, active form of divinity.

There is one more, highly concrete and specific meaning for *viṭaṅkaṉ* at Tiruvarur; this is the name given the small *linga* of precious stones that sits in a silver casket to the right of Tyāgarāja-Somāskanda. As in other Śaiva shrines, notably Cidambaram, this condensed embodiment of the god is an object receiving ritual attention (noon and evening anointings, *abhiṣeka*).[13] Like the main icon, it can also move outside.

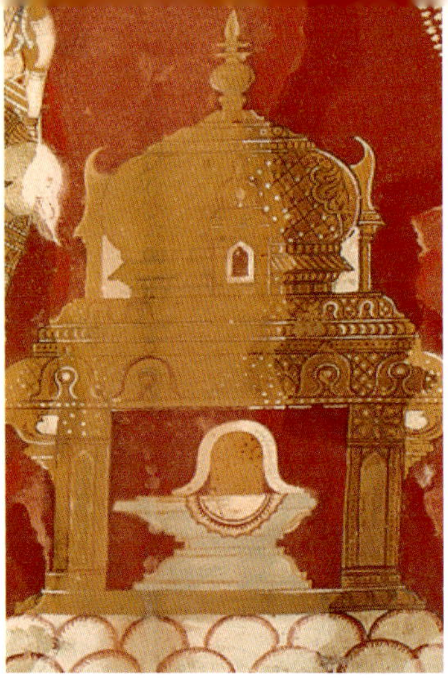

We can now understand why, in Chola times, Vītiviṭaṅkaṉ is a preferred name for the god of Tiruvarur insofar as he manifests himself not inside the temple but in the outer periphery of the village street. Thus Cekkiḻār, in his *Pĕriya Purāṇam*, describes the moment when Śiva appears to the king known as Manunītikaṇṭacoḻaṉ, who has just driven his chariot over his own son because the latter had unwittingly driven over a calf:

taṇṇaḷi vĕṇ kuṭai ventaṉ cĕyal kaṇṭu tariyātu
maṇṇavarkaṇ maḻai pŏḻintār vāṉavar pū maḻai
pŏḻintār
aṇṇalavaṉ kaṇṇ ĕtirey aṇi vīti maḻa viṭai mel
viṇṇavarka ṭoḻa niṉṟāṉ vītiviṭaṅkappĕrumāṉ (130)

When they saw what the king, in his compassion, had
done,
his subjects wept, and the gods showered flowers.
God, Vītiviṭaṅkappĕrumāṉ, showed himself
seated on his white bull to the king's eyes
as the gods gave worship, right there in the street.

The poet has selected the epithet deliberately and highlighted it by leaving it to the end of his verse. When Śiva acts in the larger realm of Tiruvarur town, he is Vītiviṭaṅkaṉ, "the one who reaches the end of the street." Such usages occur commonly in the medieval texts emanating from Tiruvarur.

Let us briefly review the iconic features of Tyāgarāja as he appears today to his worshippers. The image, installed in the *pūṅkoyil* or *deva-sabhā*, with an unusual standing Nandi positioned before him, is of Somāskanda-Śiva, the god together with Umā and their son, Skanda/Murukaṉ; but the child is entirely hidden by the so-called *Tyāga-parivaṭṭam* cloth, itself covered by flowers and ornamentation. Indeed, most of the *mūrti* itself is also hidden by this cloth; what one sees is the head of Tyāgarāja and Kŏṇṭi, his consort, who stands beside him to the right. Only at two points in the year, in Mārkaḻi Tiruvātirai and at Paṅkuṉi Uttaram—is the veil removed to reveal the god's left foot (in Mārkaḻi) and his right foot (during Paṅkuṉi Uttaram).

Tyāgarāja wears a set of long floral garlands (*tiruppaṇi*) as well as a necklace of skulls, said to belong to the Brahmās of many aeons. A high vertical crown is framed on either side by outward-facing crescent moons (called *kaṅkai* or Gaṅgā, on the left and *vĕṇpiṟai*, to the right). He wears two immense circular earrings made of *cĕvvanti* flowers (*cĕvvantittoṭu*) or, if *cĕvvanti* is not available, of jasmine and campak. To the left of the god, a small *liṅga* (*bhūmi-tattva-liṅga*) adorns a dark blue silk cloth. A dark unguent, *kṛṣṇa-gandham*, which is applied to the deity is referred to as *Tyāga-vinoda*, "Tyāgarāja's delight." Two swords, *vīra-khaḍgam* – said to be the signs of Tyāgarāja's kingly role in Tiruvarur – outline the iconic tableau from below the *ratna-siṃhâsana* on which the god is ensconced. (This throne, with its 32 lion's legs, is also known as *mantra-siṃhâsana* and *śrī-pīṭha*; as we shall see, Tyāgarāja's body is said to be fashioned from *mantras*.)[14] Patañjali and Vyāghrapāda, of Cidambaram fame, stand at the base of the throne. There are other strong links to Cidambaram as well: Like Naṭarāja, Tyāgarāja enjoys six annual *abhiṣekas* (two of them outside his shrine, in the Tevâcirayaṉ *maṇḍapa*). We will return to this theme. We have already mentioned Tyāgarāja's special fondness for *cĕnkaḷunīr* flowers (Skt. *kalhāra*), although these are no longer plentiful at Tiruvarur.[15] The back of the image, covered with golden *kavacam* and with long, jewel-studded plaits of hair (*jaṭā*), has its own special beauty: hence another current name for Tyāgarāja, *Muṉṉilum mummaṭaṅku piṉṉaḷakar*, "he whose back is three times more beautiful than his front."

Particularly favoured is the evening service to this god, *antikkāppu*, which also gives him one of his beloved names, *Antikāpp'aḷakar*, "Beautiful God of the Evening Prayer." Anyone who has seen this moment will attest to its overwhelming sensual and emotional power. Vast numbers of jasmine blossoms, roses, and other flowers are offered to the god, not woven into garlands as in other temples, but blanketing him entirely; hence the name *pūṅkoyil*, "flower shrine," for this site. In earlier times, *devadāsīs* would dance and sing outside the window, *tiruccālakam*, in the south wall of his shrine, while flautists played outside the northern window, *tiruccāraḷam*. The celestial *apsaras* Rambhā is said to have scattered flowers before Tyāgarāja day after day.[16] The priests used to wear crowns and a long silken *aṅgavastram* to perform the *antikkāppu*, as if they were enacting Indra's role. We should also mention the rare *Pañcamukha-vādyam*, a five-fold drum (the five heads tuned to the *svaras ri*, *ga*, *ma*, *dha*, and *ni* respectively) played during the evening service, the same instrument that Viṣṇu played for Śiva's dance in heaven.

But the culminating moment of the god's ritual year is surely his progression (*ulā*) on his chariot, (*āḷitter*) perhaps the largest of all temple chariots in the south, through the streets of Tiruvarur during the Spring Festival in May. In this guise, Tyāgarāja enacts his primordial identity as Vītiviṭaṅkaṉ, the god who, "nesting" in the streets, moves through the farthest reaches of space, thus opening up and shaping a liveable space for himself and his devotees.

Mucukunda, the Monkey-faced Chola

3 According to the Tiruvarur tradition, Tyāgarāja's presence at this shrine derives from the active role of the Chola king Mucukunda. We will follow his story, step by step, as we see it portrayed in the murals.

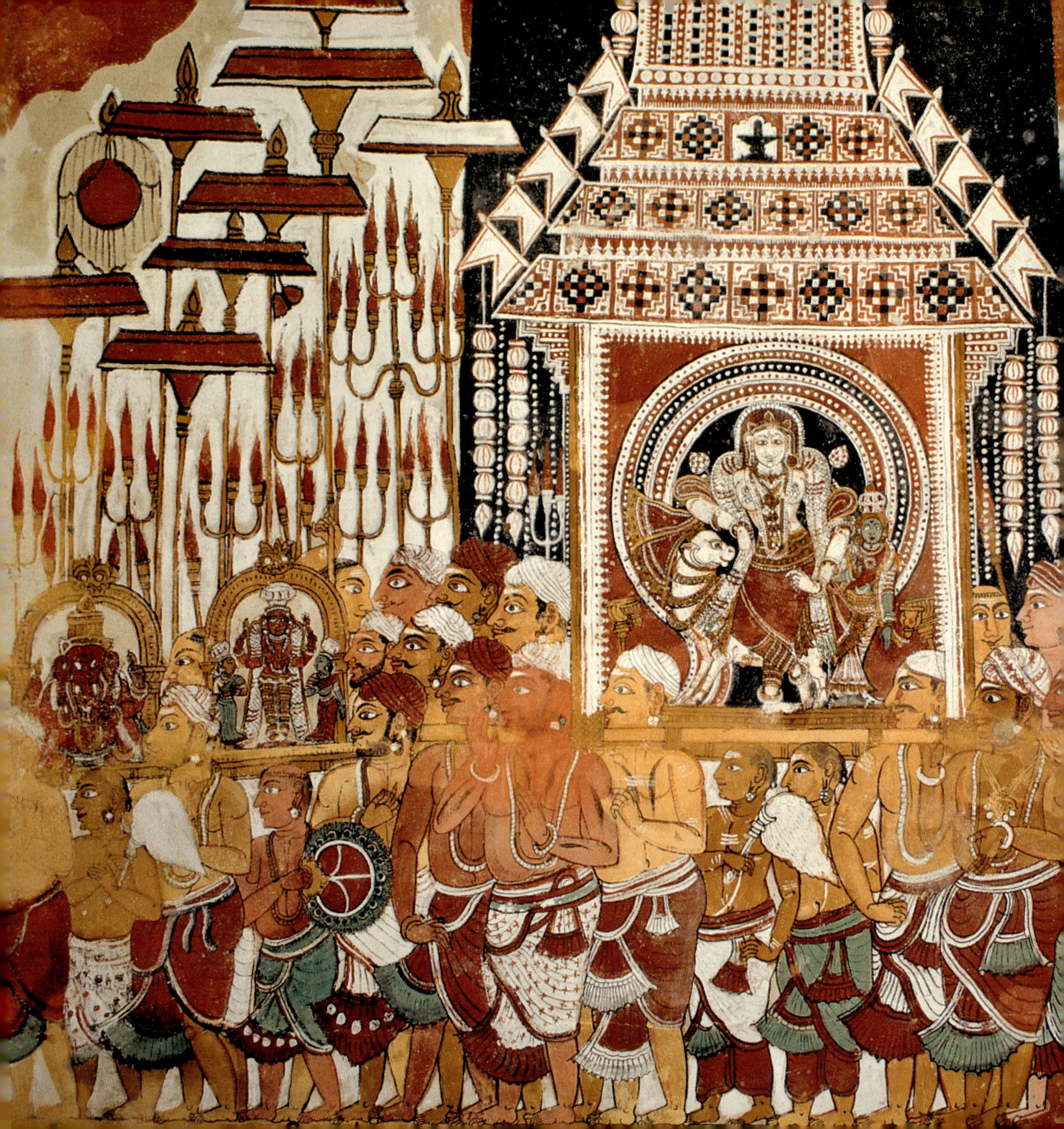

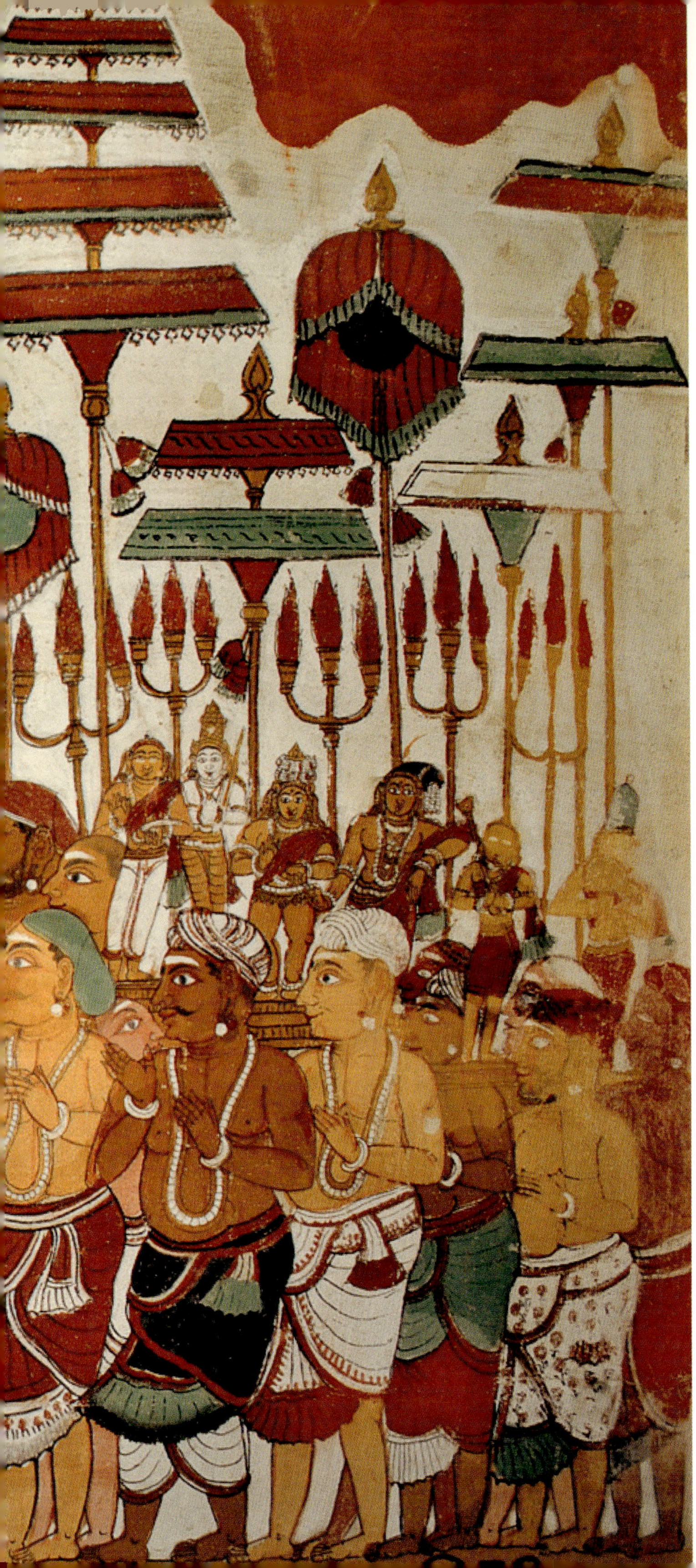

First, however, we need to identify this figure and trace his history through the classical sources.

A famous Mucukunda appears in several Sanskrit *purāṇas* at a particular moment in the life-history of Krishṇa. This Mucukunda helped the gods in their ongoing wars with the *asuras*, and in recompense he was granted an unusual boon – that he would enjoy a long, uninterrupted sleep, and that anyone who disturbed him would be burnt to ashes. A demonic figure, Kālayavana, pursued Krishṇa into the cave where Mucukunda was sleeping peacefully; Kālayavana wrongly thought the sleeping hero was Krishṇa, so he kicked him and woke him up. Mucukunda, understandably irritated, burned the demon to ash with his glance. When Mucukunda discovered that Krishṇa was standing before him, he worshipped him humbly; and the god blessed him and sent him to the celestial worlds to enjoy many heavenly pleasures; he also promised that Mucukunda would eventually be reborn in a good family and would retain his memories from earlier births. When Mucukunda came out of the cave, he saw that human beings were of very short stature and thus he knew that the Kali Age had begun.[17]

Mucukunda is a kind of Rip Van Winkle, sleeping through the transition from one age to the next. He bridges a major temporal gap. The *Mahābhārata* also knows him as a mighty conqueror who overcame Kubera with the help of his priest, Vasiṣṭha.[18] But in the Tamil region, this regal Mucukunda, with his link to Krishṇa, was eventually assimilated into the Chola genealogical lists. *Cilappatikāram* 6.14-17 speaks of an unnamed king who received five halls (*manram*) from Indra in gratitude for his protection of Amarāvatī. The medieval commentator Aṭiyārkkunallār (twelfth or thirteenth century) identifies this king as Mucukunda. Note the theme of carrying off to our world some pieces of Indra's natural realm. Several Chola-period sources make the identification more explicit. Thus in Cayaṅkŏṇṭār's *Kaliṅkattupparaṇi*, in a chapter devoted to the royal Chola genealogy (*irāca pārampariyam*), we hear of

pŏru tuṟaittalai pukuntu mucukuntaṉ imaiyor/
puram aṭaṅkalum araṇ cĕytu puranta pukaḻum

..."the great distinction won by Mucukunda who entered the battlefield and thus saved the whole heavenly world" (189).

Similarly, Kampaṉ mentions, again in a genealogical list, put into the mouth of Viśvāmitra at the Mithila court, a king with bejewelled crown and garlands who, like Dharma itself holding a sword, saved the gods' city when the very patient gods were locked in battle with the (apparently impatient) demons (1.717). The commentators' tradition refers this verse to Mucukunda, who is preceded by Mandhātṛ and succeeded by Śibi. In Ŏṭṭakkūttar's courtly *ulā*s there are elliptical references to a Chola king, perhaps Mucukunda (no name is given), who went without sleep in order to safeguard Indra's world,[19] a nice complement to the image of the soporific ally of Indra's whom we know from the Sanskrit *purāṇa*s. (I refrain from discussing the *Īṭṭiyĕḻupatu* attributed to Ŏṭṭakkūttar and containing a version of the Mucukunda-Tyāgarāja story, because of the uncertainty about this work's provenance and date.[20])

Note that none of these references says anything about a monkey's face, nor is there any link to Tiruvarur. Only much later, in the post-Chola centuries, did the Tiruvarur tradition fasten upon Mucukunda as the hero of the Tyāgarāja story as we now know it. No doubt the already existing narrative about an early, proto-Chola Mucukunda, the protector of Amaravati who brought Indra's halls to earth, served as a convenient point of departure for the story of Tyāgarāja's arrival on earth. A human mediator was definitely necessary, for reasons that will soon become clear. The monkey's face, linked to Tamil *mucu*, "langur," turns up for the first time only in the *Kantapurāṇam* or its closely allied Sanskrit text, the *Śiva-rahasya-khaṇḍa*, which give us canonical accounts of the Tamil Murukaṉ mythology as it crystallized in the northern Tamil country around the fifteenth/sixteenth centuries. Opinions differ as to the relative priority of these two texts, but they agree in establishing a close connection between Mucukunda and Lord Murukaṉ and in deriving the Tyāgarāja cycle from this linkage. Mucukunda, born with a monkey's face in the royal line of Hariścandra, is said to have been invited to the wedding of Murukaṉ and Tĕyvayāṉai at Tirupparankunram. Murukaṉ gave this king, ruling at Karuvur, nine famous warriors, including Vīrabāhu, who would become Mucukunda's father-in-law; these heroes turn up in the Tiruvarur murals, their names inscribed on the painted figures.[21] Mucukunda married Citravalli and continued the line of kings; their wedding is the prelude to Mucukunda's adventure with Tyāgarāja, narrated almost as an afterthought, but in a lucid, logical, and relatively detailed version.

Later Tamil *Purāṇas* offer other traditions about Mucukunda: thus at both Tirupperur and Tirimurttimalai in the Konku country we find a story about a *gandharva* named Vidhūma, cursed by a woman (whom he desired) to become a monkey (*mucu*); when this monkey threw *bilva* leaves on a *Śiva-liṅga* on the slopes of the Himalaya, Pārvatī cursed him to keep his monkey's face in his next birth as well, but Śiva, who saw the *bilva* leaves as an offering, made him king over the whole universe. Born as Mucukunda Cakravarti, this great ruler saved the gods from a malevolent demon. However, one day, one of the dancing-girls performing before him laughed when she saw his face.

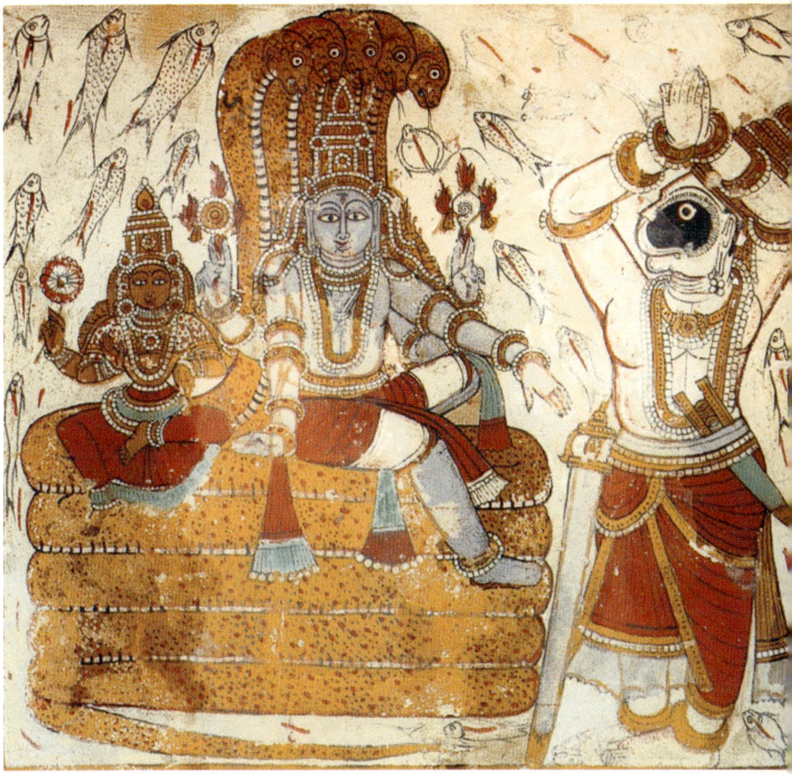

Mucukunda was so profoundly chagrined that he abandoned his kingdom and wandered over the earth in search of healing, until he bathed at the Konku shrine and at once lost his monkey's face.[22] The ancient image of Mucukunda as a highly atypical human king who rescues the gods in an emergency survives in these Western Tamil traditions. But our concern is with Tiruvarur: it is time for us to address the Mucukunda story there as it crystallized in the late-medieval poetic sources that help us to make sense of the painted murals.

How Tyāgarāja came to Tiruvarur

4 The most complete version of the Tiruvarur Mucukunda story appears in two cantos, the *Tiyākarājaccarukkam* and the *Tiruviḷāccarukkam*, of Campantamuṉivar's sixteenth-century Tamil text, *Tiruvārūrppurāṇam* (1592).[23] This is the version we will follow here, with occasional glances at three other medieval versions: Kacciyappacivâcāriyar's *Kantapurāṇam*, the Sanskrit prototype or précis of the latter (*Śiva-rahasya-khaṇḍa*, see above),[24] and Maṟaiñānacampantar's *Kamalâlayacciṟappu* (1547). Campantamuṉivar's text antedates the painted murals by a little less than a century. Another seventeenth-century text, perhaps close in time to the paintings, is the famous blind poet Antakakkavi's *Tiruvārūr ulā*; it is entirely possible that the painters knew, and in some sense even illustrated, this lovely poem. Later versions of the story, mostly from the other *viṭaṅka-sthalas*, also exist—for example, Parañcotimuṉivar's *Vetâraṇiyappurāṇam* (seventeenth century), and Tiricirapuram Mīṉāṭcicuntaram Piḷḷai's *Nākaikkāroṇappurāṇam*, composed in the mid-nineteenth century. In general, the many *purāṇic* tellings in Tamil are in close accord.

There was a monkey, actually a langur, *mucu*, living on Mount Kailāsa. Perched on a *kūviḷai* or *vilva* tree, he showered its blossoms on Śiva and Umā, happily playing beneath it. Umā was irritated by this intrusion, but Śiva corrected her: the monkey was carrying out an act of worship. Śiva therefore took away his animal delusion and imparted pure, complete knowledge (*muntai mā maruḷ akaṟṟi vāl uṇarvu muḻut' aḷittaṉaṉ*, 13). He also informed the monkey that he would be born as a human being, a great king in Manu's line. The monkey was a little nonplussed: how would he continue his worship? "Don't worry," said the god. "I will take possession of you there as well."

So the *mucu* became a Chola king appropriately called Mucukuntaṉ. We know from other sources, notably the paintings, that he retained his monkey's face even as he ruled the world from his capital at Karuvur.[25] He was a very good king, and his subjects thrived, entirely free from poverty, war, theft, and other common depredations. Rain fell at the proper time. In Śiva temples, worship followed the Āgamic rules without fail.

This is our king, the real hero of the story, the true founder of the Tiruvarur cult, as shall see. We have to leave him for a moment, at home in the Tamil country, and turn to problems in the divine sphere. In particular, two recurrent difficulties have to be resolved. Gods, like human beings, long to have children and grieve when they cannot conceive. And gods are continuously threatened by their eternal rivals, the *asuras*, who often achieve transient but still alarming victories. The Mucukunda story weaves both problems, which may, after all, be variants of a single, more deep-set blockage in reality itself, together as the backdrop to Tyāgarāja's arrival in Tiruvarur. Since the story is enacted year after year, a repeated sequence, we can perhaps shift at this point to the present tense, the proper temporal mode for the paintings as well.

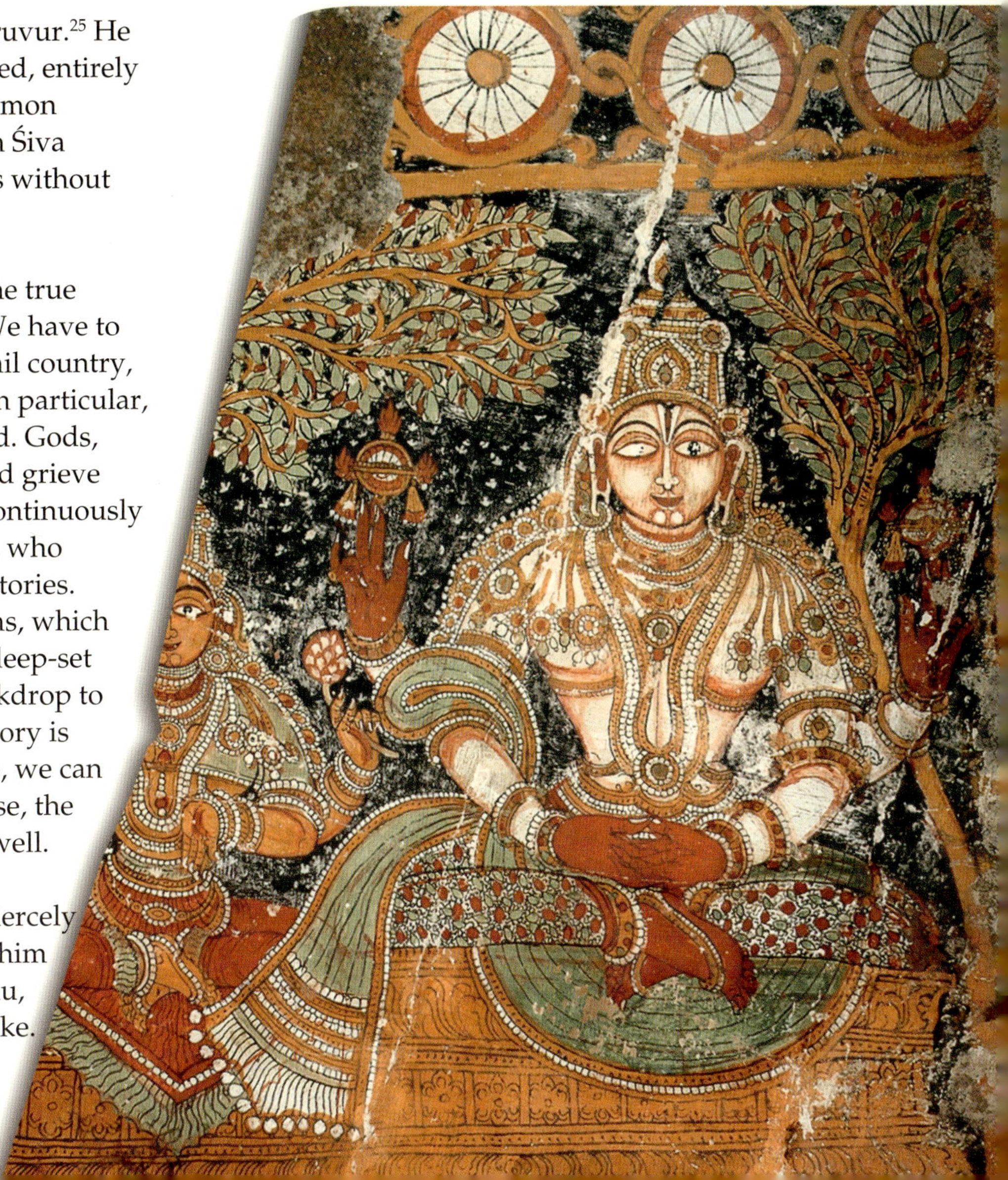

Viṣṇu has no child. He worships Śiva, in a fiercely disciplined regimen (*tapas*). Śiva appears to him together with Umā. So far so good. But Viṣṇu, so close to realizing his hope, makes a mistake. He addresses Śiva alone, the solitary male god, begging him for a son; and Śiva grants the request. But Umā is incensed (we already know she is very sensitive to such matters). She curses Viṣṇu that the son born to him will die. With her husband, she immediately disappears. Built into the Tyāgarāja origin-myth is the insistence that without attending to the female dimension of intra-divine reality, nothing creative can endure.

Viṣṇu is grief-stricken. He thinks hard. He has an image made of Śiva together with Umā and their son Skanda, a *Somāskanda-mūrti*, and in his desperate longing to find a way out of the curse, he worships this triple image of Śiva.[26] Again the god appears, together with Umā and Skanda-Murukaṉ. This time Viṣṇu makes no mistake. First he bows to Umā, then to her husband. The goddess has a prior claim. Let us remember this moment, for it speaks to the composition and cultic organization of Tyāgarāja-Somāskanda and to this deity's natural history.

Umā relents. She cannot cancel her curse; such words have a life of their own. But she can ameliorate its effects. The son born to Viṣṇu, Pradyumna, the embodiment of Manmatha, desire, will be burnt to death by Śiva's third eye; then the god will revive him. Relieved, Viṣṇu can now converse freely with Śiva, who asks him what more he wants. Viṣṇu's request: "Lord, stay here, joyfully, in the three-fold image, joined with Umā and Kantaṉ, so that I may worship you and live each day (59)." Śiva is willing to make this *Somāskanda-murti* his primary home: "Why insist on Kailāsa? (60)" Viṣṇu happily takes the image back with him to the serpent couch spread over the Ocean of Milk. There, having enshrined the image in the golden temple that is his heart (*nĕñcam ām pŏṉ aṅ koyiliṉ akattu vaittu*, 61), Viṣṇu enters into his yogic sleep; and in that state

Candramauli [= Tyāgarāja], moving with the slow
steady movement of Viṣṇu's breathing,
danced in place on Viṣṇu's breast.[27]

The phrasing is important. Tyāgarāja is fixed in place, yet he moves rhythmically, up and down, according to the in-breaths and out-breaths of his sleeping host. This movement is a dance, which will later be known as the *ajapā-tāṇḍava*, the "soundless dance." It is at the very center of the Tyāgarāja concept, a defining feature for this god who adapts himself to the physical and psychic processes of his devotee, the organic rhythms of the latter's life. The epithet Candra-mauli ("Moon-Crowned") may also be significant, for the most mobile form of Tyāgarāja is the festival image known as Candra-śekhara, the main focus of his progression through space. In any case, the first segment of our story is complete. As promised, Viṣṇu's *pūjā* bears fruit in the form of his son, Pradyumna-Manmatha (83).

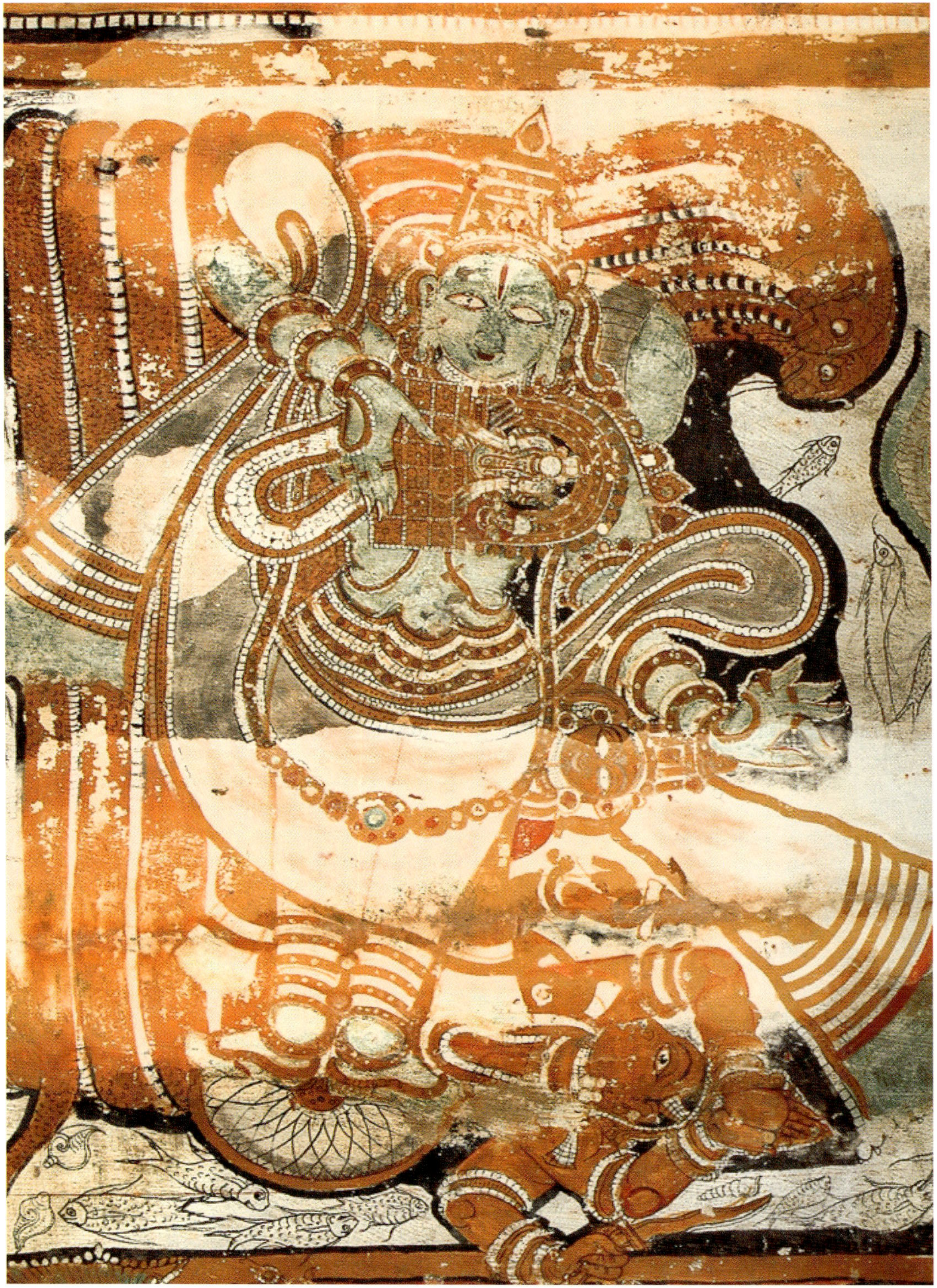

So now we have the image: a practical, accessible solution to a blockage in the domain of physical continuity through procreation. Śiva appears as Tyāgarāja in *his* generative mode, a family god joined to (literally "mixed in with", *kalantu,* 59) his wife and son. In this enhanced state, he is in constant movement, the very image of breath itself as a process infusing the cosmos with life. Still, he is far away, on Viṣṇu's breast. How are we to bring him to earth, where he is sorely needed? For this move to take place, our monkey-faced king has to act. The conditions of his engagement emerge out of another crisis in the cosmos.

Indra is attacked and defeated by the demon Vāṟkaliyaṉ, a newcomer to these *Purāṇic* contests.[28] In his distress he seeks Viṣṇu's help. Viṣṇu tells him (according to Campantamuṉivar) that if he worships Somāskanda, the image on Viṣṇu's breast, the enemy will be defeated, and very magnanimously, Viṣṇu hands the image over to Indra, who takes it away to his world. With Tyāgarāja's help, Indra defeats Vāṟkali. Tyāgarāja lives for many ages in Indra's heaven, where he is worshiped daily, without fail. Maṟaiñāṉacampantar changes the sequence: first Viṣṇu recommends to Indra that he perform a severe penance, in order to defeat his enemy; and when this tactic is successful, the victorious Indra comes back to ask Viṣṇu for the Tyāgarāja image (369-370). The result is the same: the god has shifted residence. Fortunately for *our* world, or rather because of the merit Tiruvarur itself acquired by performing *tapas (Tiruvārūrppurāṇam,* 74), after a long time Indra faces a far more severe challenge, this time from a better-known demonic foe named Vala.

Initially, things go poorly, because Śiva has set his heart on Tiruvarur. Indra once again flees ignominiously from the battlefield. Again, he urgently needs help. This time he turns to Mucukunda, from the world of human beings; and Mucukunda immediately sets off with his army to save the gods. The war is described in profound detail. Millions die on both sides. In the best tradition of Tamil battle-poems, ghouls, meat-eating demons and demonesses dance the *kuravai* dance on the corpses they are about to devour (95). (The paintings, incidentally, show the same morbid delight in the imagined experience of combat.) Ultimately, the battle is determined by an extended duel between Mucukunda and Vala, which leaves Vala unarmed and helpless, like an elephant without a tusk or a defanged snake (159). To save Indra's honour, Mucukunda gallantly steps aside and allows Indra to deliver the *coup de grâce* with his *vajra.* Suitably grateful, Indra seats Mucukunda on his elephant and flies him to Amaravati to be feasted and rewarded. Mucukunda makes a triumphal entry into heaven, regally adorned in his honour. The celestial

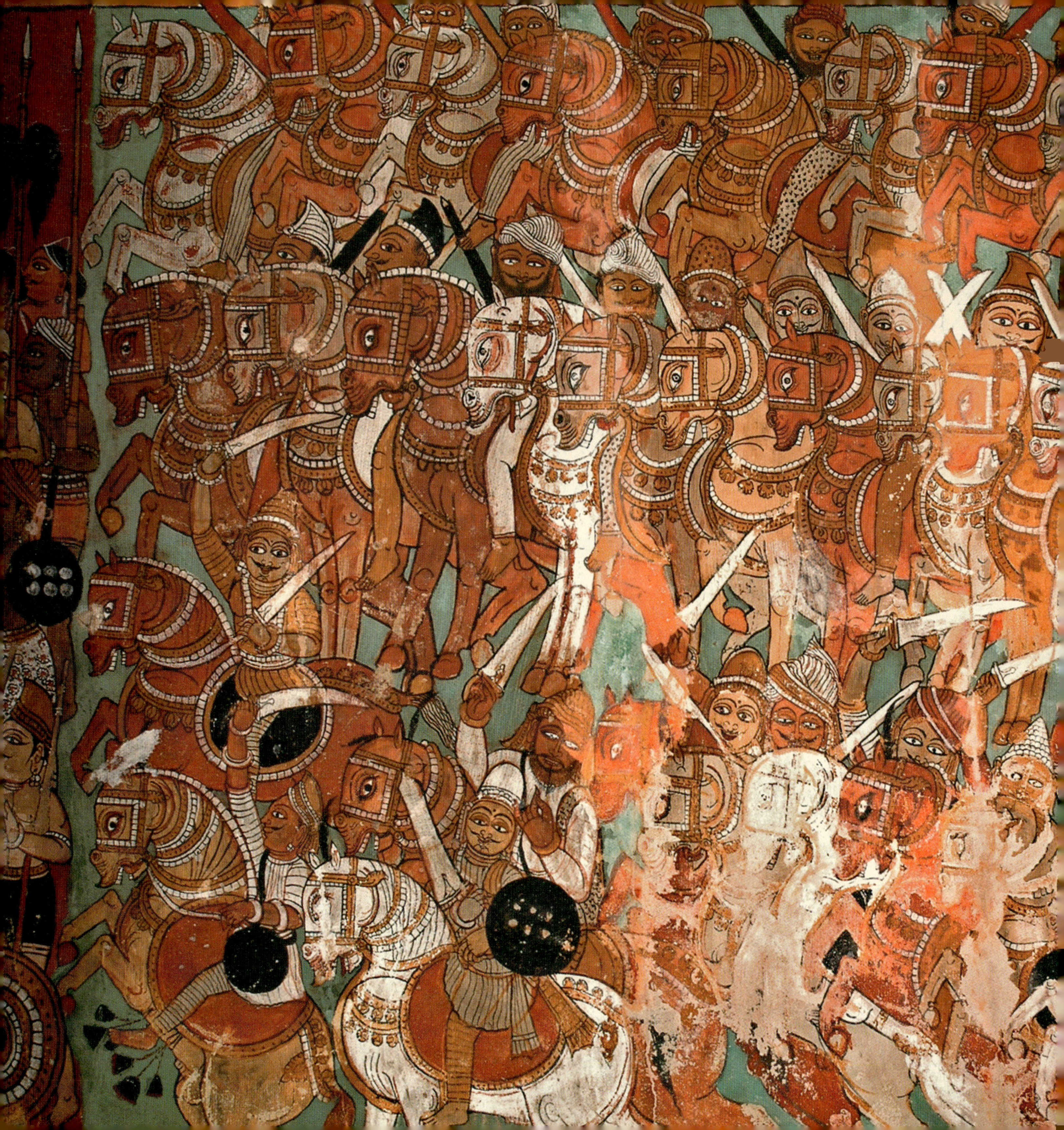

women crowd around the windows of their palaces to get a glimpse of this hero who has saved their world.

Indra seats Mucukunda on a throne in a well-appointed *maṇḍapa*. "Nothing in the entire cosmos would be a commensurate reward for what you have done," he says, and, leaving the king to reflect on this somewhat open-ended thought, Indra rushes off to bathe, dress, and perform his daily worship of the Tyāgarāja image in his *pūjā-maṇḍapa*. For his part, Mucukunda also completes his daily worship, and then makes his own way to Indra's *pūjā-maṇḍapa* where he, too, can bow to Śiva-Somāskanda (199). Here is the critical moment when God chooses to act. He shows himself, together with Umā and Skanda, just as if he were on Mount Kailāsa, to the king, making sure that Indra cannot see this revelation (*intiraṉ tĕrint' iṭā vaṇṇam*, 207). Fortunately, Mucukunda is perfectly attuned to the event: *muṉṉai niṉaivu yāvaiyum uṇarntaṉa' ṉirupar tam pĕrumāṉ*, "that king of kings intuitively understood everything **before** [Śiva had to speak] (207).

It is a profoundly interactive moment, the god's wish dependent on the king's empathic grasp. Mucukunda melts down (*urukiṉāṉ*), as is customary in such circumstances. He weeps, forgets himself (*taṉai maṟantaṉaṉ*); his senses fuse into one; whatever cumulated ills or mistakes he may carry from the past are immediately consumed; he sings, he dances. He is like a calf embraced by the mother cow after an absence (209). Passionate desire fills him from within (*uṇṇiṟaint' ĕḻu kātaloṭu*, 210). And now Śiva can speak to him, once again without allowing Indra to hear:

tec'uṟu cĕlvav ārūrt tirunakar kŏṭu poy ĕmmai/
pūcaṉai puritiy ĕṉṟāṉ pukaḻ maṟai tanta vāyāl...

"Bring us to the luminous town of Ārūr
and worship us there," said the mouth
that once uttered the Vedas (211).

Our poet allows himself an aside: If this God, this *mūrtti*, who had received endless service from Indra himself in the golden world of the gods, had a strong desire to move his home to the Parāśakti site (*parācattiyĕllai*), who can encompass the perfection of Ārūr (212)?

The god's tone is almost plaintive, as if he were trapped, locked away in the golden cage of heaven; he is, as it were, conspiring with Mucukunda, planning a daring escape. This spacious deity needs his own, intimate, irreplaceable space, and he knows where to find it. As if to highlight this bold request, for all its exotic starkness, the poet repeats the key phrase: What great merit must this king have accomplished if the god, who had been worshiped by both Viṣṇu and Indra, was able to say to him: "Take us away" (*kŏṭu poy*, 214)!

Śiva disappears back into the golden image. Indra knows nothing of what has transpired. Can anyone know the extent of God's playfulness (*māyam*, 125)? Taking leave of the god, Indra leads Mucukunda to his palace and summons the Kāma-dhenu to provide a suitable repast. After dinner, Indra removes all the king's ornaments and jewels and adorns him with new ones, with his own hands. He rewards Mucukunda's soldiers and tells them: "You are *my* retinue, and my relatives, now." Clearly feeling a little smug, relaxed, Indra embraces Mucukunda and, with a great show of courtesy (*mukamaṉ kūṟi*, 220), asks him if there is anything else he would like. "Lord," says the king, seeing his opportunity, "give me that spotless god whom you worship" (*aiya nī pūcaiy āṟṟum amalaṉait taruti*, 221).

"That great, godly *mūrtti* was made and worshipped by Mukunda/Viṣṇu," Indra replies. "If he agrees, I will give it to you." Perhaps the similarity in name has some effect. Mucukunda rushes off to the Ocean of Milk to request Viṣṇu's permission, which is granted at once. The king hastens back to Indra's heaven. By this time, Indra has thought of a last-minute stratagem for keeping the precious image in his own world. He has Viśvakarmā, artisan of the gods, produce six more Somāskanda images, exactly like the first one. These he shows to Mucukunda, one by one.

Mucukunda realizes what Indra is up to. "This isn't the one" (*ivar alar*), he says, six times. Indra reluctantly shows him the seventh icon, the one who dances on Viṣṇu's breast, his anklets ringing with incomparable Vedic notes (*uvamai tīr curutiyarava kiṇkiṇik kāl ŏru tirumūrtti*, 224). This god looks at Mucukunda's face and says, not allowing Indra to hear: "**We** are the *mūrtti* you desire" (*nī virupp'uṟṟa mūrtti yām*, 224).

An inaudible whisper, that Mucukunda at once understands. Today in Tiruvarur people say that Tyāgarāja smiled at Mucukunda at this moment. That is why they cover everything except the face of this god. Some say that Mucukunda asked the "real" Tyāgarāja to step forward, and the god agreed. In any case, as in the Nala-Damayantī story that perhaps underlies this episode, the beloved male, obscured by a series of exact replicas of himself, has a great need to be recognized and known. As Nala knows himself through Damayantī's unerring choice, thereby achieving some minimal degree of stable, continuous selfhood, so Tyāgarāja emerges fully into existence with Mucukunda's help. A certain epistemic collusion, a process of increasing certainty and connectedness, shape the successful conclusion. Damayantī's greatness

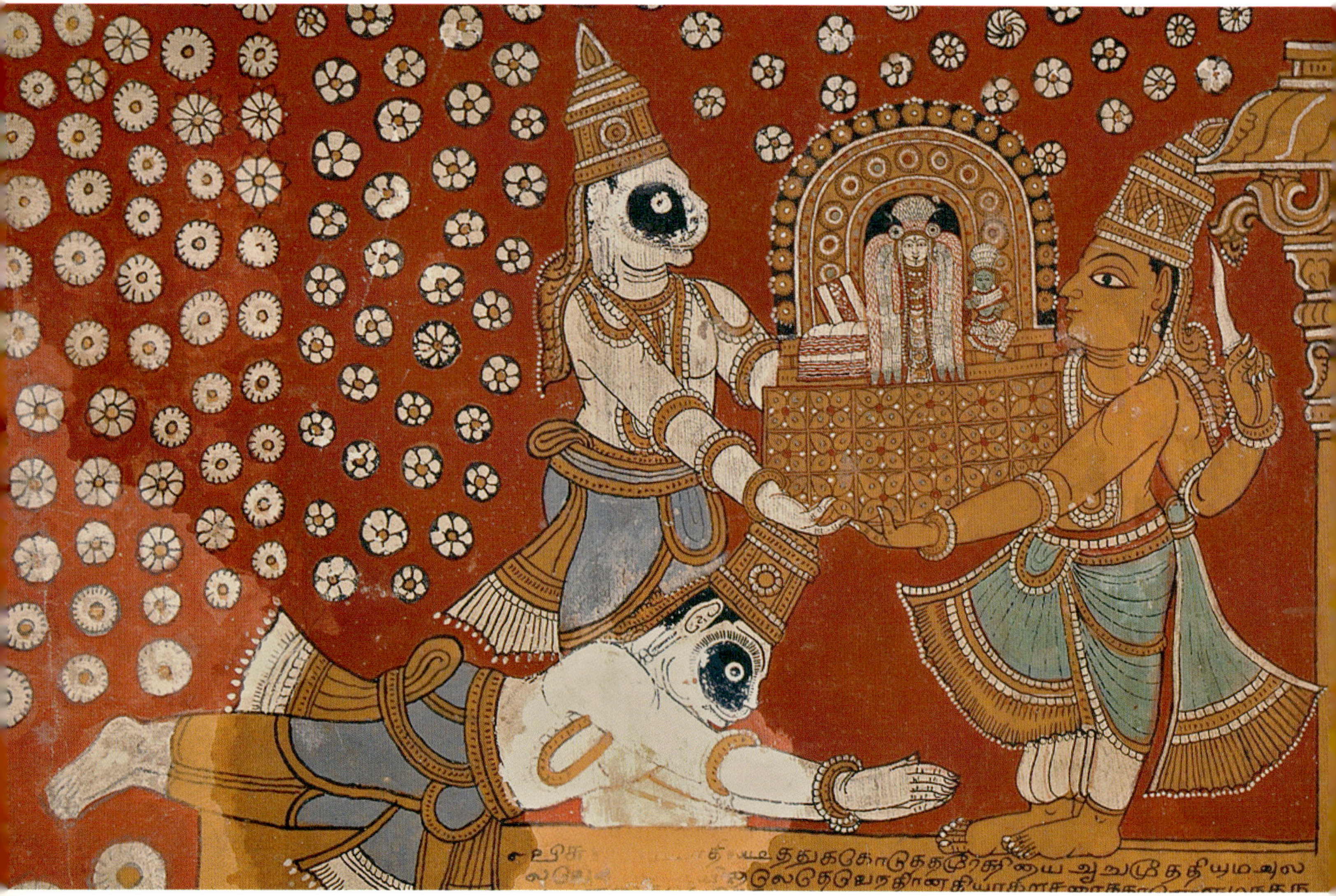

lies in choosing the human lover over other candidates who are immortal and who could perhaps make her immortal; Tyāgarāja's loving nature is revealed by his insistence on being chosen by the human devotee who will bring him down to earth. There are, it seems, distinct advantages to being human and to the world human beings inhabit. The image gives a sign, and the devotee points to what, or who, is real. The moment is an intimate one, deeply interactive and interdependent, entirely rooted in a certain level of supra-semantic, intuitive seeing and knowing.

"Give me this image," says the king. Indra transfers Tyāgarāja to Mucukunda and hands over the other six images, too. With his ministers and troops, Mucukunda takes his leave and heads for Tiruvarur. He invites Viśvakarmā to build a golden temple for the new god to the south of Valmīka-nātha, the Lord of the Anthill in the Ārūr *mūlasthāna* (233). On the Atta [= Hasta] day of Māci month, in the Vaivasvata *kalpa*, Mucukunda has Tyāgarāja installed in his new home (234).

Indra's relinquishing of the Tyāgarāja image, however necessary it may have been for *our* sake, living as we do on earth, is seen as profoundly un-innocent. To part with such a *mūrtti*, no matter what the circumstances may be, is a tragic lapse. The *Śivarahasyakhaṇḍa* (5.7.57-59) and the *Kantapurāṇam* (6.23.120-121) tell us that, because of the burden of *pāpa* inevitably consequent upon Indra's act, Indra came as an untouchable Caṇḍāla to worship Tyāgarāja at Tirurvarur. A ritual vestige of this tradition survives today in the Paṅkuṉi Uttaram festival, in which a Paṟaiyaṉ sits before the festival image on an elephant during the procession and is allowed into the temple itself, as far as the flagpole. The office of this "elephant-riding Paṟaiyaṉ" (*yānaiy eṟum pĕrum paṟaiyaṉ*) is explained orally by a version of the *svayaṃvara*-motif, in which not Mucukunda but the watchman-ancestor of today's functionary successfully identifies the Tyāgarāja icon in Indra's heaven from among the set of seven.[29] Paṟaiya integration into the main annual festival reflects a perception of the Tiruvarur community as a single whole held together by the god who maps out a habitable domain, including the interlocking boundaries of organic social space.

We should note that the *Kamalâlayacciṟappu* version of our story, altogether a much leaner, more laconic narrative, lacks the *svayaṃvara* episode entirely. Mucukunda asks Indra for Tyāgarāja and, once Viṣṇu's permission is obtained, receives the image (*kolamayam*, an unusual technical term preferred by this text) and departs for Ārūr (372-374). He installs Tyāgarāja in the Hasta *nakṣatra* during the *kṛṣṇapakṣa* of Māsi month, to the south of that Ultimate Being (*pŏruḷ*) who lives in the anthill (*puṟṟu*, 375). There are some signs that Campantamuṉivar knew and utilized his predecessor's text (or possibly both were dependent upon an earlier, common version). Both *Kantapurāṇam* and *Śivarahasyakhaṇḍa* recount Mucukunda's agonizing trial and his successful recognition of the true image. By the end of the sixteenth century, when Campantamuṉivar composed his *Tiruvārūrppurāṇam*, the *svayaṃvara* theme had clearly become canonical. Tyāgarāja revels in the recognition granted him by his royal devotee, as he will expect similar acts of identification by us, more ordinary pilgrims. We, too, make a choice, as we await his sign.

An entire canto of the *Tiruvārūrppurāṇam* is devoted to the next ritual performance: Mucukunda invites all the gods and all human kings to celebrate Tyāgarāja's procession to the Tevâciraya *maṇḍapam*, the site of our seventeenth century paintings, and thence, on a chariot fashioned by Viśvakarmā, through the streets of the town (*ulā*). This is the Paṅkuṉi Uttiram (*brahmotsavam*) festival, from the flag-hoisting on the Hasta-nakṣatra day in Māci, when Tyāgarāja was installed in his shrine, to the Uttara-nakṣatra of Paṅkuṉi.[30] On the very day of the god's installation, announcements are sent off to the furthest corners of the cosmos. Viṣṇu and Kamalā, Brahmā and Sarasvatī, Indra and Pulomajā, and the other gods and goddesses arrive together with the *dikpālas*, the sun and the moon, the asterisms, Vasus, Maruts, serpents, Mahākāli, the seven Kaṉṉiyar, rivers, sages, Rudra-gaṇas, Brahmins, Tamil kings, non-Tamil kings, and many women. Tyāgarāja receives his first *abhiṣeka* and awaits the moment when he will set off on his golden chariot for his *ulā* (*pŏṟ ratam ter meṉ maruk' ulā pota ppuri taru tiruviḻā*, 6). At the sound of the drums, Mukunda-Viṣṇu and the other gods together with the sages approach the jewel-studded *gopuram*, the entrance to the shrine. Now, with Umā, mother of the worlds, and Murukaṉ with his great lance, Śiva, in his *utsava-mūrti*, Candra-śekhara (*intu-cekaraṉ*, 44) sets off, seated on his hero's throne (*vīra-ciṅkâtaṉam*, 15), exiting the main, golden gate. There is a tremendous noise of conches, flutes, and other instruments, like the vast din at the time of the churning of the ocean. Viṣṇu, Brahmā, and Indra, with their consorts, are at his side. Famous Śaiva devotees, Agastya, Vyāghrapāda, Patañjali, and the divine sages, Sanaka and others, walk beside him. The *apsaras*, Urvaśī, Tilottamā, and others, dance in the streets before him; Tumburu and Nārada play their vīṇās; there are clouds of incense, and golden parasols, with inlaid emeralds and rubies, to hide the sun; lamps are held aloft on silver and golden pillars. King Mucukunda scatters gold in the streets, as if it were rain, a gift to poets and Brahmins. Nandin, in the very middle of the throng, keeps order with the help of his golden staff.

The procession eventually winds its way back through the *gopuram* to the *Tevâciraya-maṇḍapam* (57-58).

This is the template for the entire festival: each day Mucukunda brings the god out into the streets (*ulā vara cĕytu*, 60) on his chariot and has the proper rituals performed. On [Paṅkuṉi] Uttara day, there is a final *tirumañcaṉam*, and the immense crowd, covered in white ash and chanting *namaḥ śivāya*, takes the god back home to his shrine inside the temple (60-65).

Mucukunda has one more task to perform. He installs the other six Tyāgarāja images in their proper shrines: Nakai(kkaronam), Karayil, Kolili, Maraikkatu, Nallaru, and Vaymur. He celebrates their festivals as well (83). For the rest, for some eons, he rules the world while worshipping Tyāgarāja of the chiming anklets (*arava kiṇkiṇikkāl-amala-nāyakaṉ*)[31] and the Lord of the Anthill, the twin Tiruvarur deities, until the time comes when he reaches the almost unreachable state of release (85).

Before we take leave of this text, we should note the somewhat surprising balance built into Campantamuṉivar's narrative. Half is taken up with Mucukunda's story, culminating in the critical moment of choice, when he must identify the god and set him free. The second half is an ecstatic portrait, actually a re-enactment, of Tyāgarāja's festival procession, his true *raison d'être*, his central ritual task in Tiruvarur. Eighty-five lyrical verses carry the deity through his course to the edge of human space, then back into the depths of the temple, into his own deeper reaches of being. This movement, too, an annual cycle, is like the rhythm of breath, out into space, back into self. The temple breathes the god out into the world and breathes him back into its interior. The god breathes and is breathed, dances and is danced. This powerful rhythm moulds his presence at every moment, just as it gives shape to all music, that is, to language, hence to all awareness. One might say that Tyāgarāja's presence, and above all his active extroversion in procession, heals the arrhythmia built into our ordinary entropic perception. This relation of the god to healing sound, to breath in its universal dimension, needs to be further explored.

Ajapā and *Unmanī*

5 On one side, breathing inward, there is silence, stillness, emptiness, inactivity. On the other side, breathing out, a hint of sonar vibration, visibility, desire. We can also use the language of up and down, forward and back, heaven and earth, concealing and revealing, other and self. These appear, wrongly, as antinomies, an unfortunate by-product of our language. The god combines them without effort in his Ajapā dance, his defining mode.

It is not simple to disentangle the threads historically. One could say, with S. Ponnusamy, that at Tiruvarur, as at Cidambaram, "in the course of time the processional

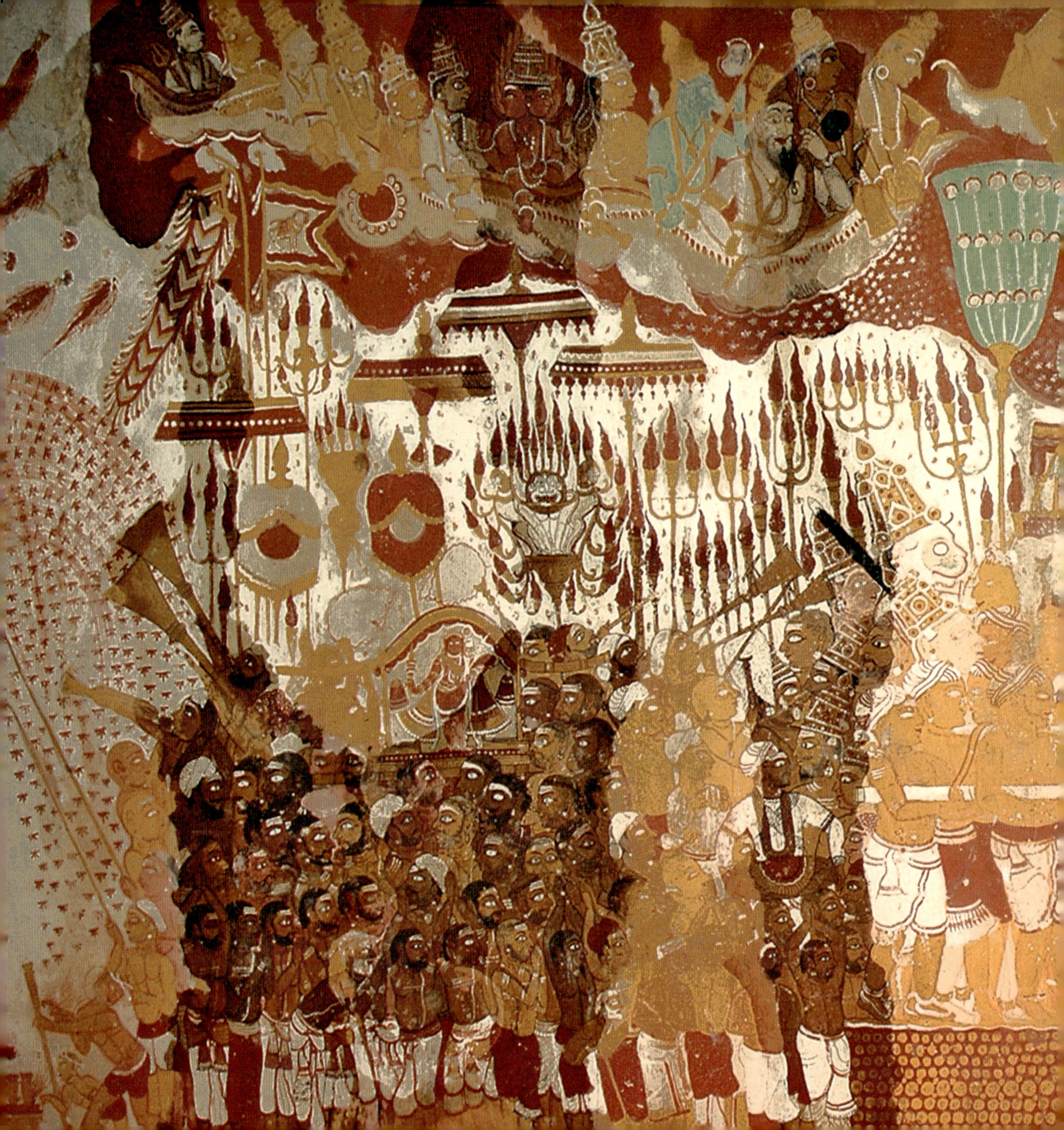

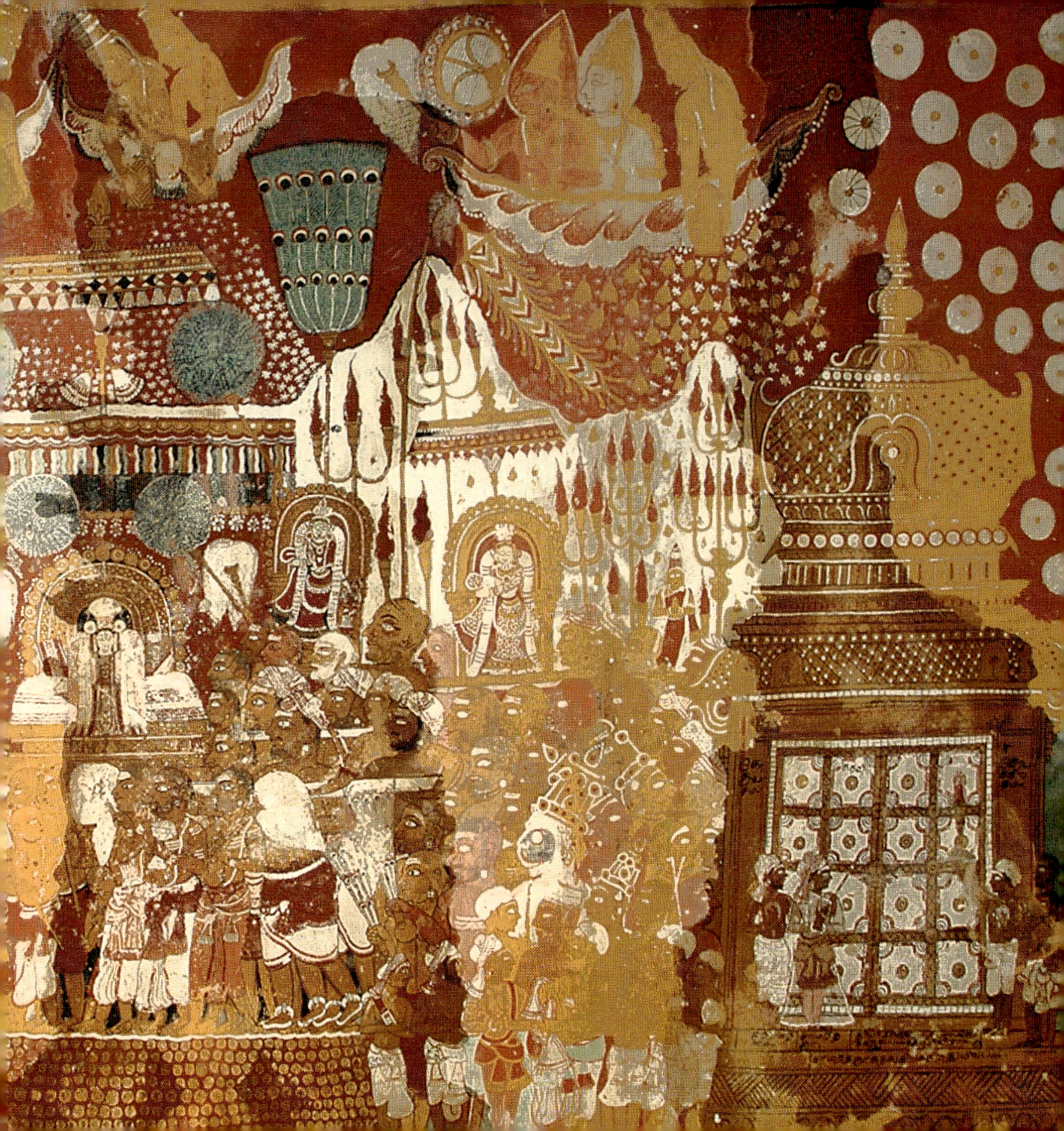

image . . . superseded the main deity in importance and popularity."[32] This assumes that Tyāgarāja was "originally" the movable festival image of Valmīkanātha.[33] But perhaps it is too much to assume. A persistent notion in the scholarly literature points to the possible presence of Viṣṇu in the closed cella behind the present Tyāgarāja *antarāla*.[34] The very existence of this empty, locked space again recalls Cidambaram and the *ākāśa-liṅga*; indeed, Cidambaram and Tiruvarur are in many ways sister-shrines, rooted in the same historical moment when the great Chola kings of the early eleventh century elevated them to a wider and more substantial public role and even modeled the new Tanjavur Bṛhadīśvara temple on the two earlier, already well-established Śaiva centers. A well-known inscription from 1030 in Tiruvarur describes the transformation of the cella, Vītiviṭaṅkar's site, from brick to stone under the aegis of Rājendra I and his beloved concubine, Naṅkai Paravai.[35] Both Rājarāja and Rājendra, and, it appears, their consorts, were devoted to Śiva as the dancer outside the *mūlasthānam* in both these shrines: Naṭarāja with his *ānanda-tāṇḍava* at Cidambaram, Vītiviṭaṅkaṉ and his *āsīna-tāṇḍava* ("Sitting Dance") in Tiruvarur.

Ponnusamy's conclusion: "In view of the association of Vishṇu with the Vīdiviṭanka concept it is probable that a figure of Vishṇu was also portrayed with the Somāskanda image. It is not known when the *garbhagṛha* [the cella behind Tyāgarāja's present seat] fell into disuse."[36] It is conceivable that the earlier form of the Tiruvarur temple complex required the presence of both great gods, Śiva and Viṣṇu, as we find them at Mamallapuram's Shore Temple, at Cidambaram, and many other ancient sites. Tyāgarāja is still offered the common Vaiṣṇava dish, *puliyora*, each day. Let us recall that the Tyāgarāja icon is said by the Tiruvarur *Purāṇa*s to have been commissioned by Viṣṇu himself; this strong assertion is unlikely to be incidental. Moreover, the Tiruvarur tradition seems to recognize that an original *Mukundârcana* ritual, linked to Viṣṇu, was eventually replaced by the *Mucukundârcana*, the liturgical rite performed today.[37] In general, the links between Tyāgarāja and a Vaiṣṇava cultic milieu are highly conspicuous.

But Mucukunda's role goes far beyond a technical, alliterative device and can be more precisely stated, at least as a working hypothesis. What we see today in Tiruvarur is a highly elaborate, strongly localized Tantric cult almost certainly drawing, again like Cidambaram, upon the *Śrī-vidyā*, and possibly coloured by a Pañcarātra reworking of the *ajapā-haṃsa* theme (see below).[38] The *Śrīcakra* is embossed on all the *viṭaṅka* images; moreover, as we shall see, this basic *Śrīvidyā yantra* reappears in surprising transformations at Tiruvarur. A recurrent tradition, not easily given to verification, also asserts that the secret *mantra* of

Tripurasundarī[39] is engraved on the Tyāgarāja icon. It seems likely that a mature, "Tantric" stage in the development of the temple was reached in the late Chola or early post-Chola centuries and culminated in an esoteric praxis documented by many sources including, with particular eloquence, the well-known *kṛtis* of Muttusvāmi Dīkṣitar (late 18th century) on Tiruvarur. By the early sixteenth century, this Tantric Tyāgarāja was firmly in place. Mucukunda, the hero of our narrative and of the painted ceiling, would then be the emblem of this profound cultural change, the royal harbinger of an esoteric structural conversion. When Mucukunda brings Tyāgarāja to Tiruvarur, he is creating a home, in effect, a stage, for a god whose body consists of *mantras* and whose consciousness is beyond the range of all conceivable linguistic form.

Mucukunda is, as we have seen, a Chola king, with an honorable place in the Chola genealogies; but nothing in the inscriptional record supports a theory of Tantric reformulation during the "high" Chola period, when the temple achieved high political visibility. More likely, the royal protagonist of cultic mutation is a retrojected image from the fourteenth and fifteenth centuries, a period of transition in which a Chola precursor could be a useful asset, as we see in several other major Tamil sites (Cidambaram, Tiruvanaikka, Tirupperur, Tirupati, etc.). On the other hand, the association of Tyāgarāja with a special form of the dance, *i.e.* the existence of a mobile, dancing deity, present in a metal icon, alongside the *mūlasthāna* god, ***does*** seem to be a Chola-period phenomenon with roots attested already in the *Tevāram patikams*. It is difficult to say, at this point, whether the dance in question is the *ajapā-naṭanam* for which Tyāgarāja is famous today.

Here are the primary elements of the mature Tantric complex of Tyāgarāja: first, as we might expect, a precise sonar presence, susceptible to further, far-reaching elaboration. Then a more articulated mantric identity; a relation to breathing, to the *haṃsa* that embodies the rhythms of breath, and to Yogic physiology; a female aspect; a geometric *yantra* and its mathematical correlates; an emphasis on human fertility or generativity. And, as we have already seen, a recurrent linkage to notions of movement (dance) and, as a derivative of movement, of space. Let us examine these elements in a synchronic overview of their mutually reinforcing, interlocking conceptual themes.

Tyāgarāja, says the *Mucukunda-sahasranāma* (416), is at the center of the stage of phonic devolution called *unmanī*.[40] We know the term (more properly *unmanā*) from the northern Śaiva tradition, in texts such as the *Yoginī-hṛdaya* (3.174): the six voids, which are also the *kalās* of the seed-syllable *Hrīṃ*, culminate (so to speak—that is, empty out) in the final void, *mahā-śūnya*, which is truth. The threshold to this final void is *unmanā*.[41] In other words, *unmanā* is the name for an extremely subtle, indeed inaudible transition within that divine process that we call "speech" or "sound." The root-syllable *Oṃ* leads the mindful practitioner through a steep ascent into these ethereal phonic potentialities: following the pronunciation of the nasal *m* one can learn to discern a resonance, issuing into silence, correlated to distinct forms of godhead and to mathematical durations. One moves from *nāda*, the sonar stuff of reality, to the end of *nāda* (*nādânta*), and then through *śakti* to the three nearly inconceivable and imperceptible levels of *vyāpinī* (the pervasive), *samanā* (still "with mind"), and, finally, *unmanā* ("out of mind").[42] If we reverse the direction, from *unmanā* "down" to *nāda* and then to the audible reproduction of the *Oṃ*, we will end up with an objectified cosmos. Of course, this linear description is rather misleading; in some sense, as with Tyāgarāja's dance, there is constant, continuous movement within simultaneity. Still, the Śaiva texts tell us that *nāda* has the duration of 1/16 of a *mātrā* (mora), that *śakti* is half of that and *vyāpinī* half as long as *śakti* (1/64 *mātrā*). *Unmanā* has no duration, since the latter is a property of the thinking mind.

One cannot "think" when one is entirely subsumed within god. *Unmanā* is a creative linguistic potentiality that pre-exists the emergence of sound itself. Being utterly empty, it is all there is. Tyāgarāja resides inside it or, in another sense, ***is*** this empty wholeness.

This should tell us something about the god's movement in and out of self. We already know that he is dancing. But we can now begin to characterize the dance more clearly. Antakakkavi tells us at the very beginning of his *Tiruvārūr ulā* (seventeenth century) that the god of Tiruvarur is "the dancer [actor] alive in the end of sound" (*nātānta meyāy naṭikkiṉṟoṉ*, couplet 2). We can begin to see what this might mean, especially in the context of Tyāgarāja's *ulā*-progression around the temple. Sound, in its most real, most subtle aspect, is classified as dance. Tirumūlar tells us in the first section of the fourth *tantra* of his esoteric masterpiece, *Tirumantiram*:

tāṇṭavamāṉa taṉiy ĕḻutt' or ĕḻutt'
āṇṭavamāṉat' aṉukkirakattŏḻil

*The unique syllable (*ĕḻuttu = akṣara*) is the Tāṇḍava dance*
*that is God's loving presence (*aṉukkirakattŏḻil*).*
*This dance stands alone, highest of all (*taṟparam*),*
a dance of pure gold. (868)

There is a tradition of commentary that identifies the "unique syllable" with the five-syllable *mantra*, *namaḥ śivāya*, although as the verse reads literally, we would be equally justified in understanding it as the *Oṃ*.[43]

In any case, this entire section goes by the name *acapai*, that is, *ajapā*, the name of Tyāgarāja's characteristic dance (*acapainaṭaṉam*) at Tiruvarur. The dance, in which the icon rises and falls in accordance with the rhythmic movement of his bearers—he is loosely tied with banana fibers to two poles and thus "appears freely to move up and down with the bearers"[44]—reproduces the vibration that generates sound out of unthinkable (*unmanā*) stillness. This is movement so subtle as to be hardly on this side of the boundary between non-existence and existence. This god is situated precisely at the site of the initial quiver within reality that gives birth to that reality and, given this situation at the point of origin of life itself, he is the deity most intimately linked with generativity *per se*. Viṣṇu is granted a living but mortal child, Manmatha, who will be burnt by Śiva and then reborn without visible body, as the direct result of fashioning and worshipping Tyāgarāja's image.

Tyāgarāja is thus a god in continuous movement classed as dance. This movement has several other, specific correlates. For one thing, the two poles to which the icon is tied are said to be the *iḍā* and *piṅgaḷā* conduits of the subtle Yogic body.[45] A cosmic metabolism replicates itself on the level of each living individual; and the primary systemic process that fuels this metabolism, on both levels, is the regular business of breathing in and breathing out. Again and again we are told by the Tamil sources from medieval Tiruvarur that Tyāgarāja's *ajapā* dance fits the rhythm of Viṣṇu's breath as he, Viṣṇu, lies at rest on the ocean of milk, with Tyāgarāja ensconced on his breast (as we can see him in the murals: see p. 25). Tyāgarāja rises with Viṣṇu's in-breath and falls with his out-breath. Breathing out, Viṣṇu exfoliates our world; breathing in, he re-absorbs it.[46] Ādiśeṣa, Viṣṇu's serpent-couch, is also breathing in and out; and this expansion and contraction, we are told, also puts Tyāgarāja into movement, as does the wave-like rising and falling of the ocean beneath them all.[47] The cosmos consists of this variously conditioned contrary movement, *pravṛtti* engagement followed by *nivṛtti* retraction. Each breath we take recapitulates the unending breathing of the universe. Since this deep, unconscious rhythm takes place at the edge of unuttered sound, to see the dancing god of Tiruvarur is to listen for the hardly audible breathing of that somewhat fictive medium we call "space."

Space is no more a given, a datum, than is time. Tyāgarāja, as we have seen, is the master of space, its creator and mapmaker who fixes its outer boundaries, who travels to its farthest limit. He inhabits this space, and retraces its borders periodically, as an ongoing pulsation that could be defined, again like time, like breathing, like movement itself, as a persistent, recurrent contraction and release.[48] In this fully

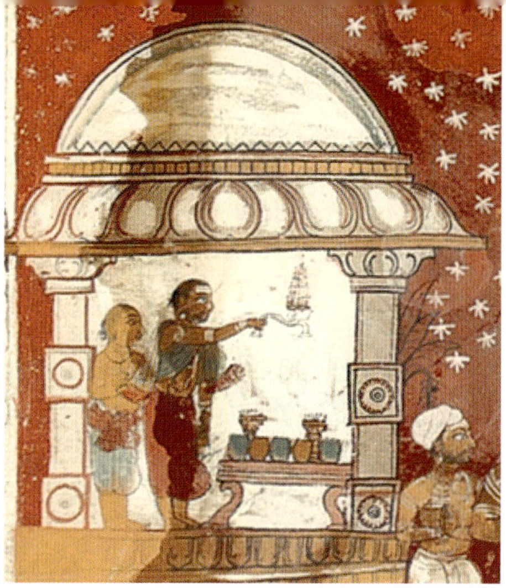

articulated Tantric cosmology, space exists only as this continuous bunching up and slackening. It is a creative, contingent ***act***, never a structural feature naively conceived to be inherent in reality. For this very reason, because it is an active movement of creative divinity, this "Tyāgarāja space" is generative in truly consequential ways. A certain tension always marks it, indeed might be said to comprise it. We can see this clearly in the fascinating retrograde vector built into the *ajapā* breath, in several distinct modes.

Take, for example, the very striking movement of the oil lamp waved in *ārati* before Tyāgarāja every evening in the *pradoṣa-pūjā*. The lamp is first whirled counterclockwise, a half circuit and then down the middle of the icon—for Ambāḷ and the son, Murukaṉ, then in three to four clockwise revolutions. The names of Śiva's five faces are recited backwards, from Aghora to Sadyojāta, the reverse of the standard order. One might see in this ritual a distant memory of the initial tension between Śiva as a solitary, holistic male and Śiva as Somāskanda-mūrti, a family deity complete with wife and son. We should recall that the Mucukunda story begins with just this problem, with Viṣṇu's worship of Śiva in the first (barren) mode and then his graduation, as a result of Pārvatī's curse, into the second (fertile) mode. The *ārati* lamp offers us a vision of both possible forms. The priest applies ash to the god in the medium of *ākāśa*, open space, which is also the domain of sound, *nāda* or *nādânta*. If we want to actualize the *nāda*, even pushing it over the brink of audibility without losing the standard modular features of this emergence out of silent potentiality into objectified vibration, we can now recite the syllable *Oṃ*, but note that along with its descent into an unavoidable linear sequentiality, this pregnant condensation of the *nāda* actually reverses the direction that would normally lead to emergence. *Oṃ* uttered, as it were, from left to right (*a* + *u* + *ṃ* + the subtle echoes and vibrations ending in silence), moves the speaker/listener backward or upward toward that *unmanā* non-moment in which sound itself goes still and thus achieves truth. We have already seen that to follow this route is, in one reading, to reconstitute the god's *ajapā* dance.

The *praṇava-mantra Oṃ* has another name intimately associated with Tyāgarāja in Tiruvarur: this syllable at once embodies and reverses, syntactically and semantically, the ancient Upaniṣadic utterance known as *haṃsa*, the "goose" flying over the watery void. A normative syntax would read *so 'ham [asmi]*,[49] "I am," or "I am he," that is, the "I" is equated to that divine whole. This is not the place to trace the long history of this utterance in the classical sources, but that Tyāgarāja is the primordial *haṃsa* is a commonplace of the Tiruvarur texts, as Ghose has beautifully shown.[50] Muttusvāmi Dīkṣitar sings to Hāṭakeśvara-Śiva at Tiruvarur, that is, the early, fixed deity whom Tyāgarāja activates by external movement,[51] as *haṃsa-rūpa cid-vilāsa*, "the play of awareness shaped as the goose." Once the identification of Tyāgarāja with the *haṃsa* is in place, a whole world of Tantric metaphysics can be invoked, combining Yogic physiology and cosmology, *prāṇâyāma*, the praxis of awakening the Kuṇḍalinī and, at the base of all of these, a theory of sonar or phonematic cosmogony and its potential soteriological reversal.[52] Tiruvarur is thus not only the site where sound graduates from latency into manifest audibility but also the "root *cakra*" (*mūlâdhāra*) in a set of seven *cakra*-shrines. It also provides, as we have seen, the primary module of God's ongoing dance of inhalation-exhalation, a creative pulsation that seems to operate constantly, perhaps simultaneously, in two contrasting directions, into the world and back into the near-silent, dormant self.

We could also say that the great temple at Tiruvarur has organized itself so as to enable an ascent, from the *mūlâdhāra* to the *brahma-randhra*, from the dispersal of breathing out to the re-integration of breathing in, from space as contraction or constriction to space as release, from the stasis or paralysis of objectification to the dance of de-objectification, and from the semantic debris that weighs so heavily upon externalized speech to the pure expressivity of pre-audible sound that begins vibrating somewhere beyond the mind. Such a cultic organization maximizes the generative, fertilizing potential of the godhead conceived as having a body made of *mantras*[53] and, therefore, as being endowed with a miraculous beauty. Conceptually (but not necessarily historically), such a deity must actually ***precede*** the stationary *mūlasthānam* god, Valmīka-nātha, who may himself be an externalization or objectification of the dancing, generative pulsation that precedes space and time. On the other hand, such a deity will naturally establish very intimate links with the Tantric goddess, Kamalâmpāḷ, whose geometric or mathematical condensation (another pragmatic model) is imprinted on Tyāgarāja's mantric body. By the time of Muttusvāmi Dīkṣitar in the late eighteenth century, this geometric *yantra* has become capable of being re-created not visually but rather aurally, in the sound-patterns of this composer's famous *Navâvaraṇa kṛtis*, an audible diagram for materializing the goddess through both musical and grammatical devices (the Sanskrit case-endings). It is in this sense that Tyāgarāja, too, is identified at Tiruvarur and elsewhere (notably Tiruvorriyur) as a grammarian, *draviḍa-vyākaraṇa-guru*;[54] the god oversees a grammaticalized cosmos at work in both mantric and musical domains (but he may also, like Murukaṉ, have a special relation to Tamil grammar per se). Both Tyāgarāja and Kamalâmpāḷ are thus entirely fashioned out of sound, although the former deliberately straddles the transition toward audible pulsation while the latter fully incorporates all the stages and modes of speech, from the highest, least accessible (*parā*) to the lowest (*vaikharī*). Kamalâmbikā, according to Muttusvāmi Dīkṣitar, is *parâdi-vāg-devatā-rūpa-vāsinī*, "embodying the forms of the goddess of speech, beginning with *parā*," as well as *hrīṃ-kāra-suśarīriṇī*, "embodied in the mantra *hrīṃ*."[55]

This matter of the transition – from one existential state to another; more specifically, from a divinity at home in the farthest reaches of the cosmos to a god who has chosen a particular terrestrial residence – lies at the heart of the Mucukunda story and of its stunning pictorial presentation on the Tevâciraya Maṇḍapa. In a strict historical sense, Mucukunda emblematically focuses the post-Chola transition toward the mature Tantric cult we have been exploring. Thematically, he shows us the very human possibility of bringing God down to earth by virtue of a powerful inner relatedness to this deity, the gift of hearing and seeing him when others cannot do so – or, differently stated, the gift of recognizing him in the midst of his ersatz replicas and thus of making a choice. Real beauty, such as Tyāgarāja's, is always amenable to such moments of choice, just as it very often demands such acts of unexpected, intimate recognition. In a way, these moments and these acts define the human being and underlie any serious claim to kingship. By the same token, it is far from trivial or accidental that Mucukunda deliberately preserves his monkey's face. We might restate the challenge implicit in this remarkable story of cultic origins in terms proper to its final, most elaborated metaphysical mode: Who, what kind of being, and under what special conditions, where, and to what potential effect, is capable of hearing the inaudible murmur that is the sign of god's deepest intent?

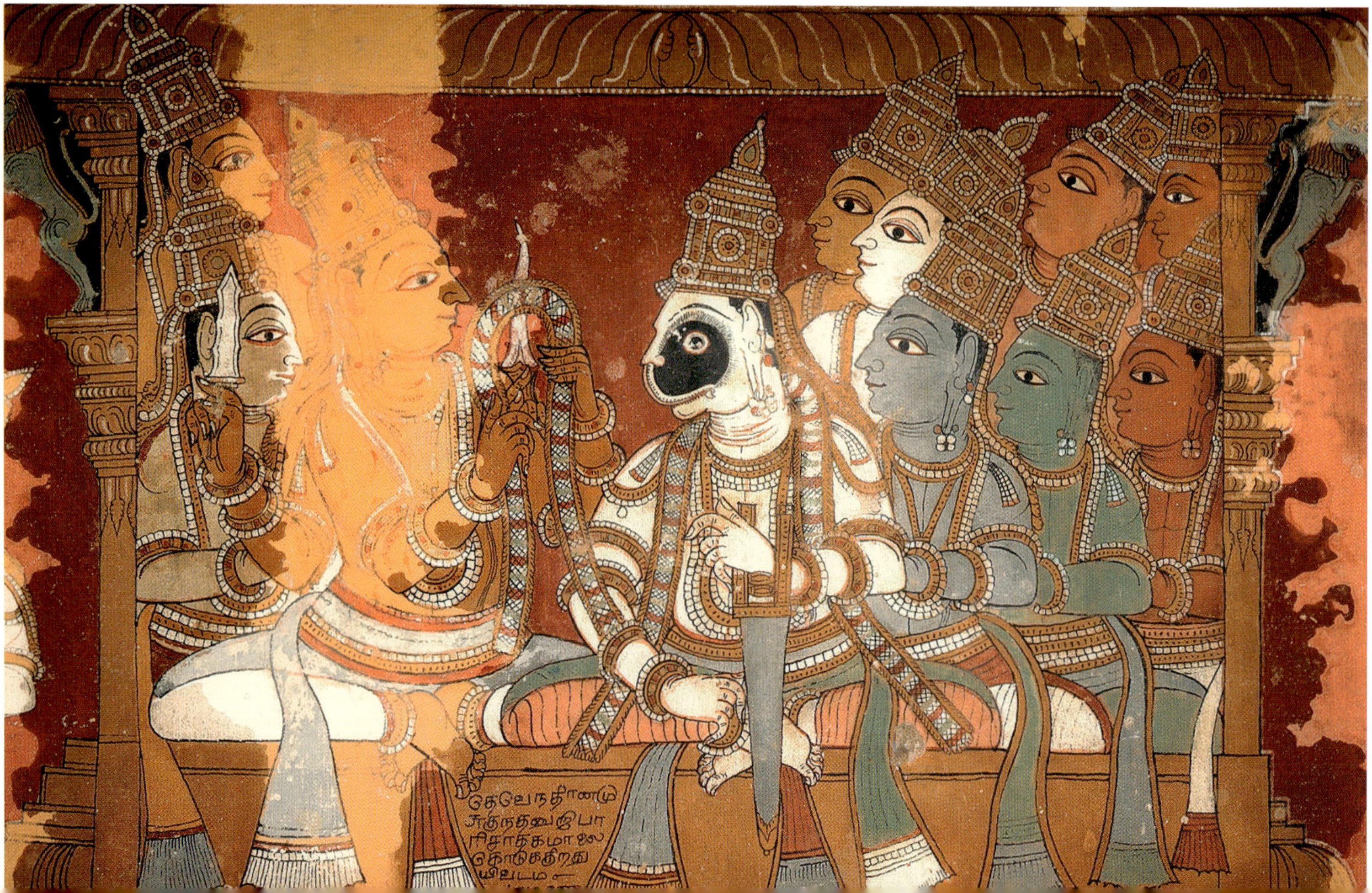

R E F E R E N C E S

[1] The *Tevāram* poet Tiruñāṉacampantar is the first to name the Tiruvarur consort-goddess Alliyaṅkotai, "with lilies in her hair" (1.105.9), equivalent to Nilotpalâmbāḷ.

[2] Thus in the *ulā*: see D. Shulman, *The King and the Clown in South Indian Myth and Poetry* (Princeton: Princeton University Press, 1985), 312-24; and Blake Wentworth's forthcoming Ph.D. dissertation on the *ulā*, University of Chicago. Rajeshwari Ghose, *The Tyagaraja Cult in Tamilnadu: A Study in Conflict and Accomodation* (Delhi: Motilal Banarsidass, 1996), 31, believes this is the context of these verses.

[3] A. Kandiah, "A Critical Study of Early Tamil Śaiva Bhakti Literature, with special reference to Tevāram," Ph.D. dissertation, University of London, 1973; and see F. Hardy, *Viraha-bhakti: The Early History of Kṛṣṇa Devotion in South India* (Delhi: Oxford University Press, 1983), 315-64.

[4] See *Madras Tamil Lexicon*, s.v.

[5] For other suggestions, see Ghose, 30-31.

[6] *Ibid.*, 32.

[7] SII 2:1; see survey of the epigraphical materials by Ghose, 32-38.

[8] The list is well-known; see *Tiruvārūr ulā* of Antakakkavi, edited with with notes by U. Ve. Caminataiyar (Madurai: Tamilccaṅka muttirācālai, 1905), 25-26.

[9] My thanks to M.C. Kanakaiah, private conversation, April 2006.

[10] *Bhīma-khaṇḍamu* of Śrīnātha (Madras: Kottapalli Venkata Padmanabha Sastri, 1901), 3.212.

[11] See translation by Velcheru Narayana Rao and David Shulman, *A Lover's Guide to Warangal: The Krīḍâbhirāmamu of Vinukŏṇḍa Vallabharāya* (Delhi: Permanent Black, 2002), pp. 50, 58.

[12] *Ibid.*, note 40.

[13] Ghose, 30.

[14] Of the seven *viṭaṅkas*, only the Tyāgarāja of Tiruvarur has this throne.

[15] My thanks to S. Gurumurthy for discussing this; see also *Civamañcari, Tiyākarājariṉ ciṟappukaḷ*, 458-60.

[16] *Ibid.*, 458.

[17] *Viṣṇu-purāṇa* 5.23-24. Cf. *Harivaṃśa* 2.58.43-67.

[18] *Mahābhārata* (BORI edition) 12.75.

[19] *Kulottuṅkacolaṉ ulā* 7-8; *Irācarācaṉ ulā* 140; *Vikkiramacolaṉ ulā* 12.

[20] Ghose has discussed this interesting version at pp. 79-89.

[21] See *Śrīskāndamahāpurāṇa* [= *Śiva-rahasya-khaṇḍa*], edited by Ceṅkālipuram Aṉantarāma Dīkṣitar (Salem, n. d.), 5.6.1-62; *Kantapurāṇam* 6.23.24-39.

[22] *Tirupperūrppurāṇam* of Kacciyappamuṉivar (Madras: Sriranjani Press, 1884), 16-17; *Tirimūrttimalaippurāṇavacanam* of Aruṇâcala Kavuṇṭar (Madras: 1936), 1.

[23] On these dates, and more detailed discussion of the two texts, see Ghose, 82-86. I have used the edition edited by Cu. Cuvaminata Tecikar (Madras: Comacuntara Mutaliyar, 1894).

[24] See discussion of these works by Ghose, 86; D. Shulman, *Tamil Temple Myths* (Princeton: Princeton University Press, 1980), 31-32.

[25] The inscriptions to the Tiruvarur murals, however, tell us that Mucukunda's capital was Ayodhyā in Kośala.

[26] *Kamalâlayacciṟappu* of Maṟaiñāṉacampanta Muṉivar (Tiruvanmiyur: U. Ve. Caminataiyar Library, 1961), 353 tells us that Viṣṇu ordered Viśvakarmā (*imaiyor kammiyaṉ*) to produce the triple image (*māyam*), according to âgamic prescriptions.

[27] *yoka naṟ ṟuyil kōṇṭ' uṟai kaṭavu' ṇeṭṭ'uyirpp' acaivāl aṉṉāṉ/ ākamīt' acaint'āṭiyey amarntaṉaṉ cantira-moli* (62).

[28] *Kamalâlayacciṟappu* 368 gives the name.

[29] The very beautiful, rather playful text was collected by Ghose, 226-227. Here the sign given by the god is a small grasshopper, *piḷḷaippūcci*, held above the true icon.

[30] It seems that originally the Spring Festival, *vasantotsavam* , immediately followed Paṅkuṉi Uttaram; it is now a ten-day ritual in the month of Cittirai, in the hot season. Nearly a third of the painted murals depict Tyāgarāja's *ulā* in what is perhaps a combined or continuous Paṅkuṉi Uttaram and Vasantotsava, in line with the original ritual cycle. See Ca. Taṇṭapāṇi Tecikar, *Tiruvārūr* (Tarumapuram: Tarumapura Ātīṉam, 1949), 75.

[31] This is perhaps Campantamuṉivar's favorite epithet for Tyāgarāja.

[32] S. Ponnusamy, *Sri Thyagaraja Temple, Thiruvarur* (Madras: Tamilnadu State Department of Archaeology, 1972), 24.

[33] *Ibid.* 23.

[34] See *ibid.* 26; Ghose, 28, 320; D. Shulman, "On the Prehistory of Tyāgarāja-Śiva at Tiruvārūr," *Art and Archaeology Research Papers* 13 (1978), 55-58.

[35] 680 of 1919; Ponnusamy, 26 and 33-34.

[36] Ponnusamy, 26.

[37] The local tradition states that because Viṣṇu-Mukunda used to chant the *sahasra-nāma* here, the Tiruvarur liturgy was known as *Mukundârccana*. Mukunda is also present in the inscriptions that accompany the Mucukunda murals.

[38] See Ghose 119; this highly speculative thesis requires serious study.

[39] See D. Shulman, "How to Make a Goddess through Visible Sounds," in Sergio La Porta and D. Shulman (eds.), *The Poetics of Grammar and the Metaphysics of Sound and Sign* (Leiden: Brill, in press); *Civamañcari*, 465.

[40] Ghose, 110.

[41] See A. Padoux, *Vāc: The Concept of the Word in Select Hindu Tantras* (Albany: SUNY Press, 1990), 96.

[42] Ibid, 94-95, 404-407.

[43] *Tirumantiram* of Tirumūlar, with commentary of Pa. Irāmanāta Piḷḷai (Tirunelveli and Madras: South India Saiva Siddhanta Works Publishing Society, 1942), 868, 883.

[44] Ghose, 125.

[45] *Ibid.*

[46] See Wendy Doniger, "Inside and Outside the Mouth of God: The Boundary between Myth and Reality," *Daedalus* 109, 2 (1980), 93-125; Don Handelman and D. Shulman, *God Inside Out: Śiva's Game of Dice* (New York: Oxford University Press, 1997), 47-48; *idem*, *Śiva in the Forest of Pines: An Essay on Sorcery and Self-Knowledge* (Delhi: Oxford University Press, 2004), 47, 65, 83.

[47] *Civamañcari*, 476.

[48] On time as obstruction and release, see Bhartṛhari, *Vākya-padīya*, *Kāla-samuddeśa* 4; D. Shulman, "Waking Aja", in press.

[49] *Bṛhadāraṇyaka Upaniṣad* 1.4.1.

[50] Ghose, 100ff.

[51] This Hāṭakeśvara, today a cave-like underground shrine within the temple, is historically linked to Hāṭakeśvara in Gujarat; the Tiruvarur *purāṇas* describe a transition from Hāṭakeśvara to Valmīka-nātha, the *mūlasthānam*. See Ponnusamy, 7.

[52] In the light of these assertions, we can perhaps understand a little more deeply the possible meaning of the rāga *Haṃsa-dhvani*, "the sound of the goose," said to have been invented at Tiruvarur by the father of Muttusvāmi Dīkṣitar, Rāmasvāmi Dīkṣitar, who may have initiated his son into the *Śrī-vidyā*.

[53] See *Tirumantiram* 880: *irukkiṉṟa mantirañ civaṉ tirumeṉi*.

[54] See Ghose 109. Tyāgarāja is specifically a **Tamil** grammarian, a natural extension of his localization in the Tamil cultural milieu.

[55] "Śrīkamalâmbikāyām": *Śrī muttusvāmi dīkṣita kṛti maṇidīpika* (Tenali, n.d.), 182.

The Paintings

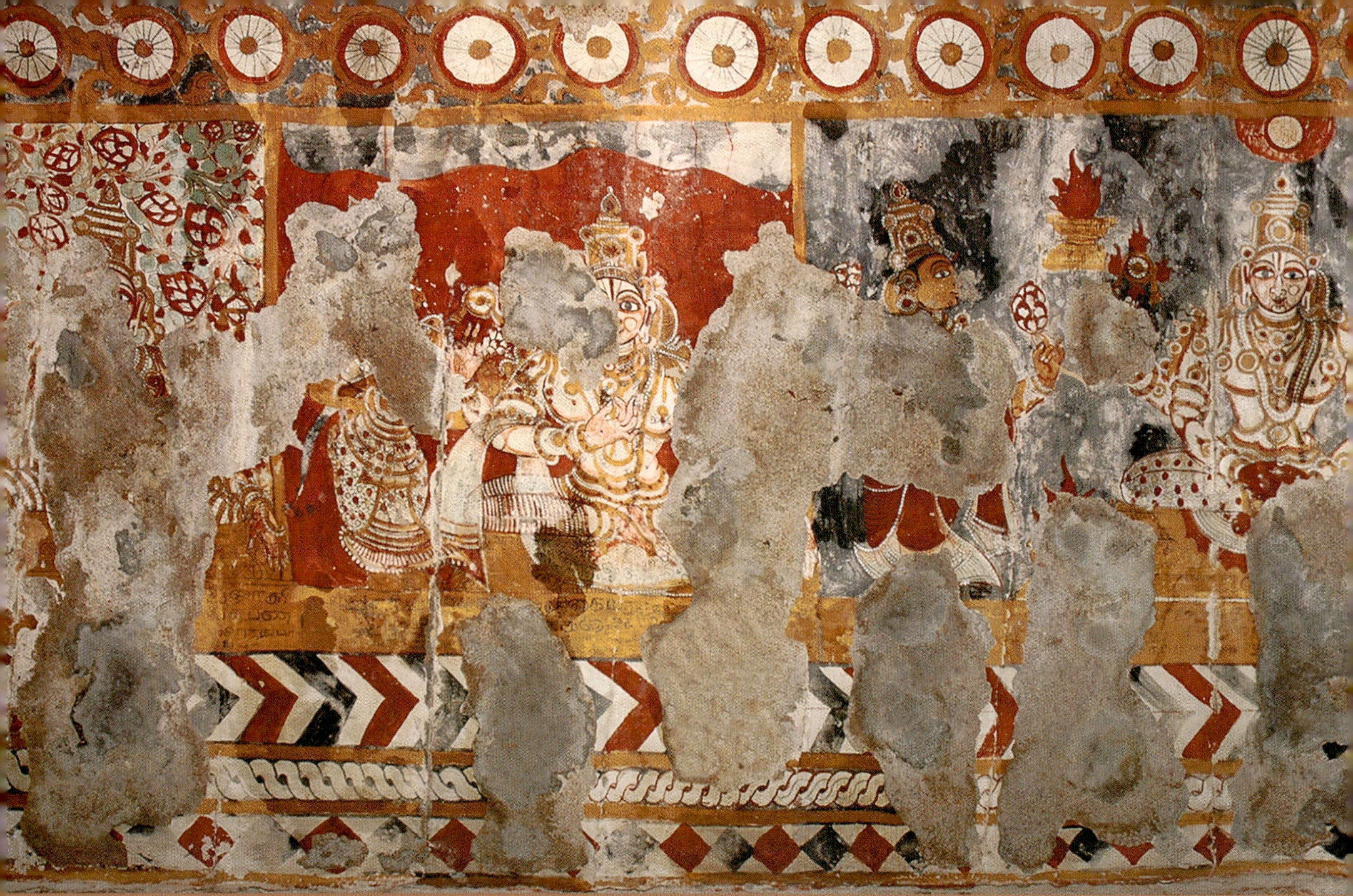

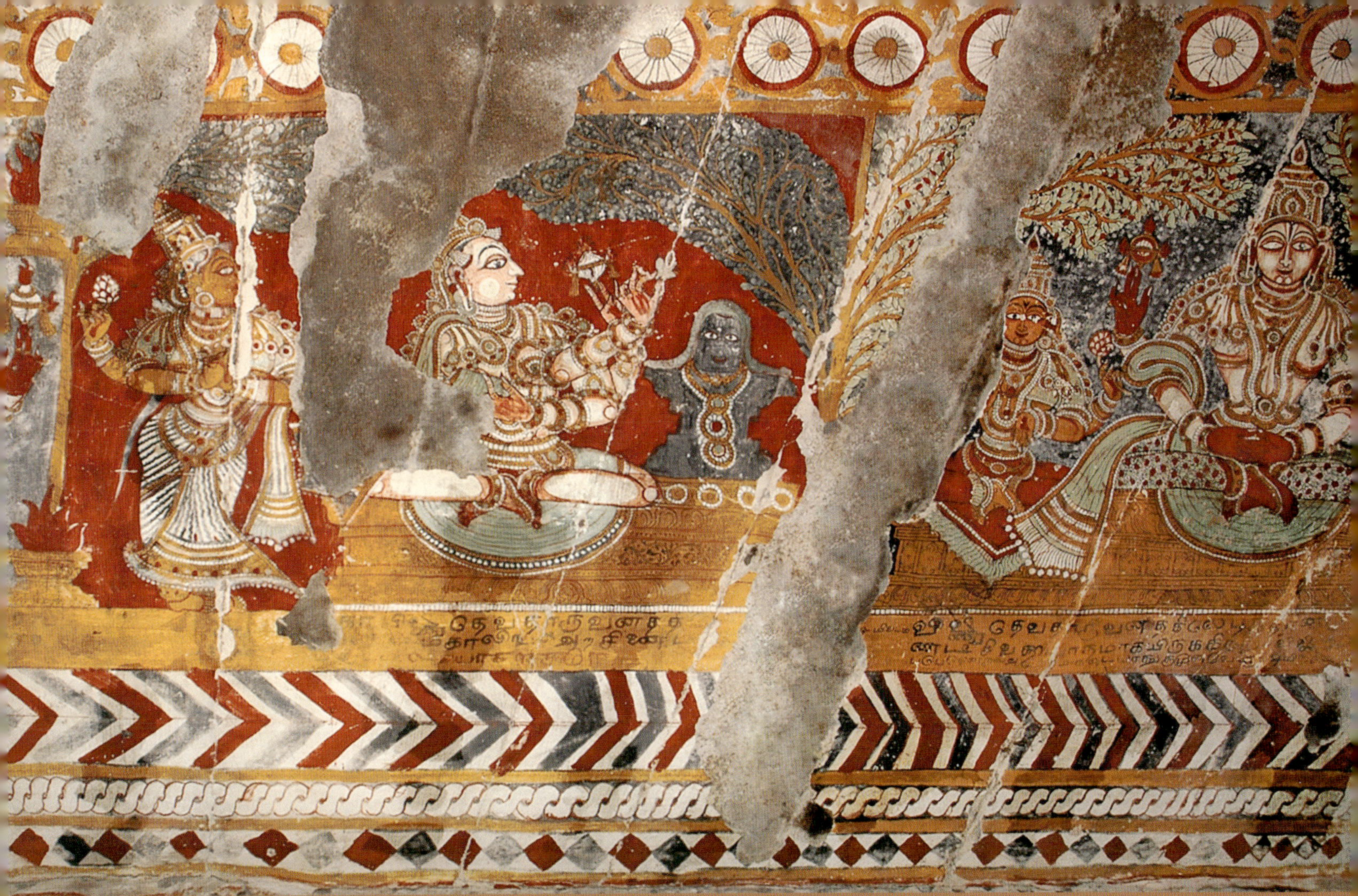

Panel 1-2, from right to left:

- *Viṣṇu meditates on Śiva in the Forest of Pines in order to be blessed with a son.*
- *Viṣṇu worships the* linga *in the Forest of Pines.*

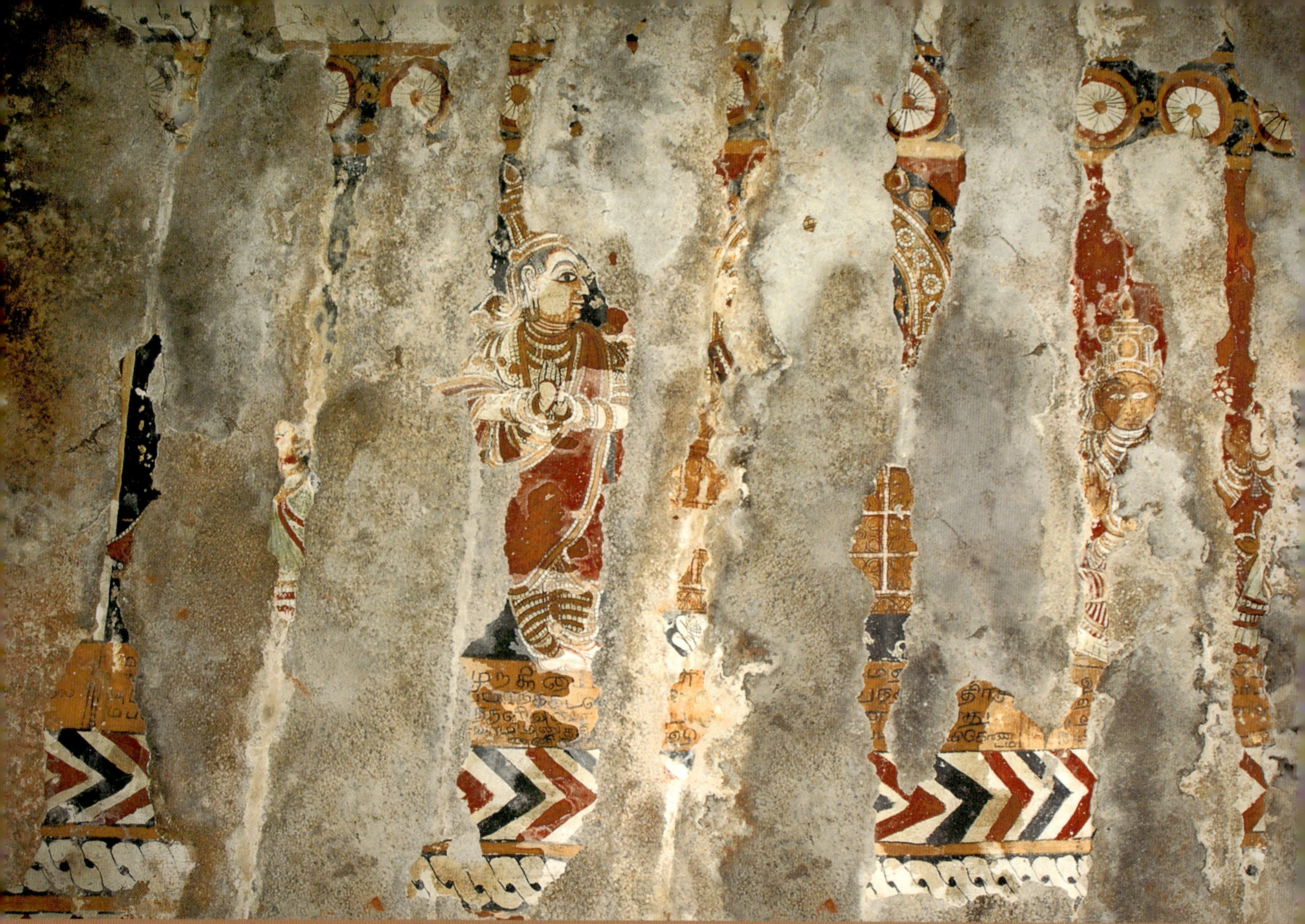

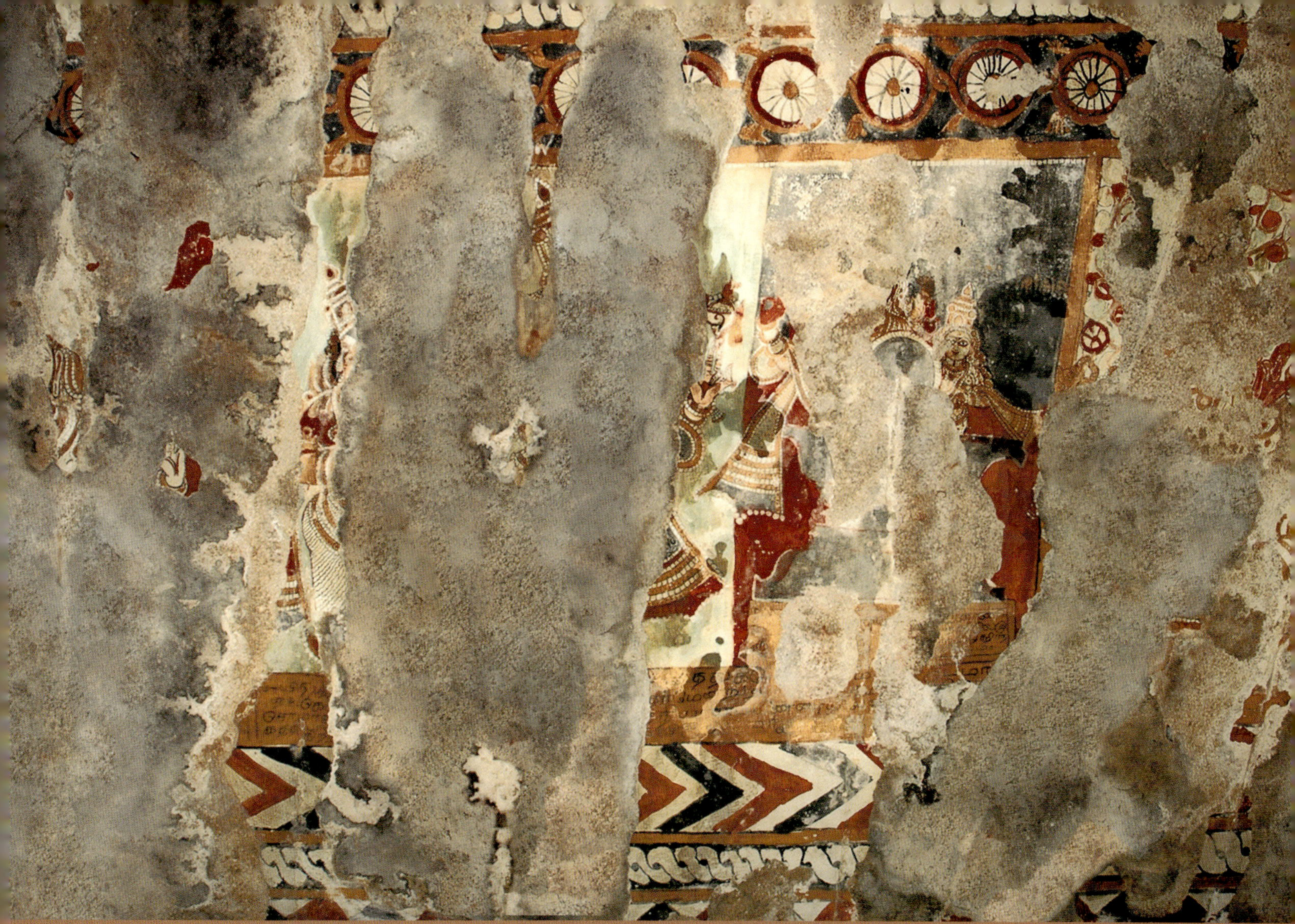

Panel 3-4, from right to left:

- *Śiva grants Viṣṇu a son. [Pārvatī curses the son to die.] Viśvakarmā makes the Somāskanda image of Tyāgarāja.*
- *The first worship of the Tyāgarāja image.*

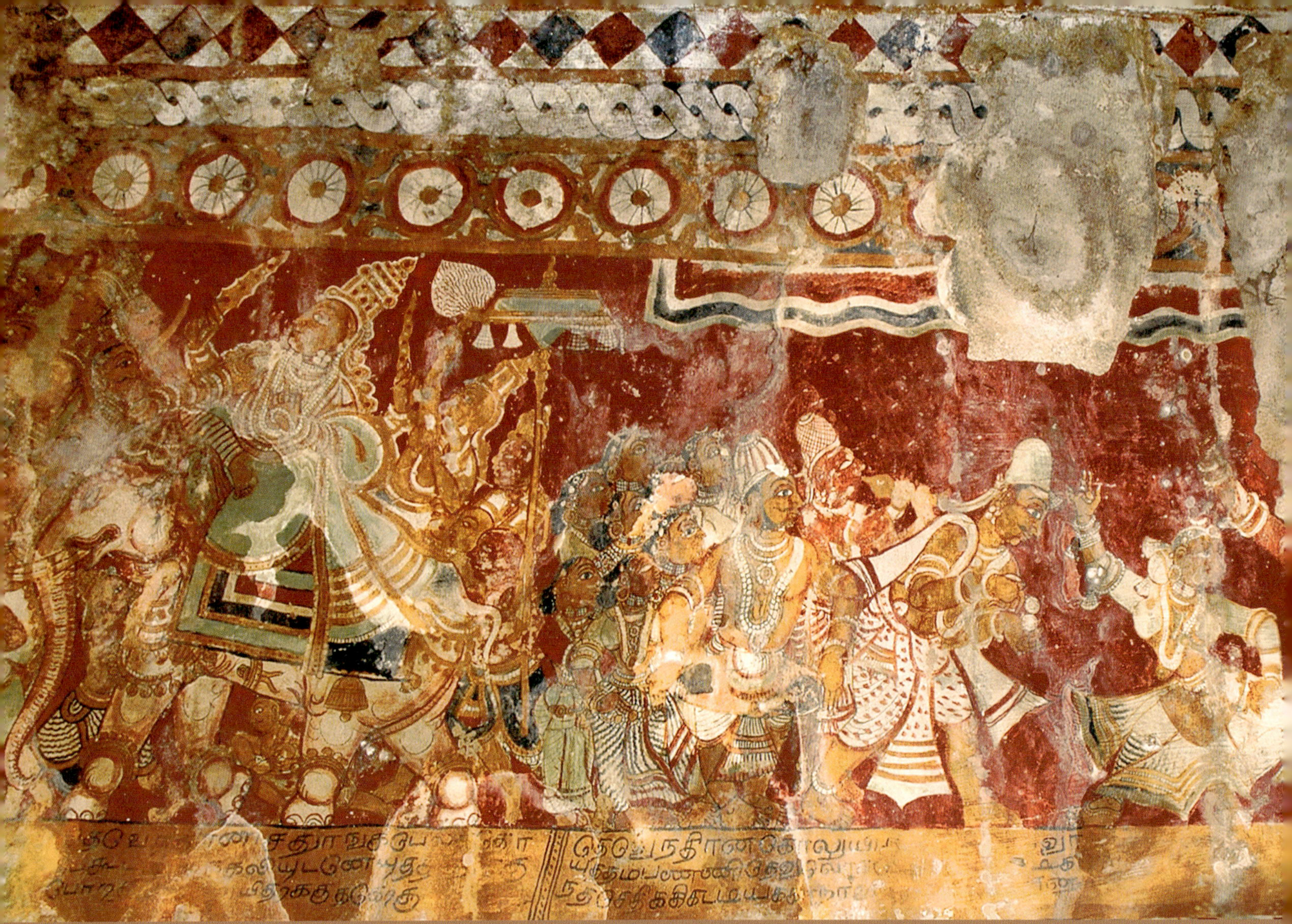

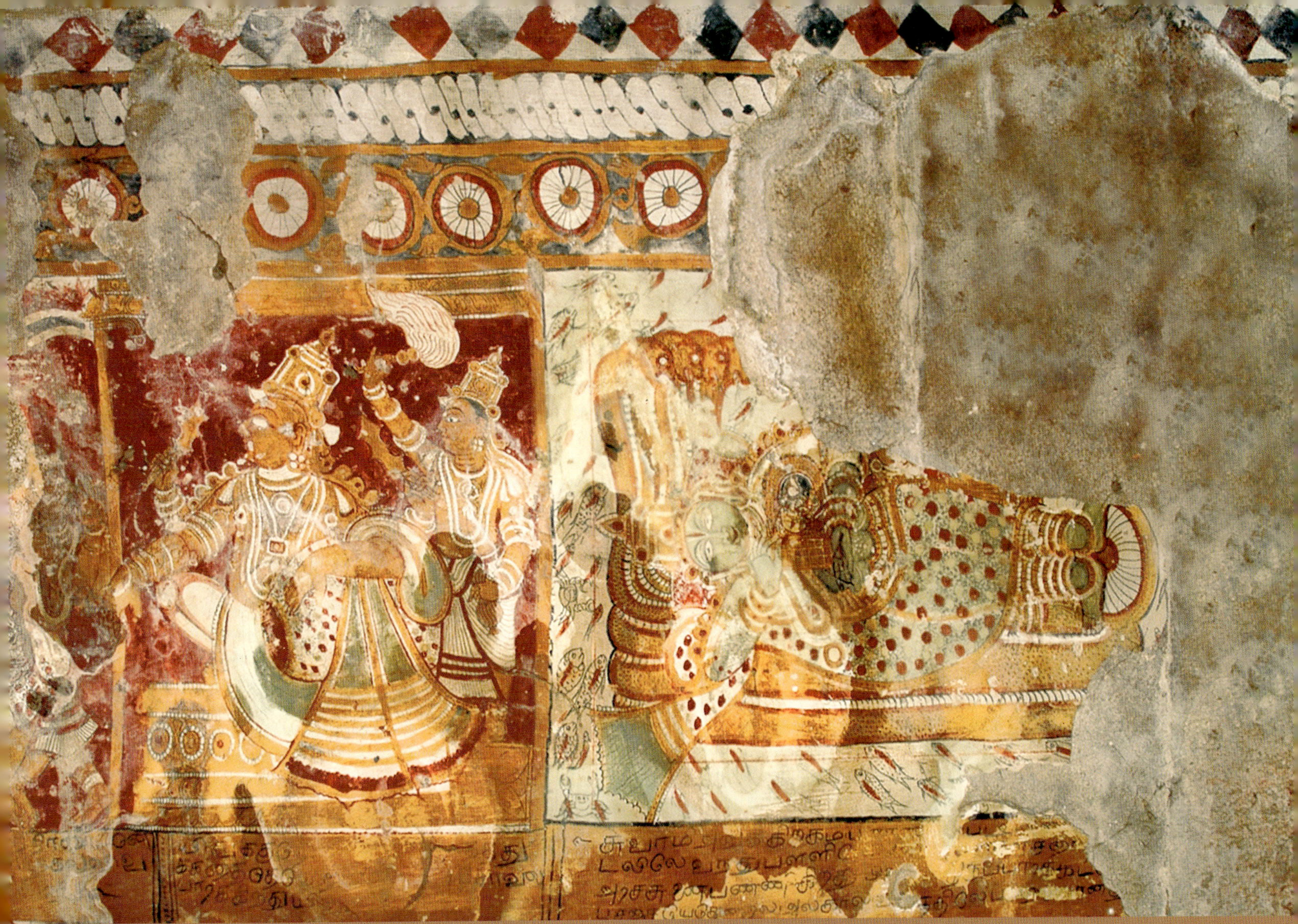

Panel 5-6, from right to left:

- *Viṣṇu worships Tyāgarāja, resting on his breast, while lying on Ādiśeṣa on the Ocean of Milk.*
- *Indra in his court.*
- *Indra watching dancers and musicians. News arrives of the demon Vārkali's threat to the world of the gods.*
- *Left: Indra sets off with his army for war.*

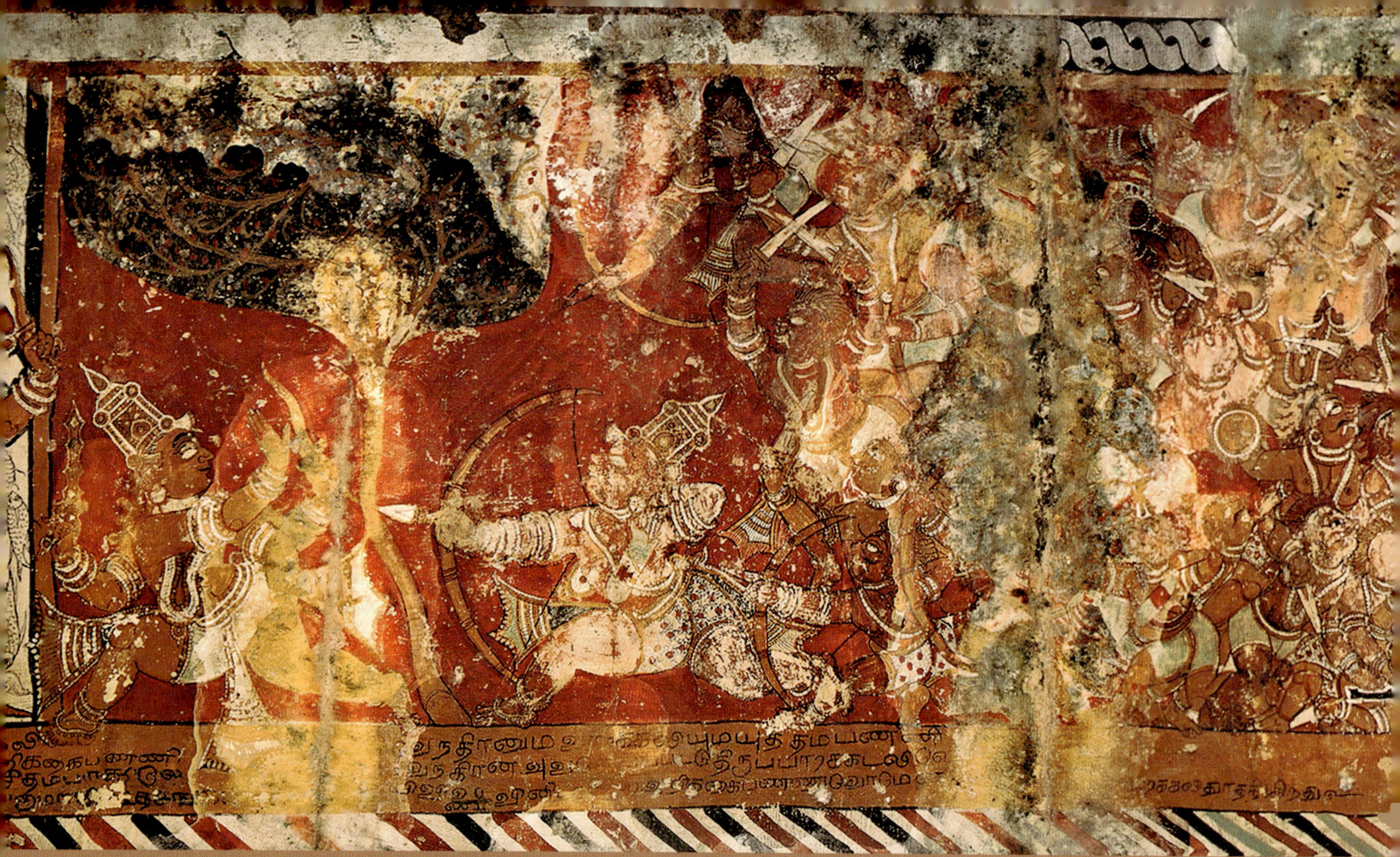

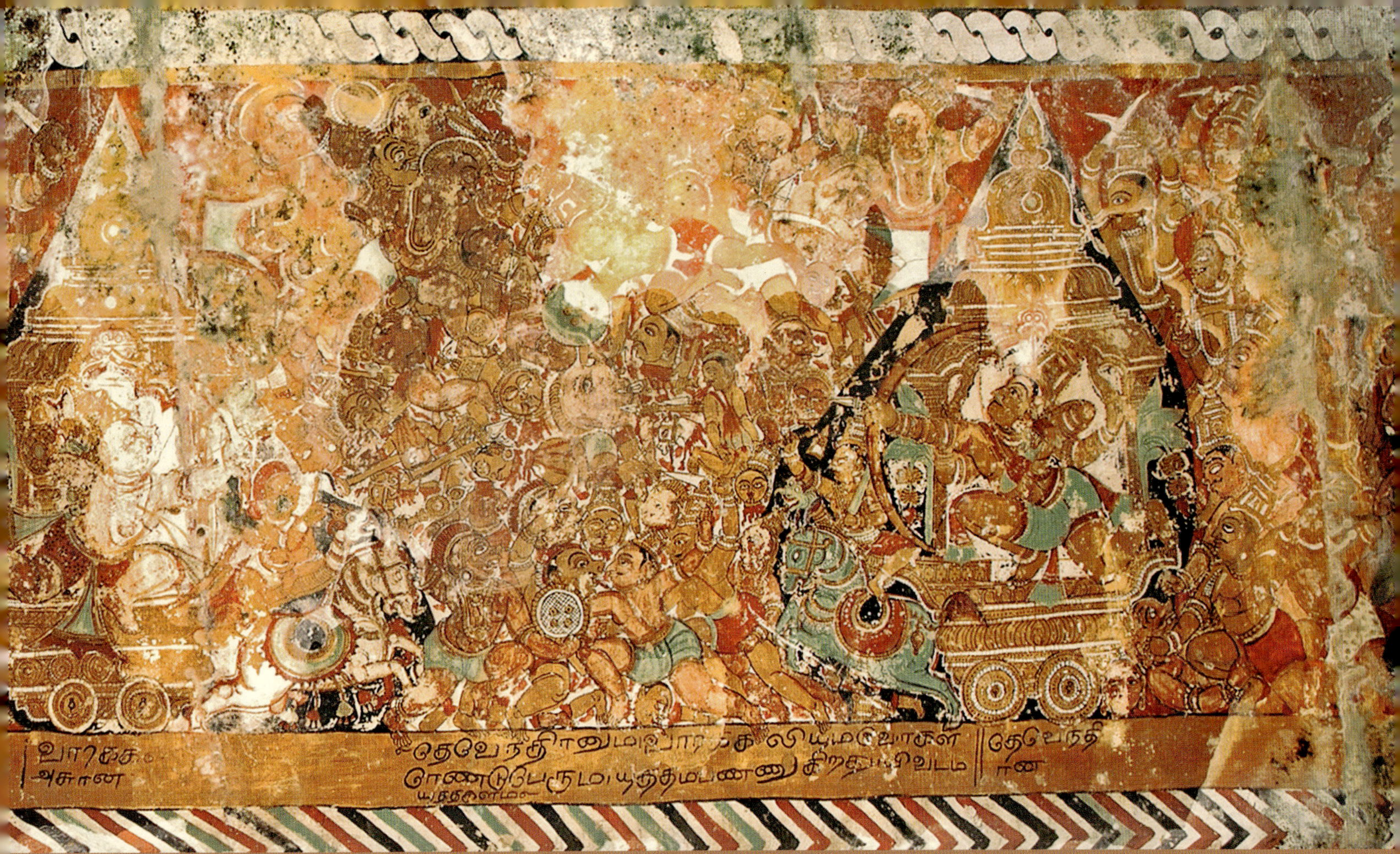

Panel 7-8, from right to left:

- *Battle of Indra and Vārkali. Vārkali defeats Indra and drives him off the battlefield.*
- *Indra's flight from the battlefield.*

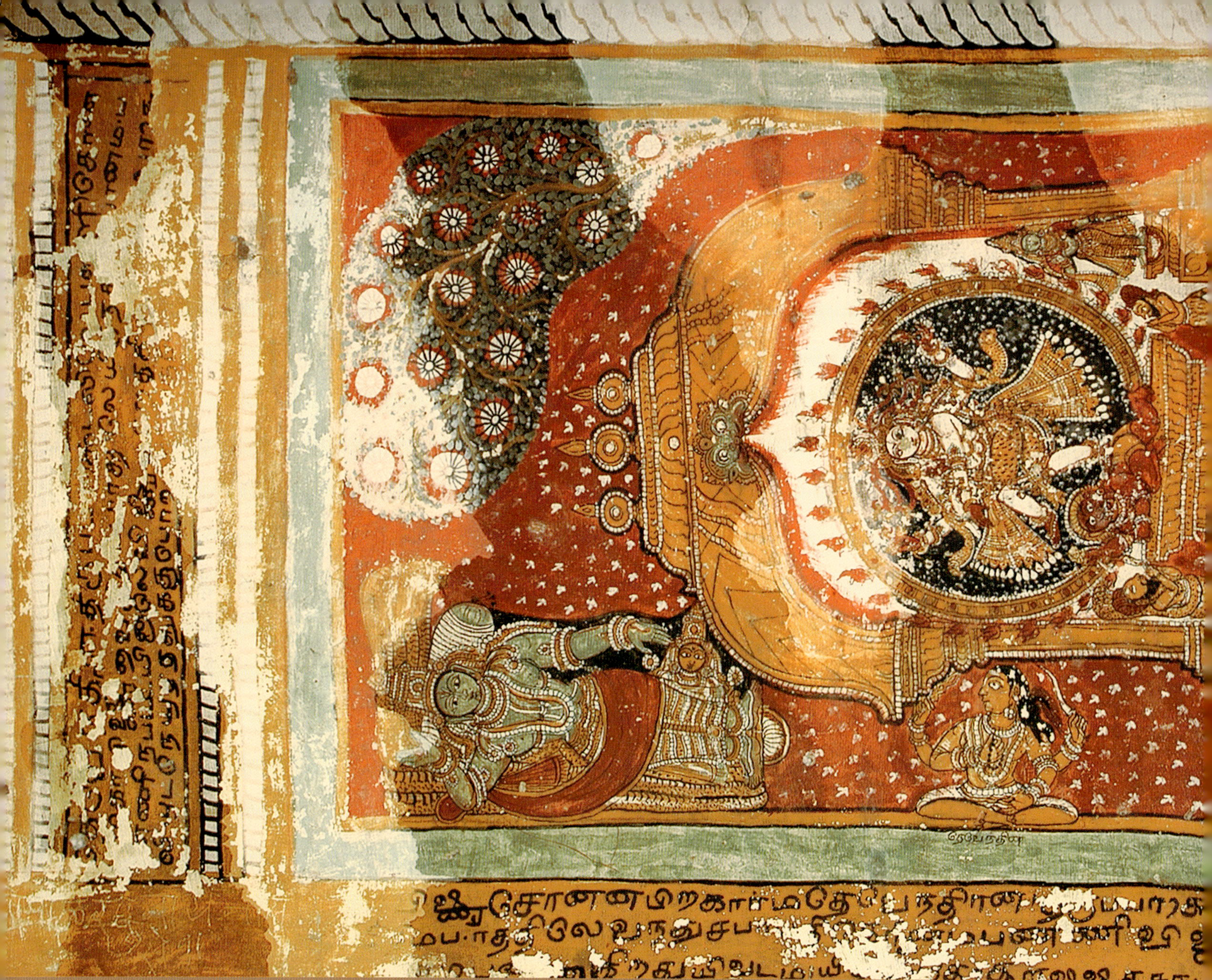

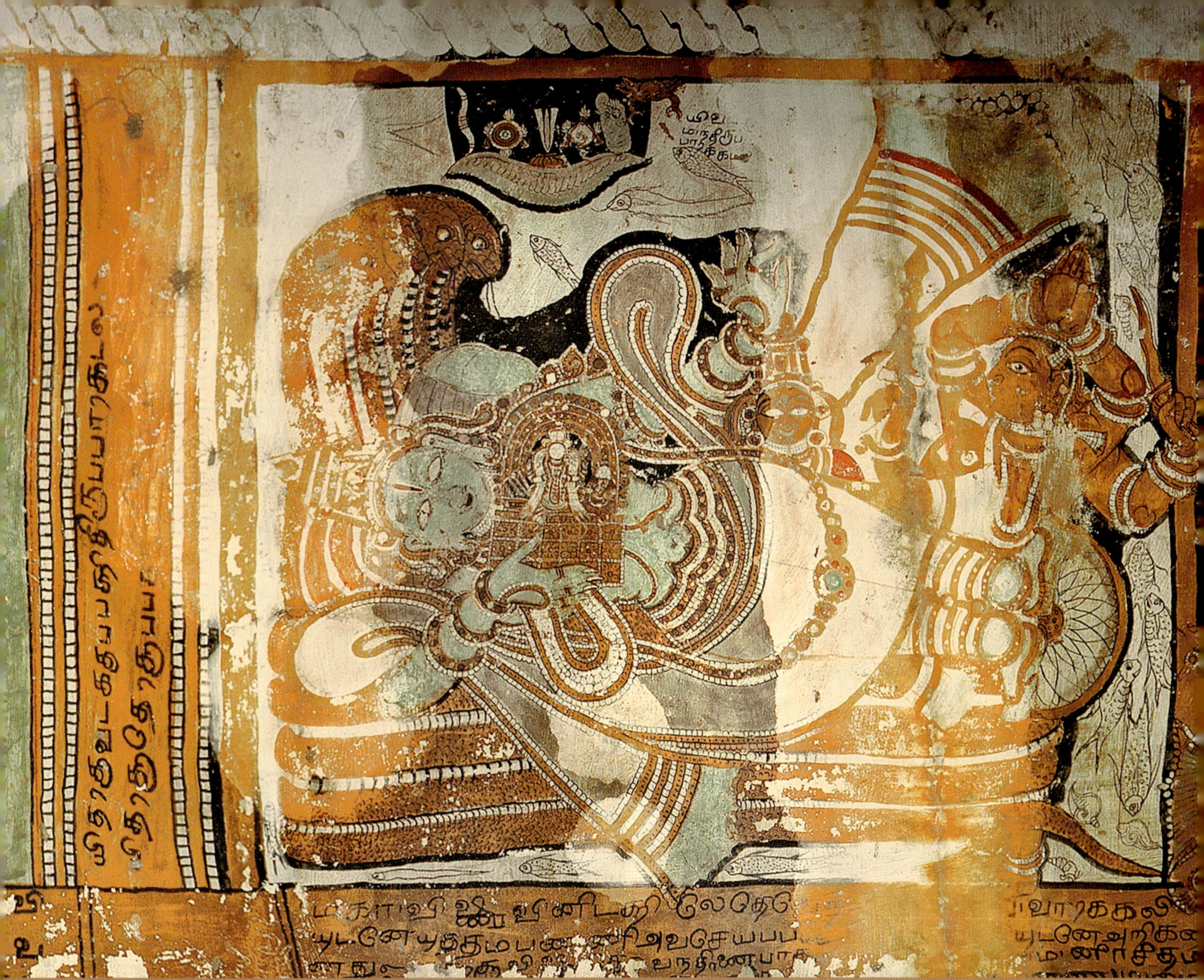

Panel 9-10, from right to left:

- *Indra informs Viṣṇu on the Ocean of Milk of his defeat by Vārkali. Viṣṇu sends him to Cidambaram to worship Naṭarāja.*
- *Indra worships Naṭarāja, the Sabhāpati, at Cidambaram.*

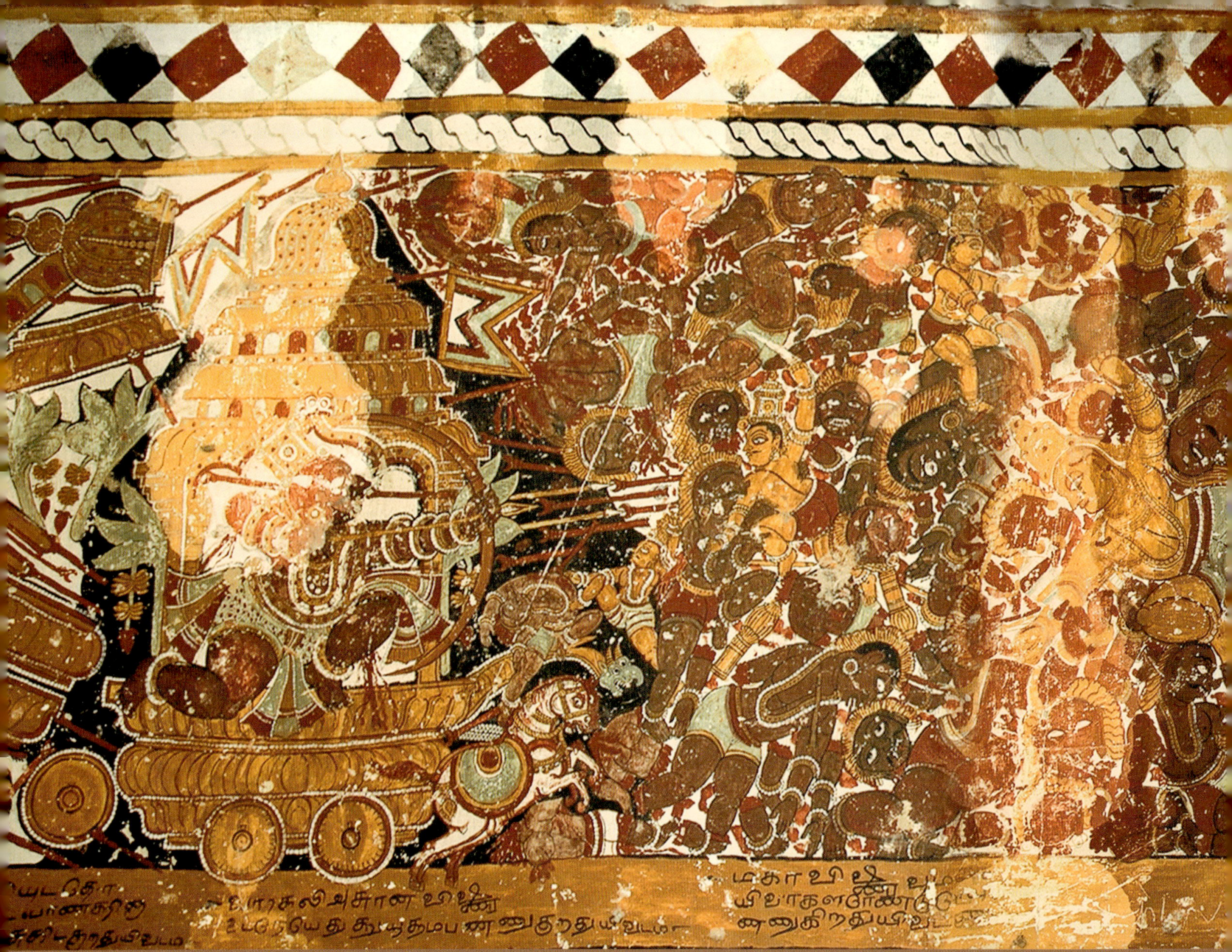

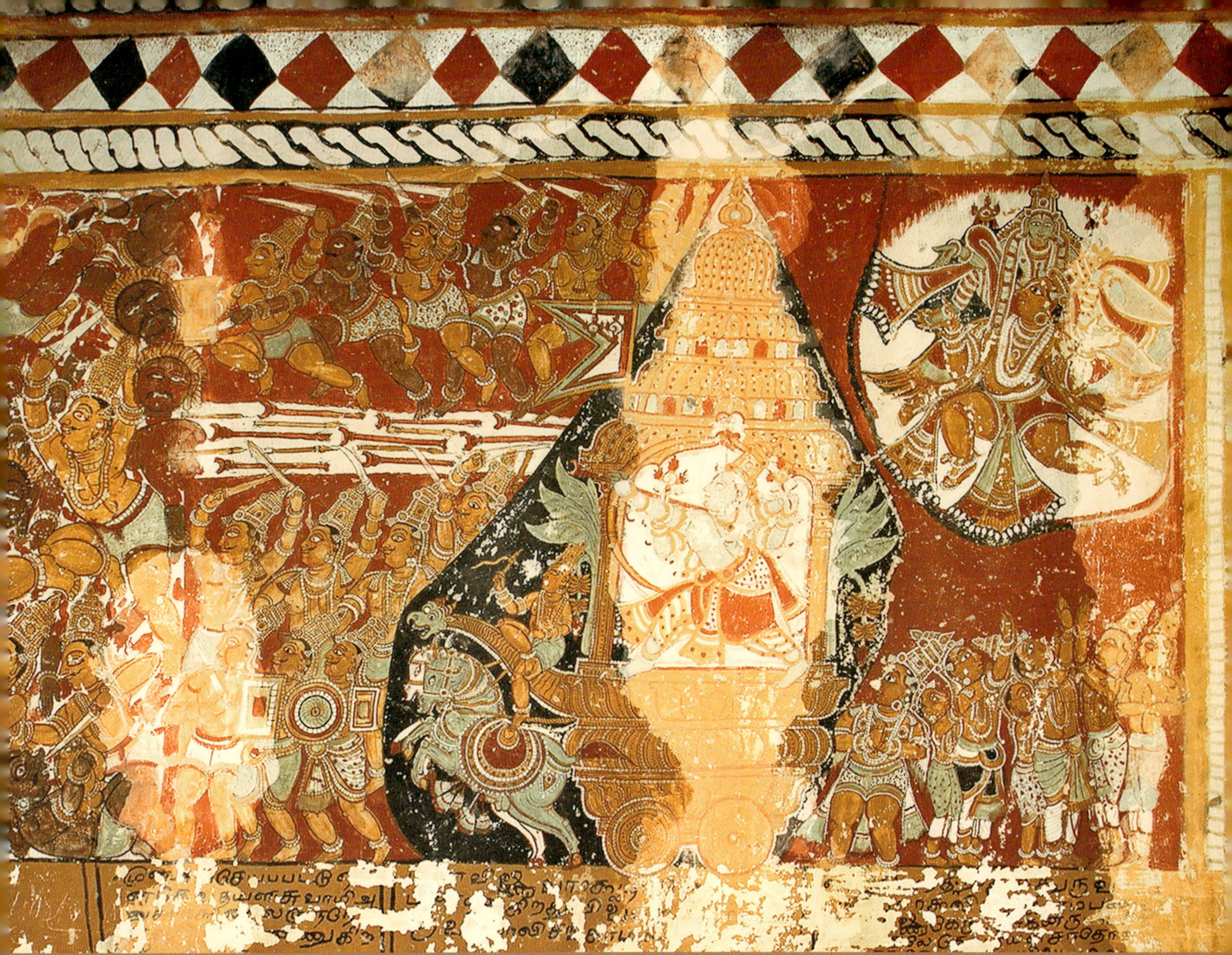

Panel 11-12, from right to left:

- *Viṣṇu's war with Vārkali.*
Far right: Indra and the gods see Viṣṇu on Garuḍa proceeding to the war and are pleased.
- *Viṣṇu fights Vārkali and the demon army.*

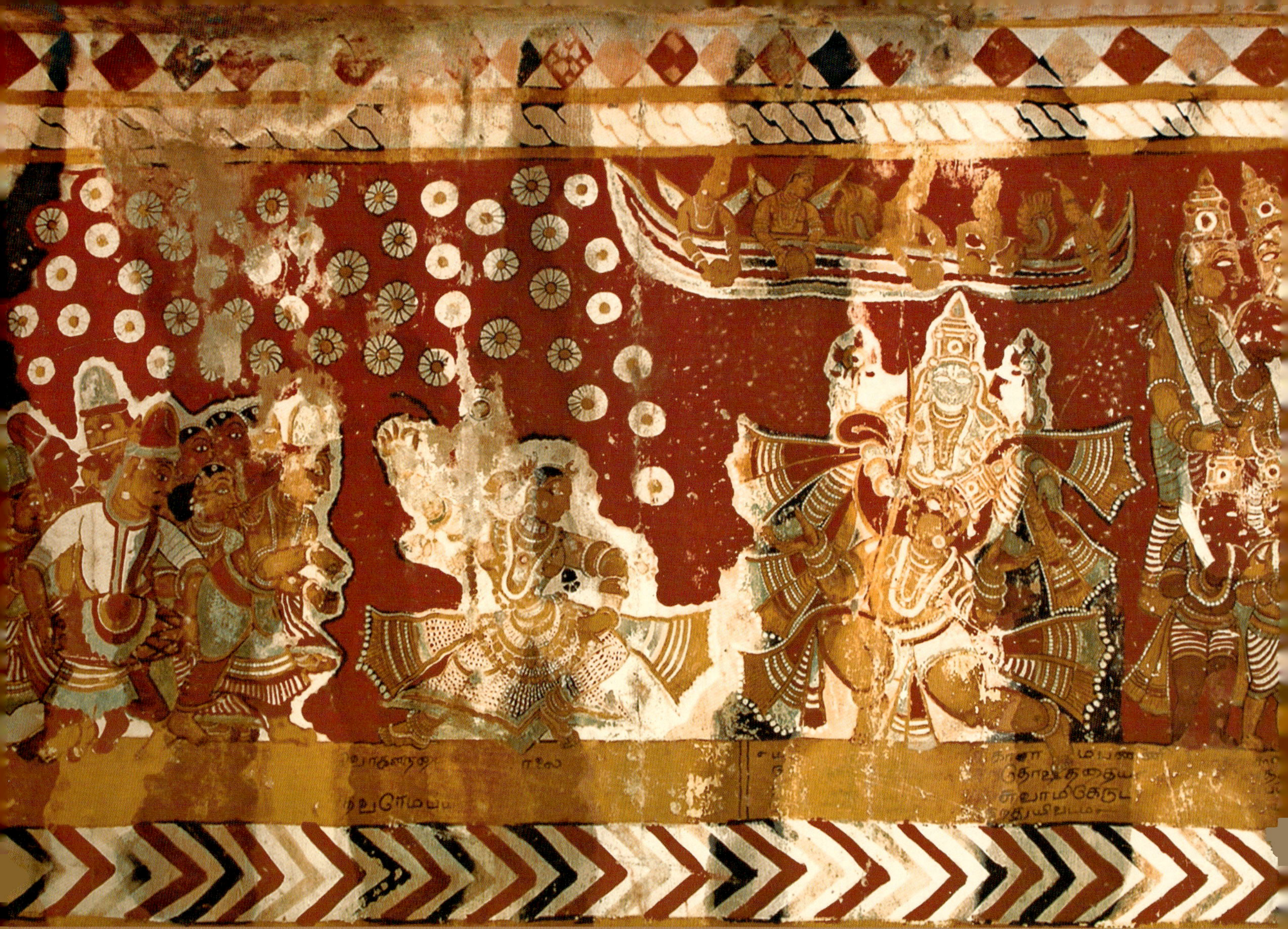

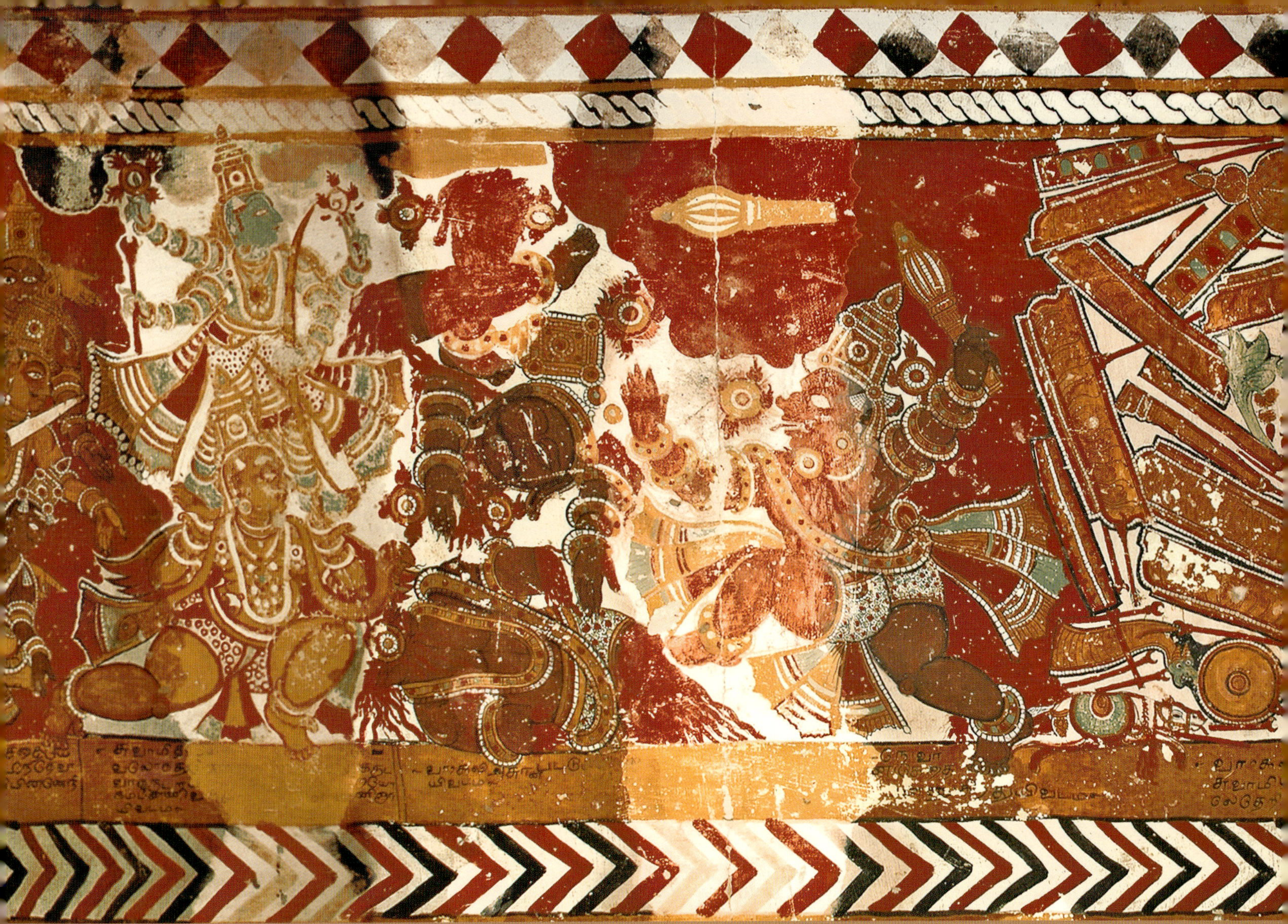

Panel 13-14, from right to left:

- *Vārkali's chariot is shattered by Viṣṇu's arrows. Vārkali flees the battlefield. Vārkali is beheaded.*
- *Celebration of Viṣṇu's victory over Vārkali. The gods pour down flowers. Dance and music in Devaloka.*

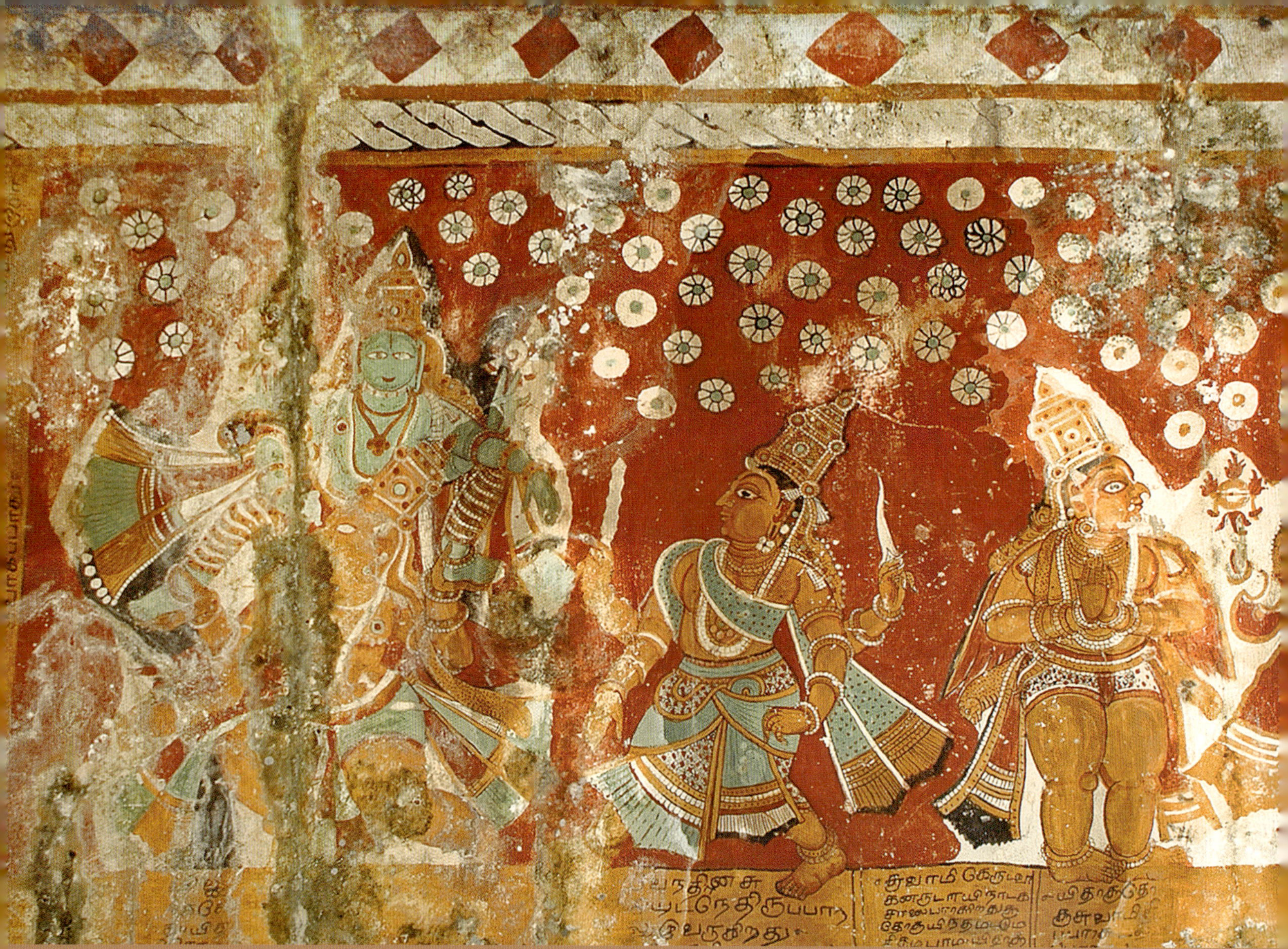

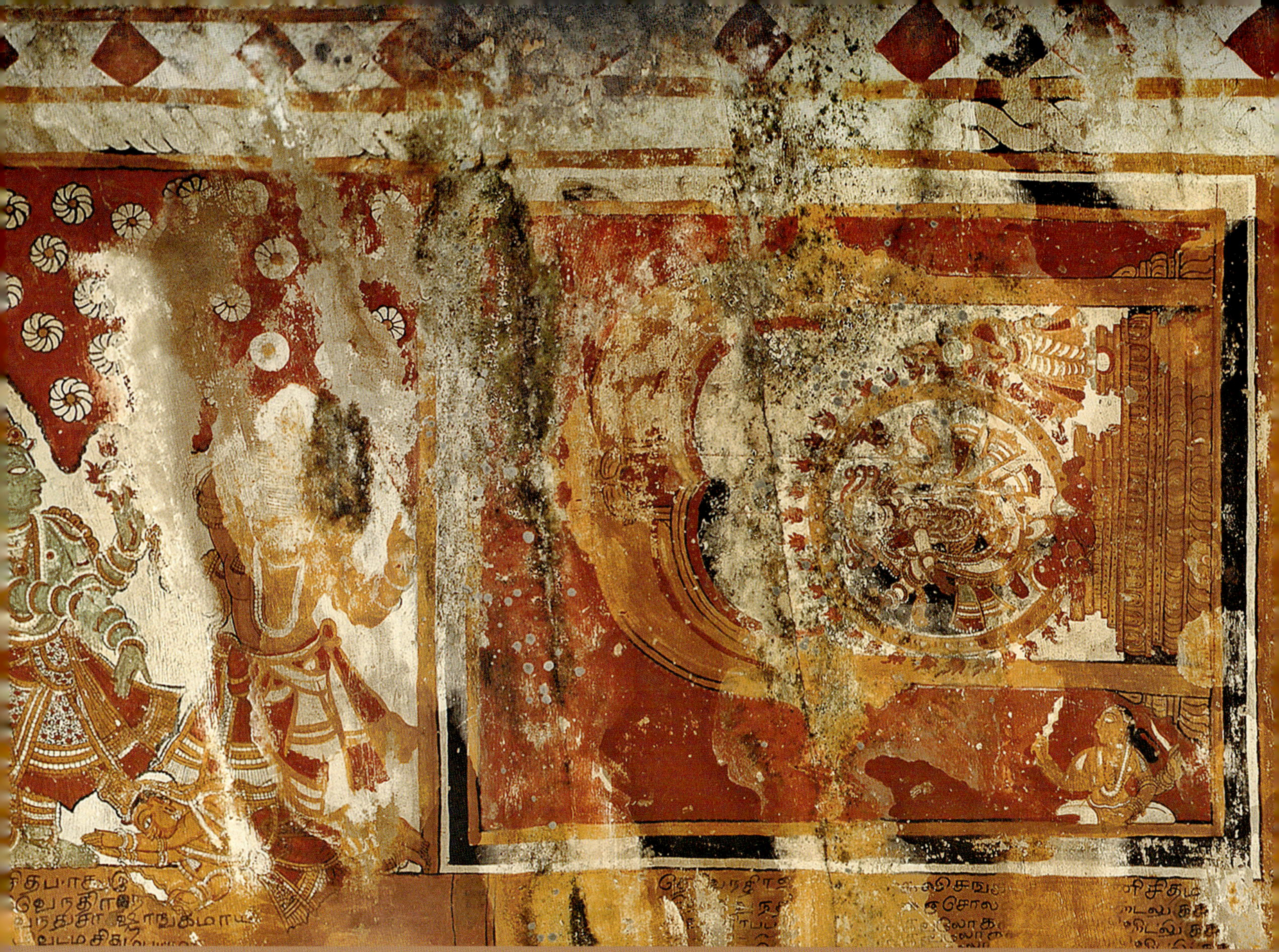

Panel 15-16, from right to left:

- *Indra returns to Cidambaram to ask that the Tyāgarāja image be transferred to his world.*
- *Indra prostrates to Viṣṇu in Cidambaram. Viṣṇu returns to the Ocean of Milk. Indra seeks him out there.*

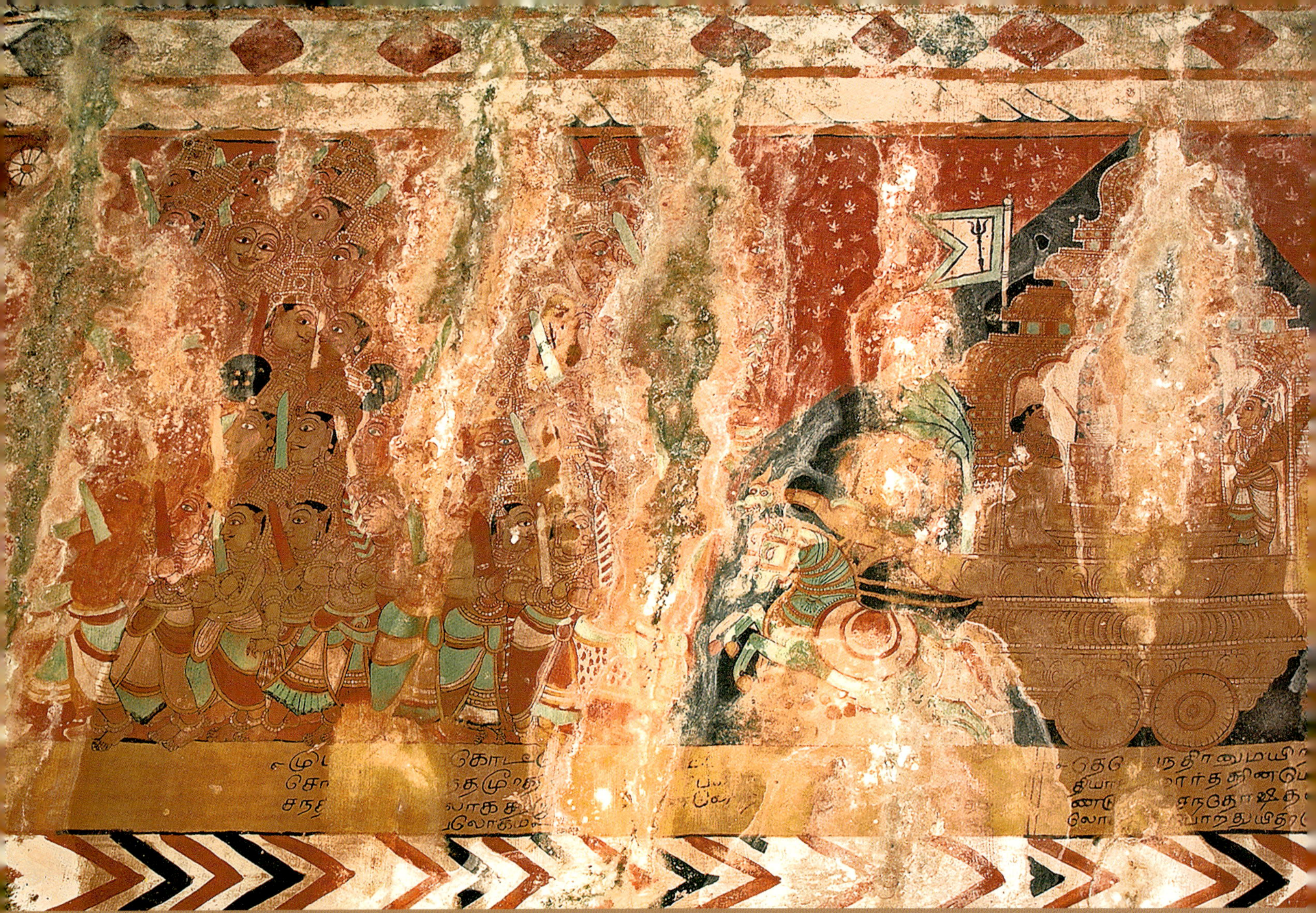

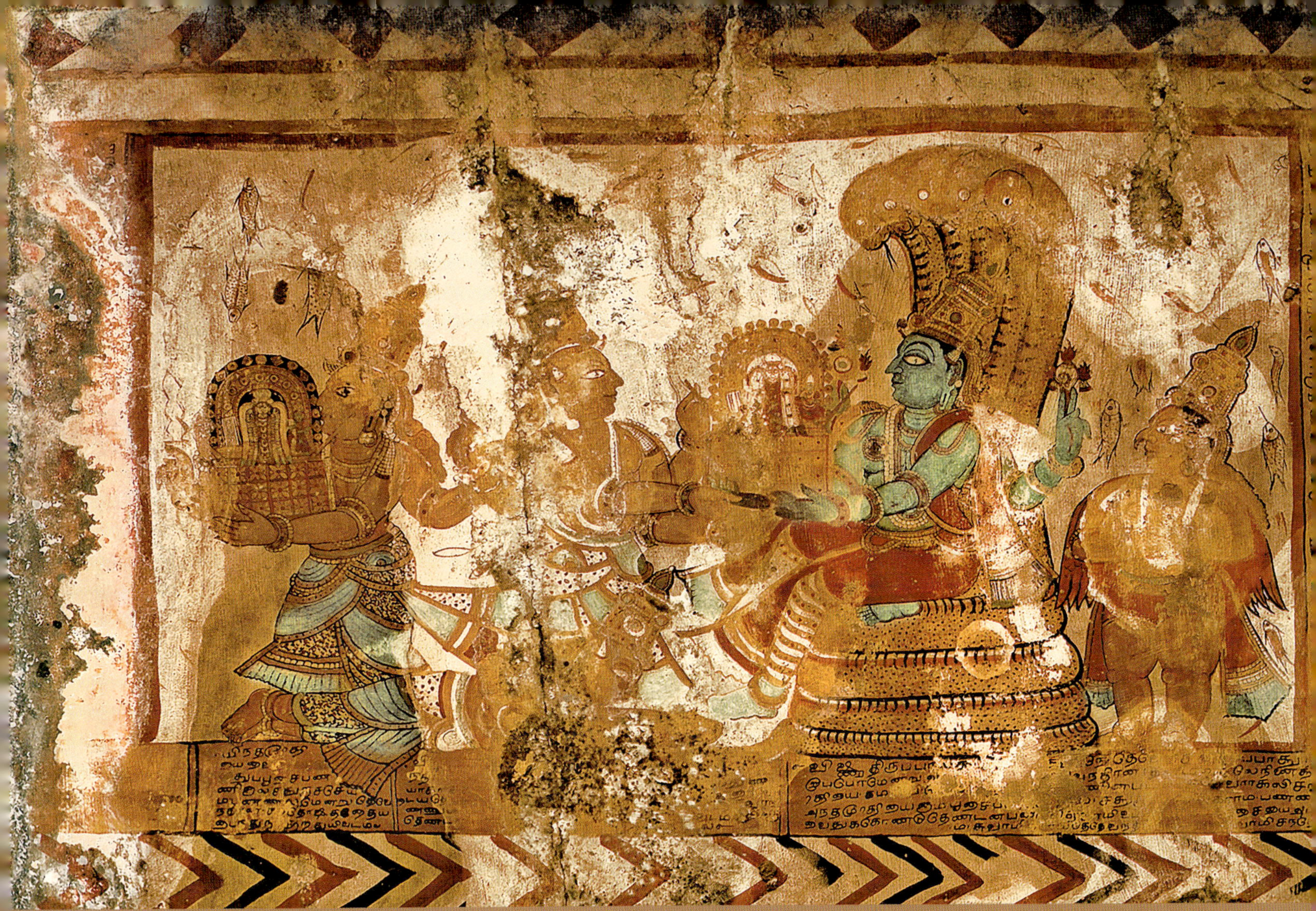

Panel 17-18, from right to left:

- *Viṣṇu hands over to Indra the Tyāgarāja icon. Indra prostrates to Tyāgarāja and takes the image to his heaven.*
- *The gods escort Tyāgarāja to heaven.*

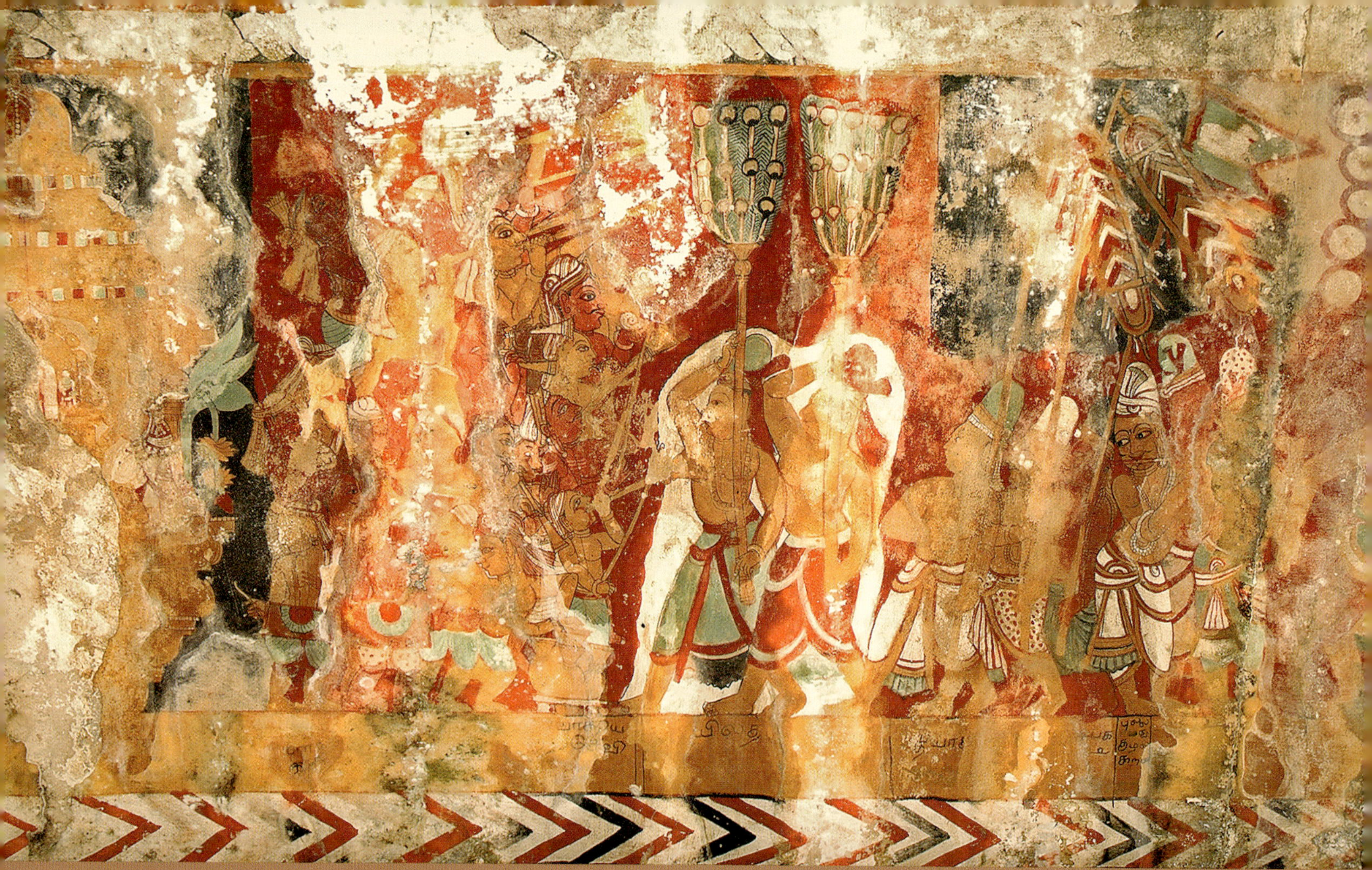

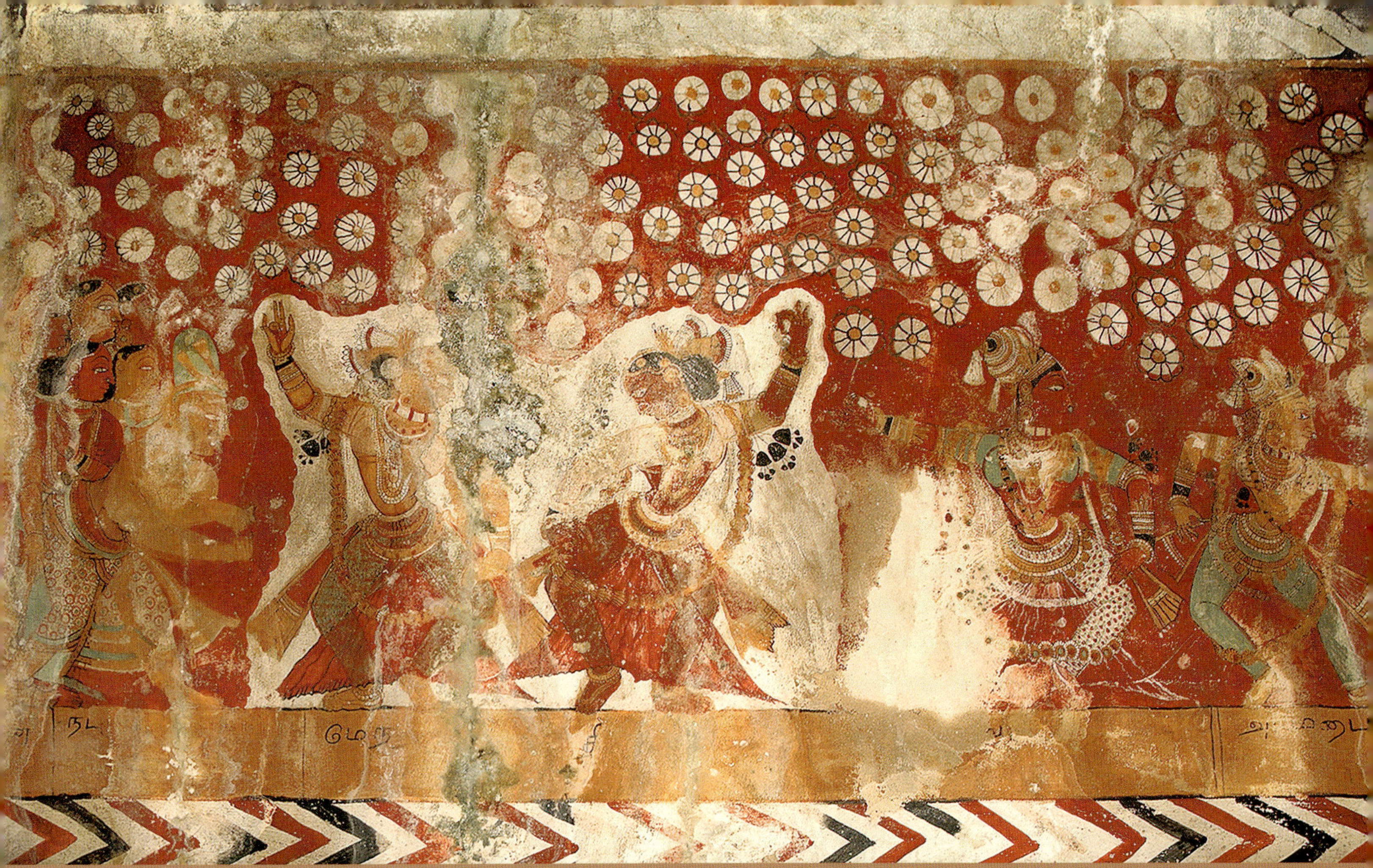

Panel 19-20, from right to left:

- *Apsaras dance to welcome the god.*
- *Tyāgarāja in procession in Indra's heaven. Musicians play before him.*

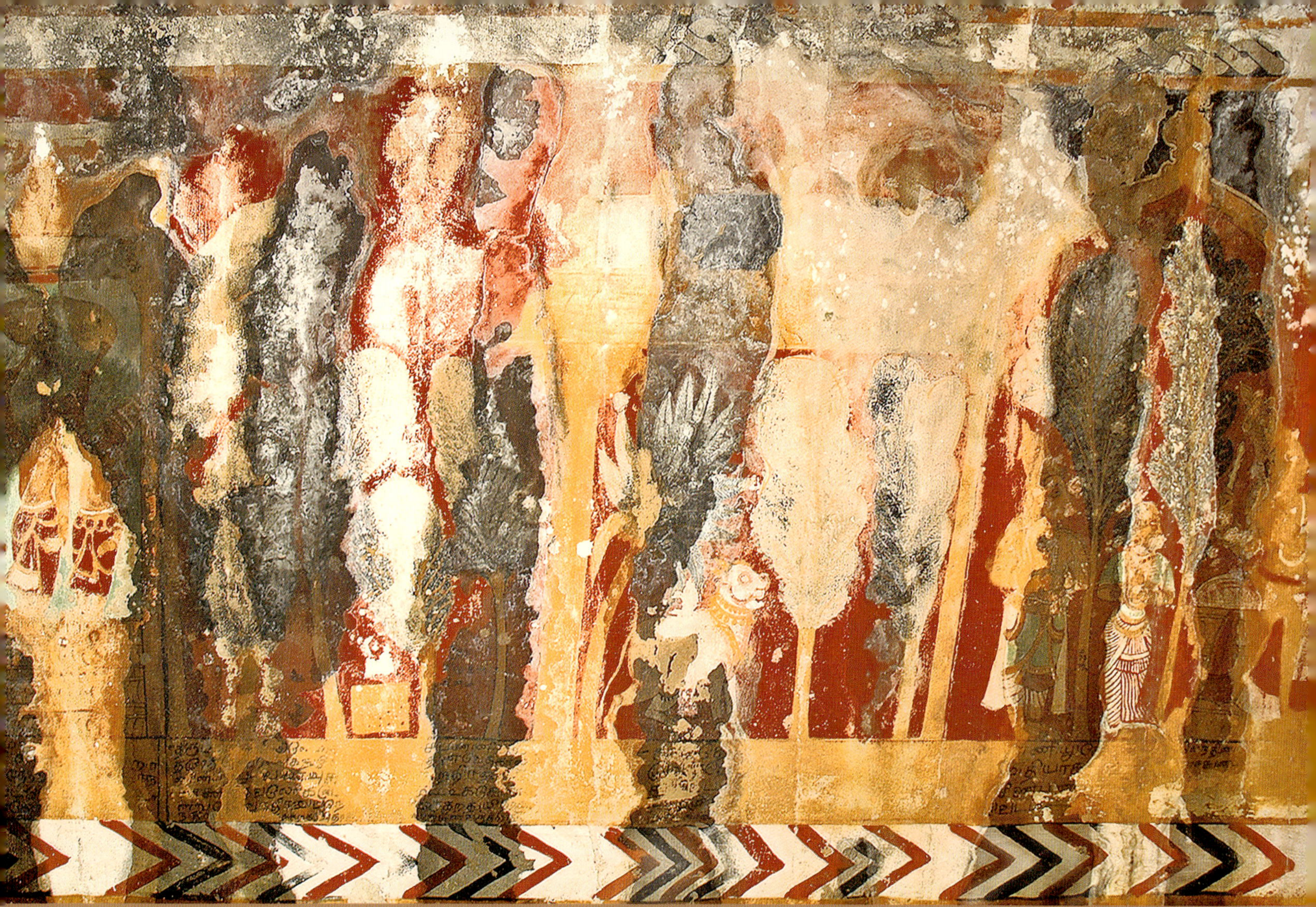

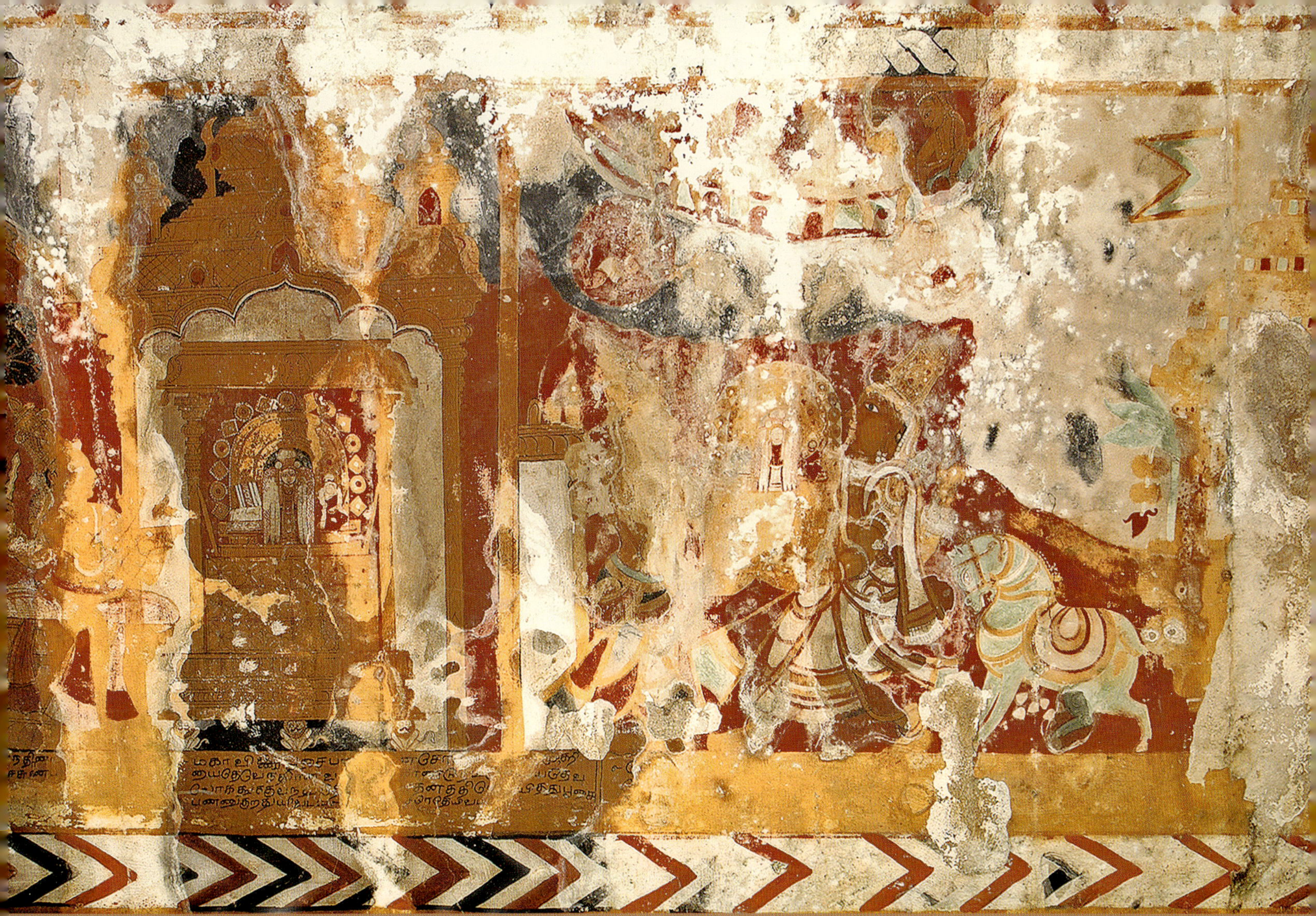

Panel 21-22, from right to left:

- *Indra installs Tyāgarāja in his shrine and worships him.*
- *Scenes in Indra's heaven. News arrives of Valâsura's attack.*

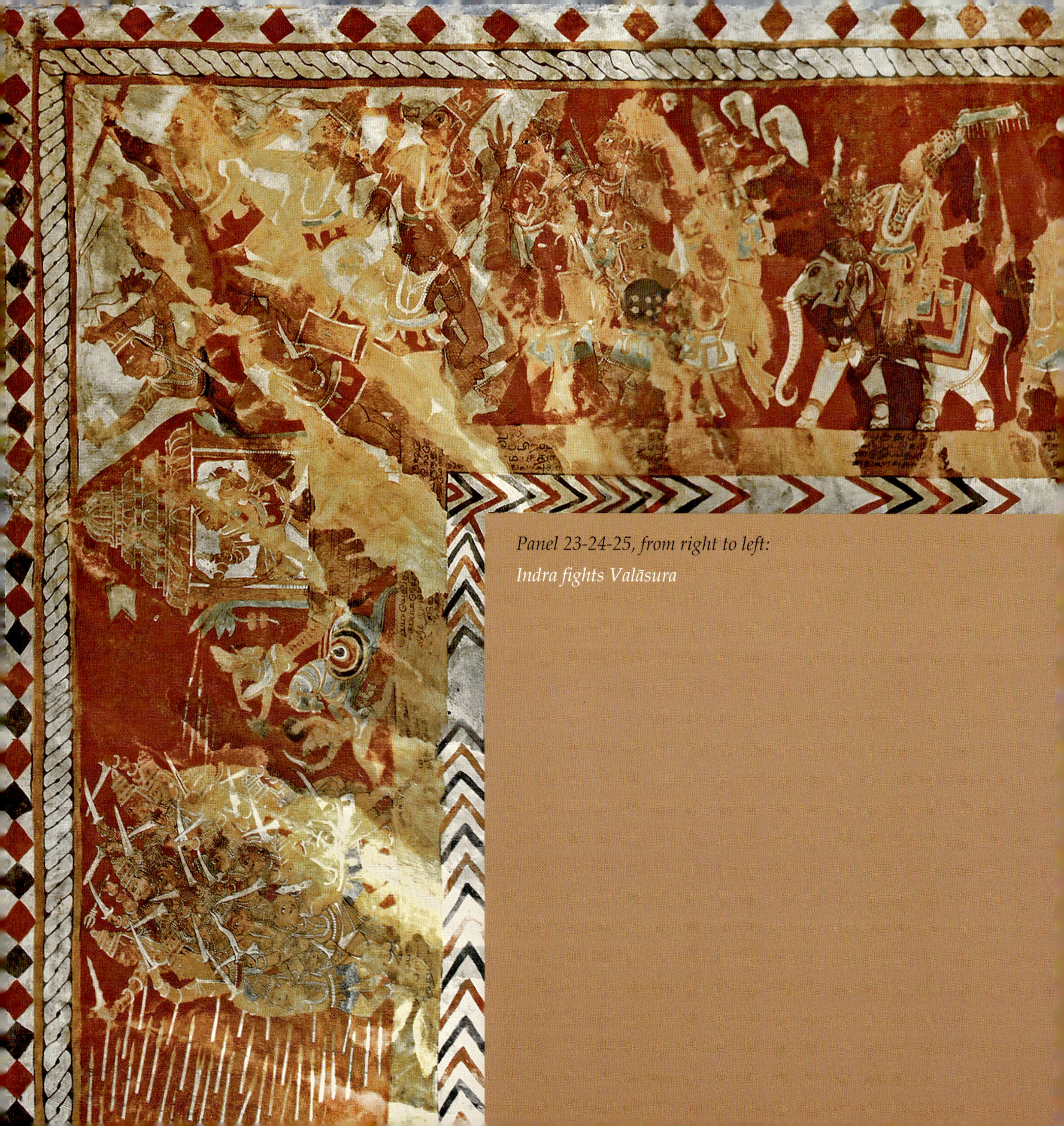

Panel 23-24-25, from right to left:
Indra fights Valāsura

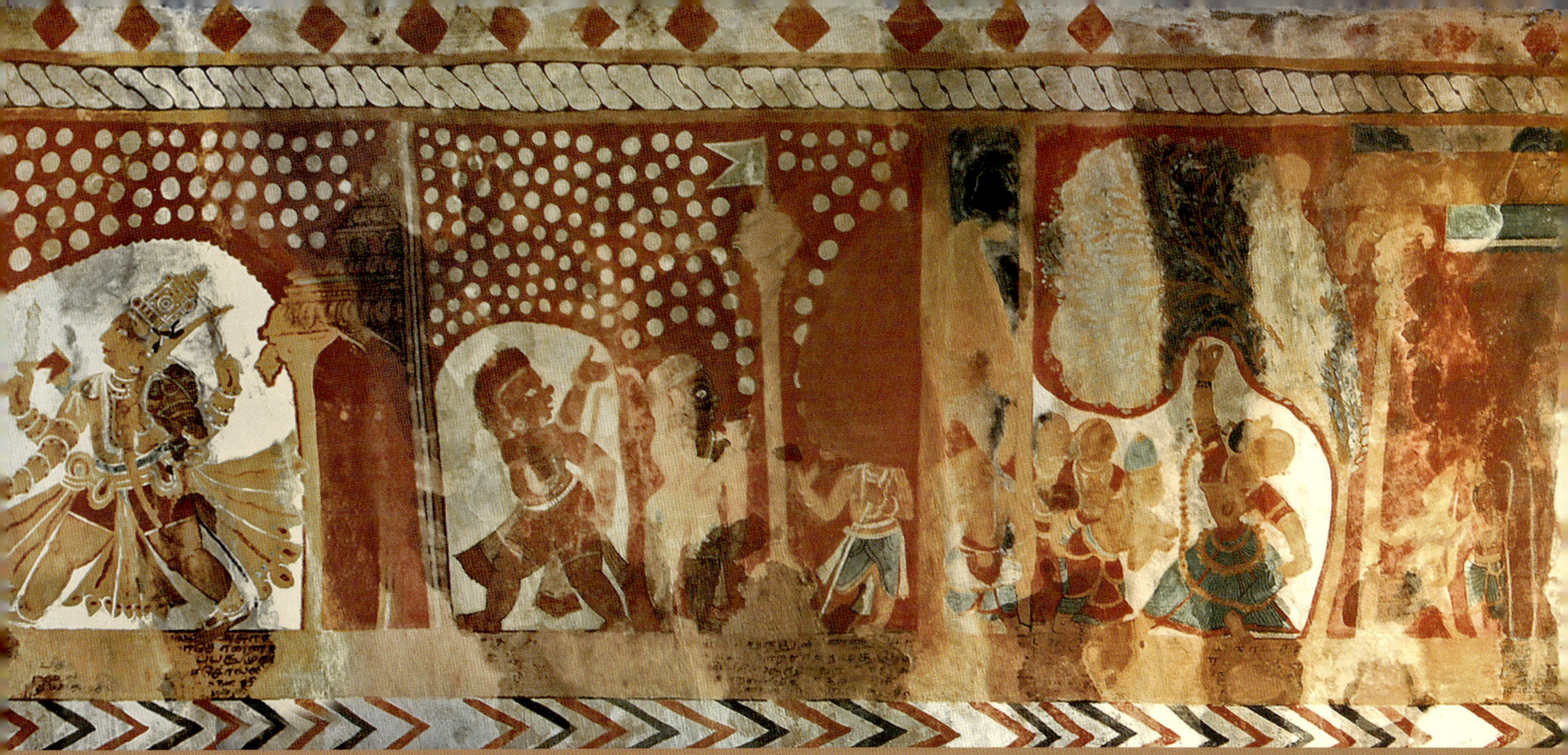

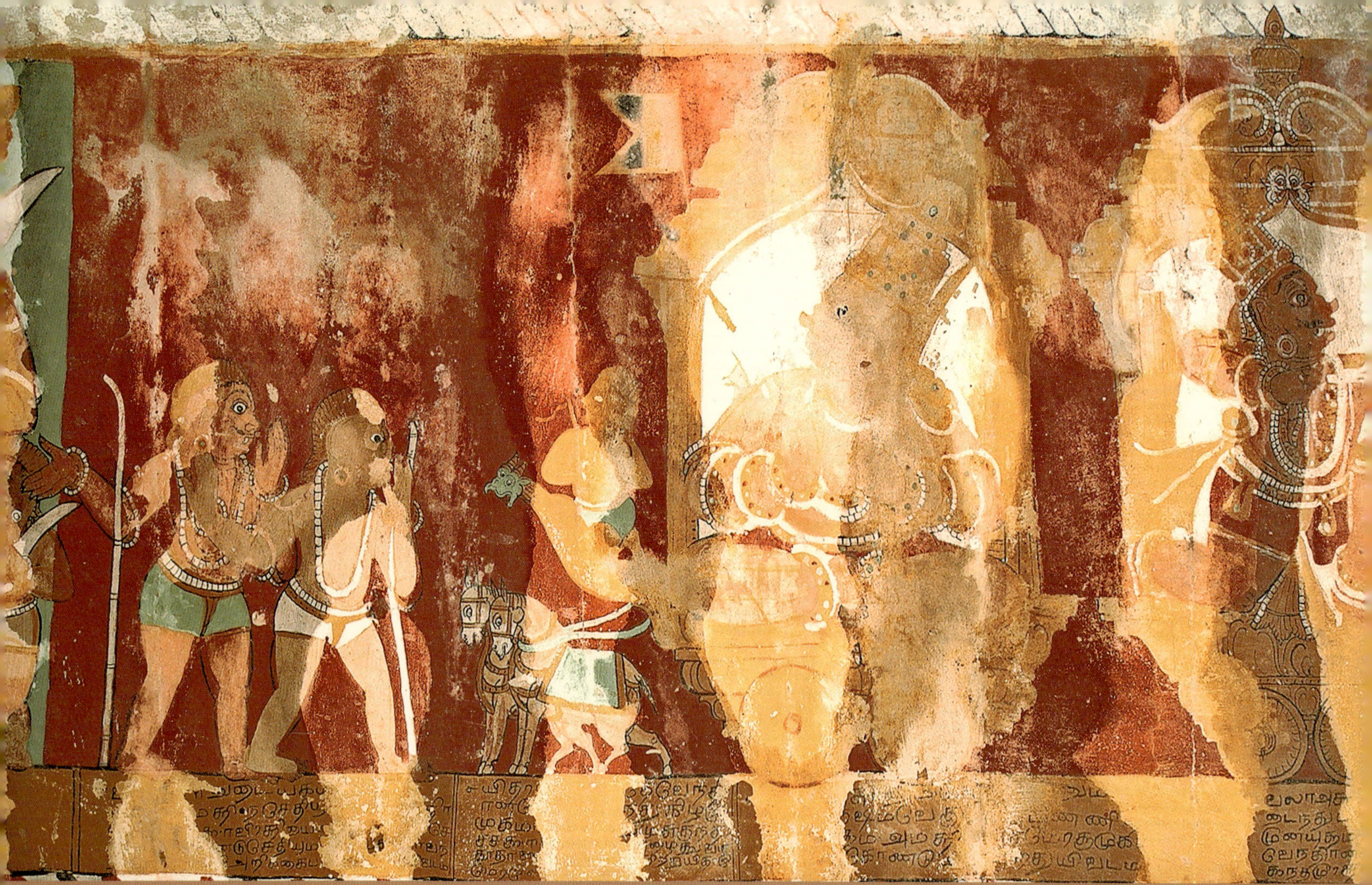

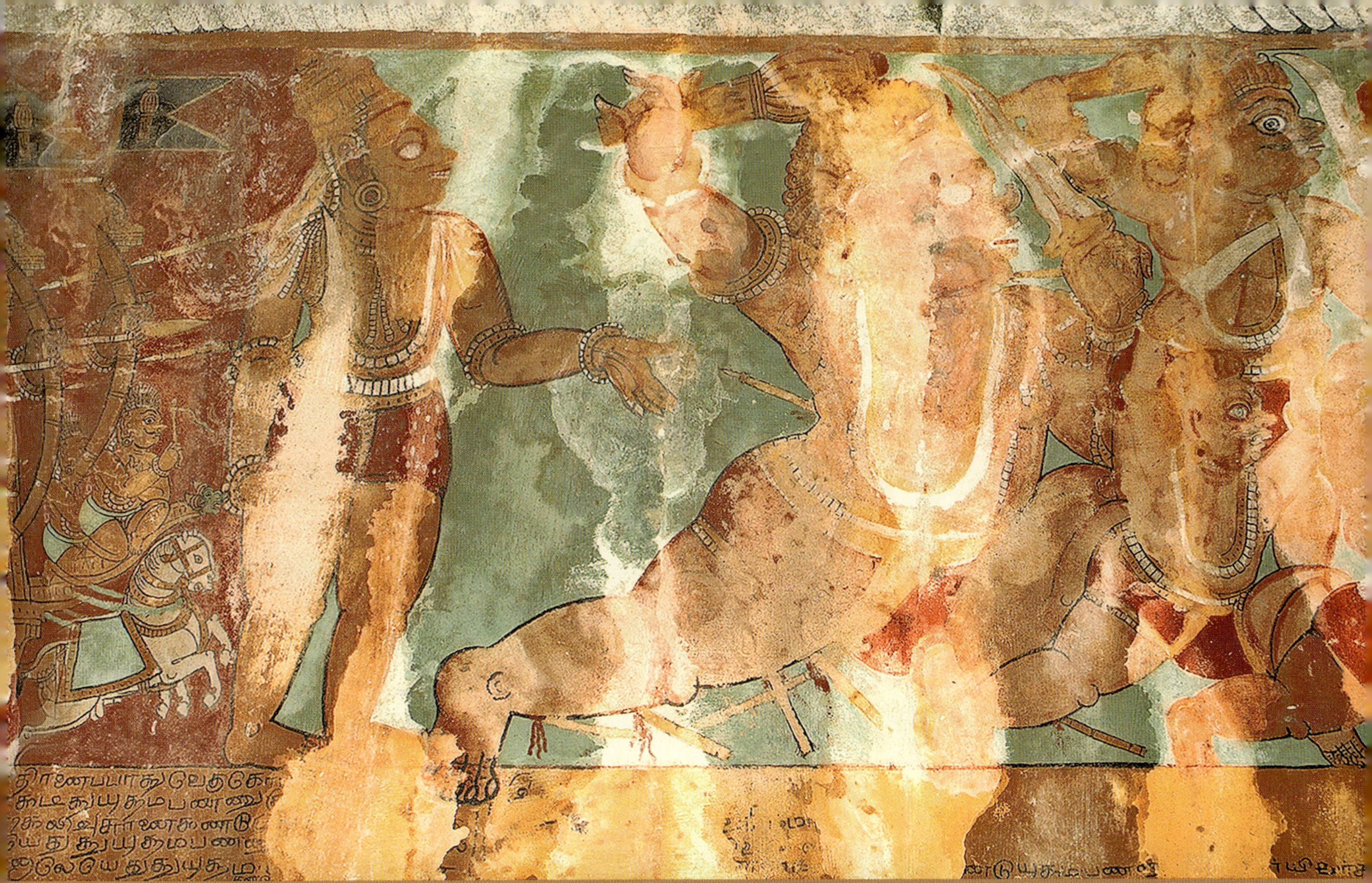

Panel 26-27, from right to left:

- *Valāsura sees Indra and, enraged at Vārkalī's death, goes to war against him. Indra fights back.*
- *Indra decides to send an embassy to Mucukunda.*

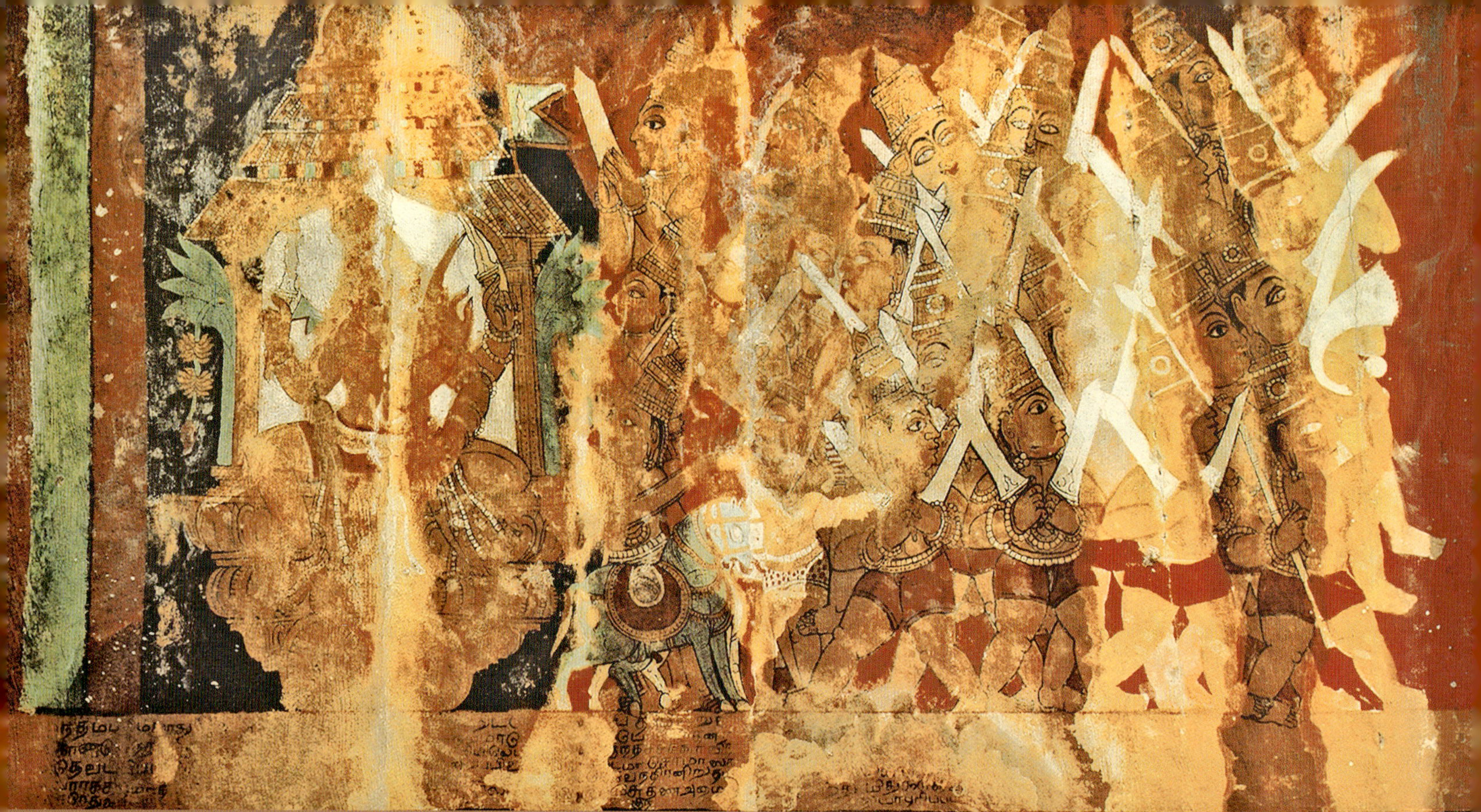

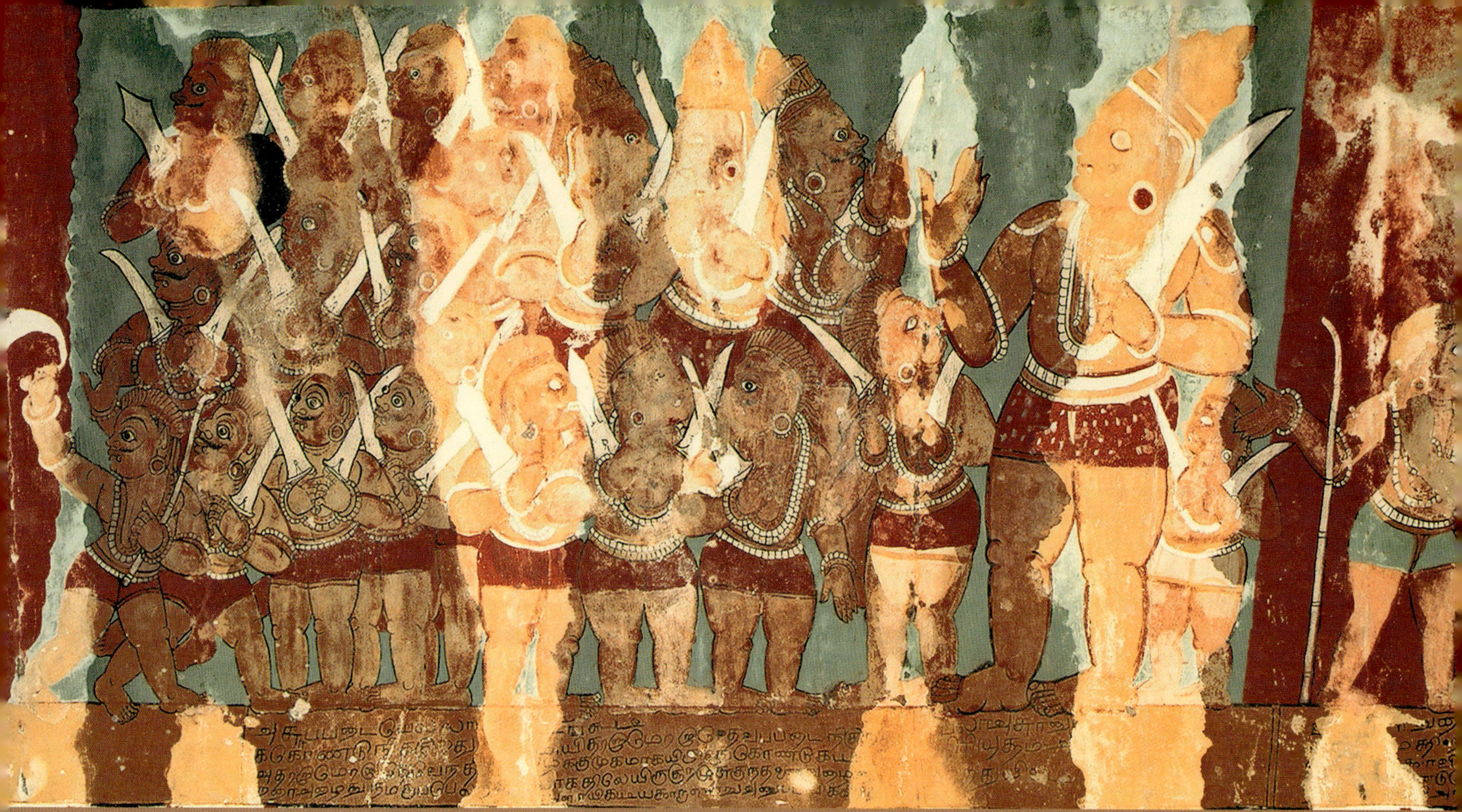

Panel 28-29, from right to left:

- *Valāsura assembles his demon army. Indra briefs his messenger.*
- *Indra's embassy sent to Mucukunda.*

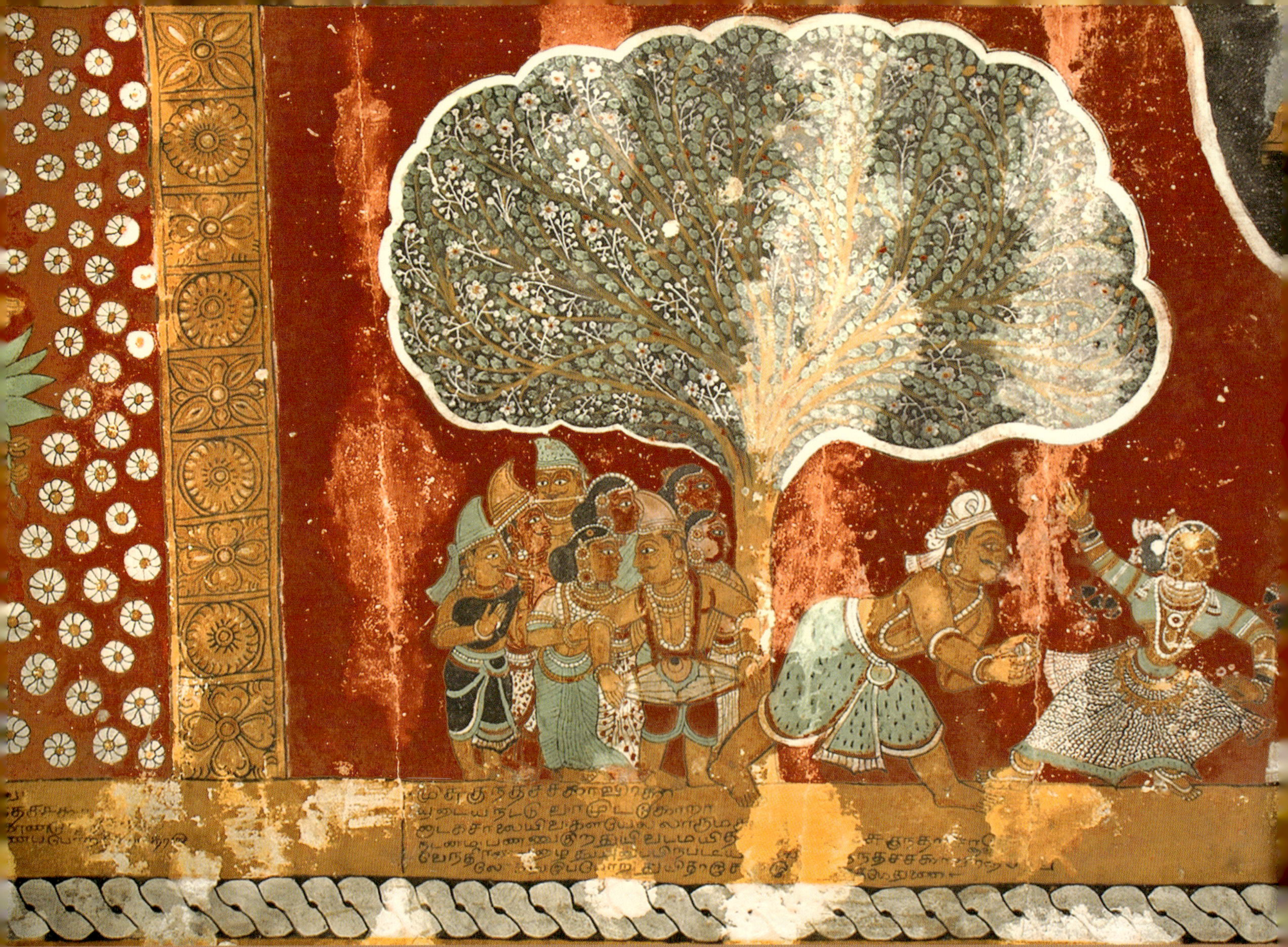

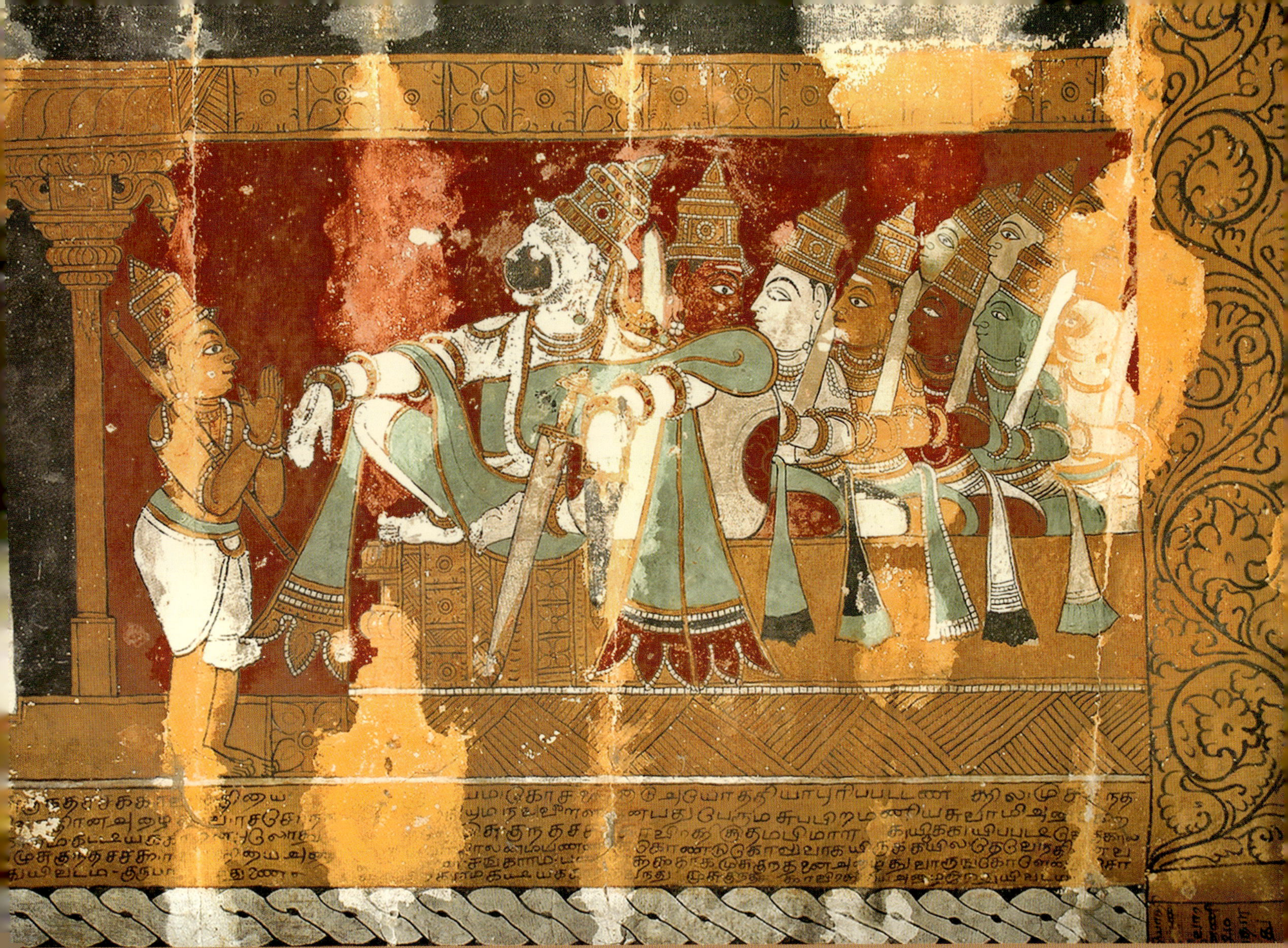

Panel 30-31, from right to left:

- *Indra's messenger at Mucukunda's court in Ayodhya.*
- *Music and dance in Mucukunda's court.*

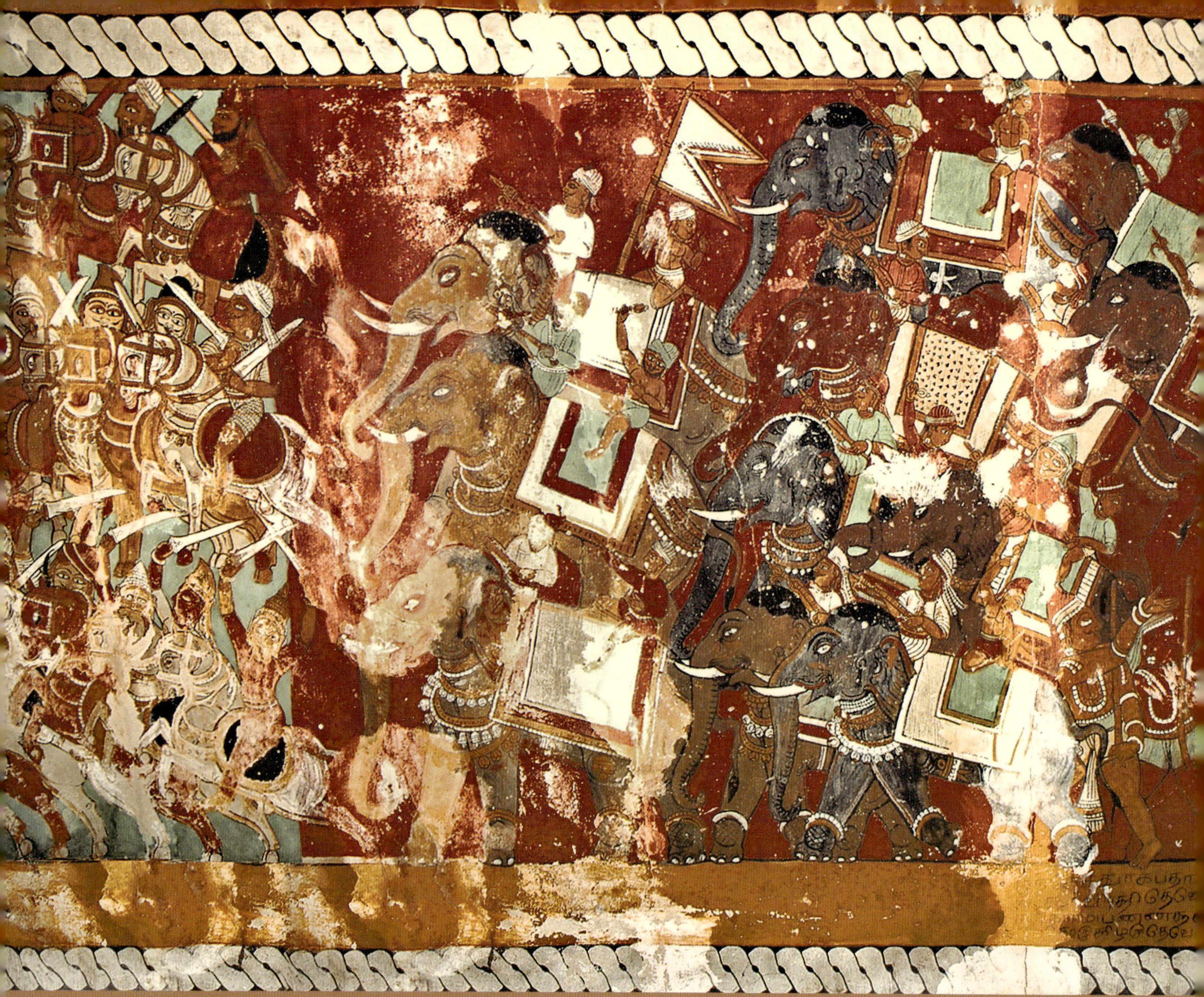

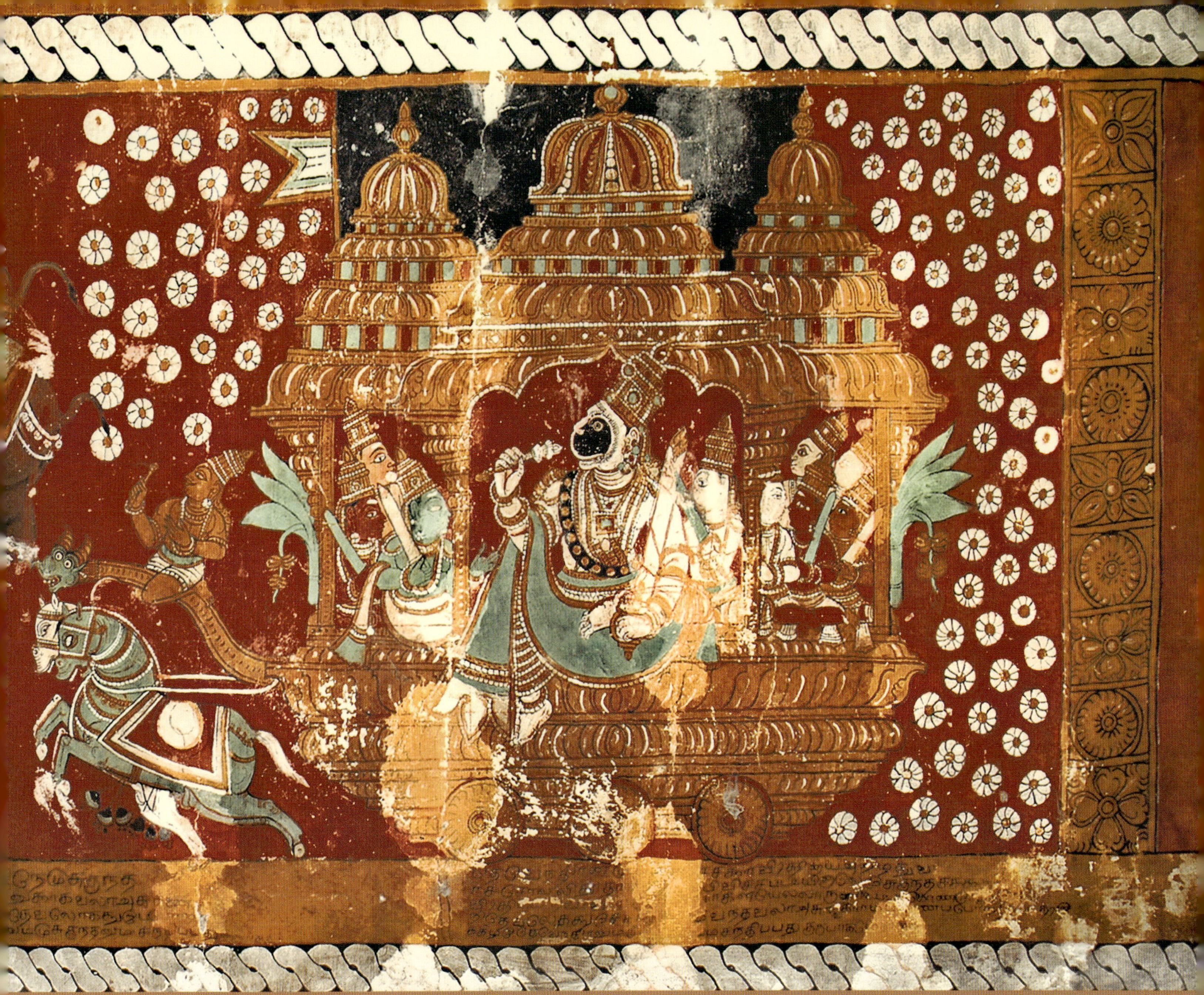

Panel 32-33, from right to left:

- *Mucukunda leaves for Indra's heaven and the Valāsura campaign*
- *Mucukunda's army: war-chariots and elephants.*

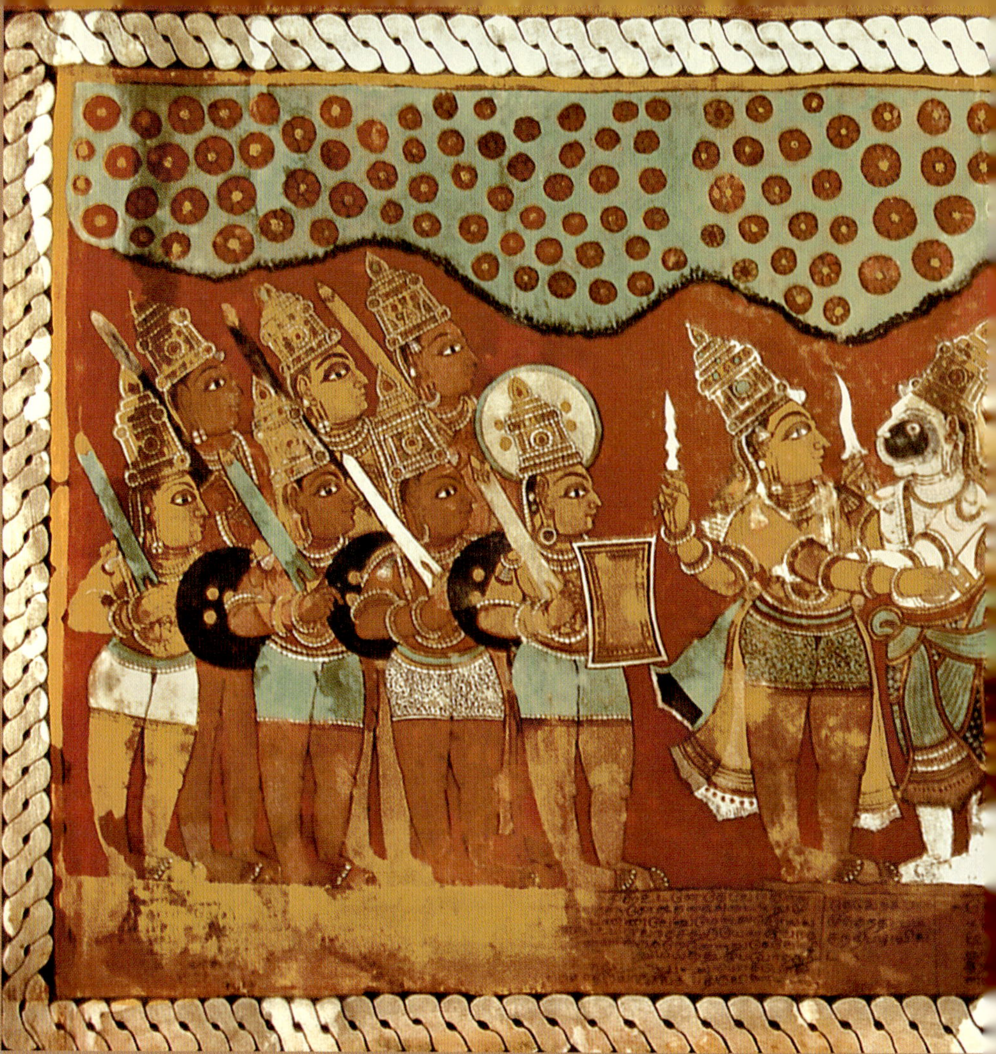

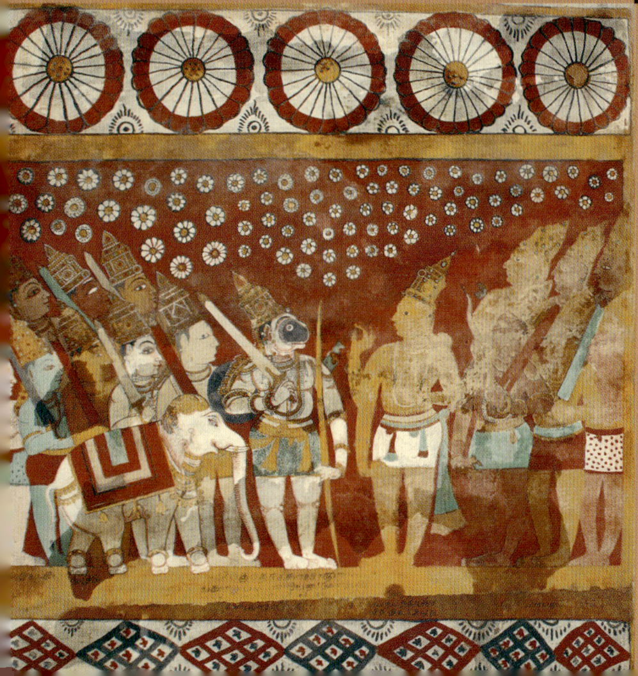

Panel 34-35-36, from right to left:

- *Mucukunda's cavalry and foot-soldiers*
- *Indra meets Mucukunda*
- *Gathering of the troops*

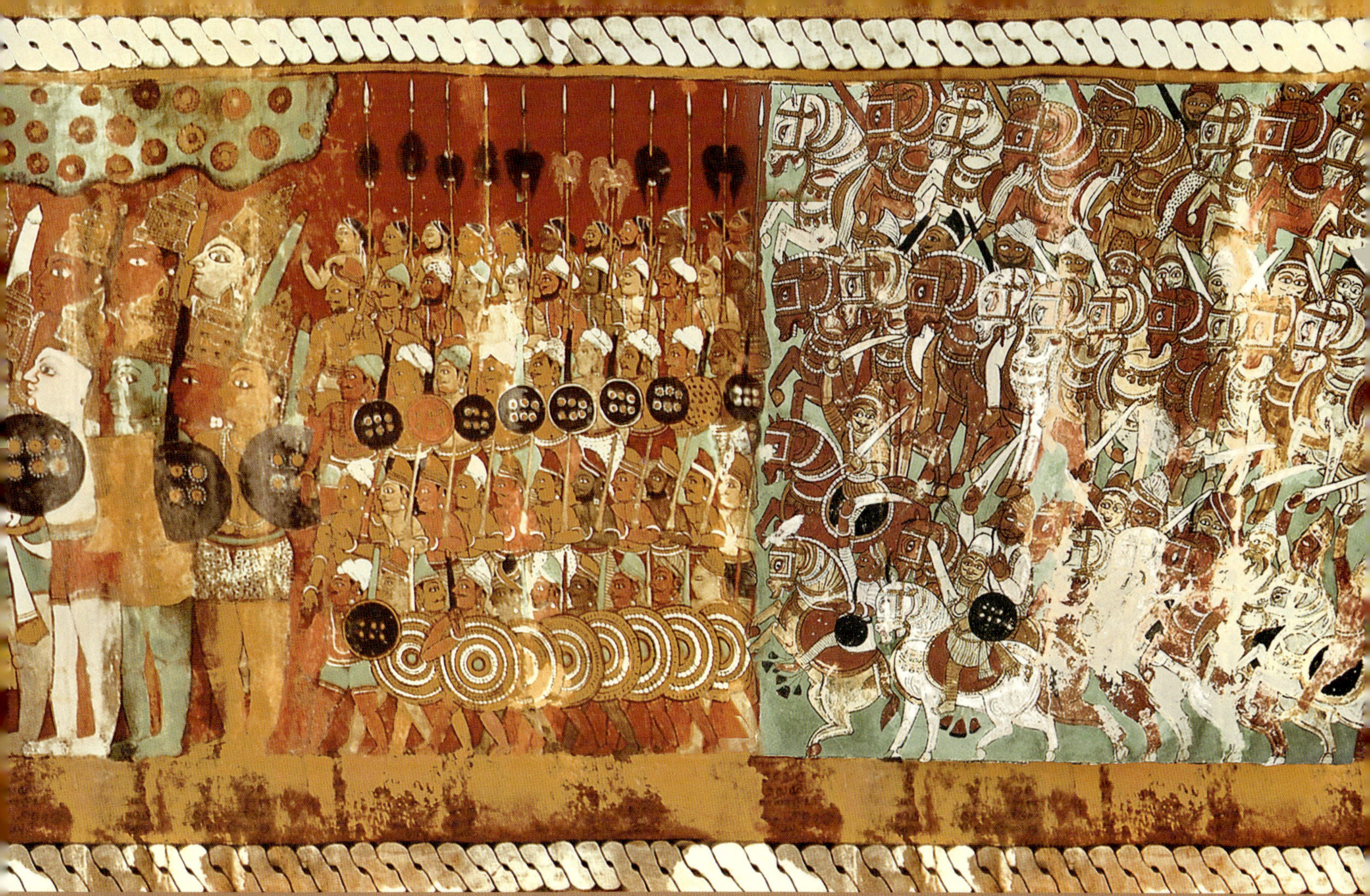

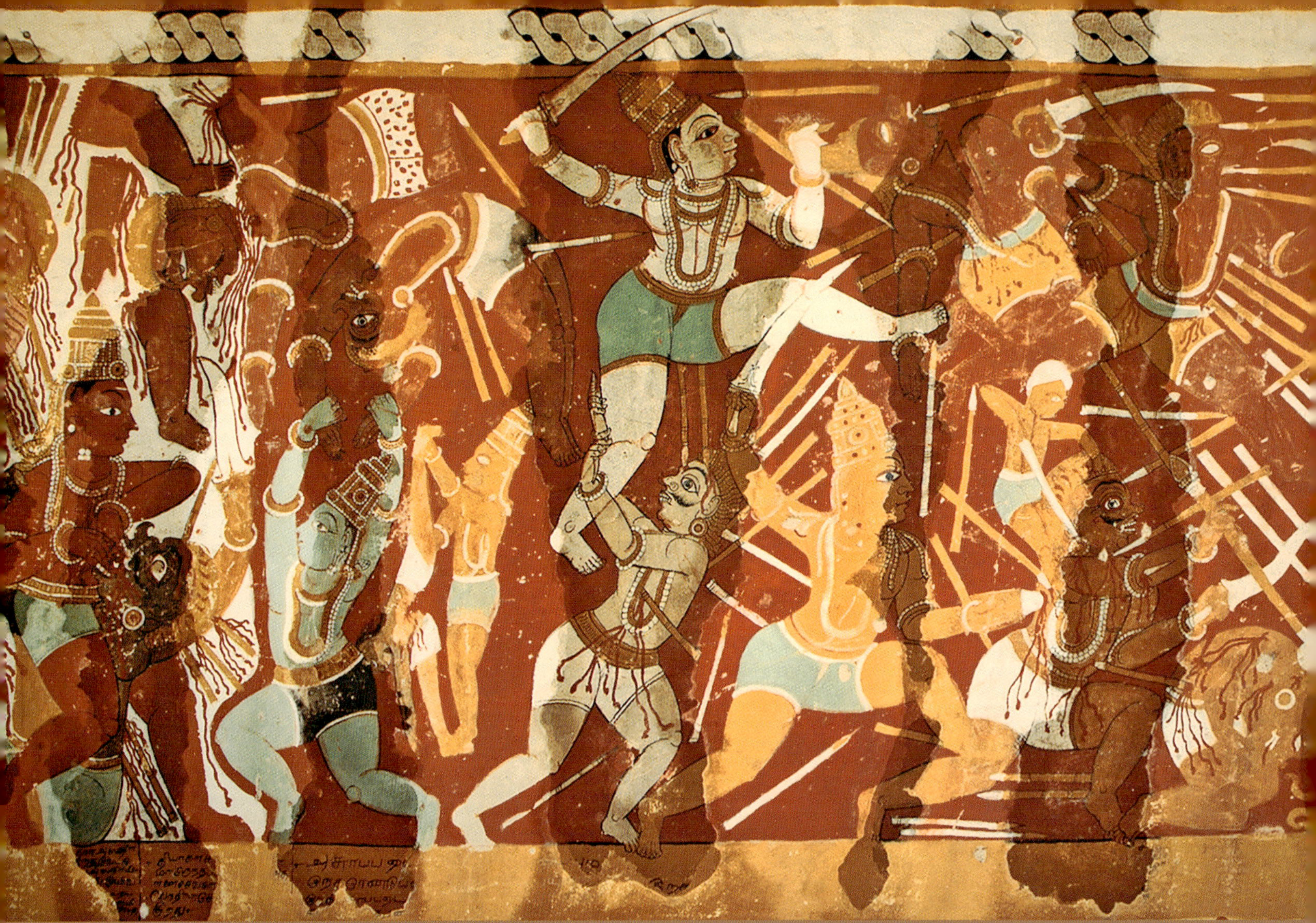

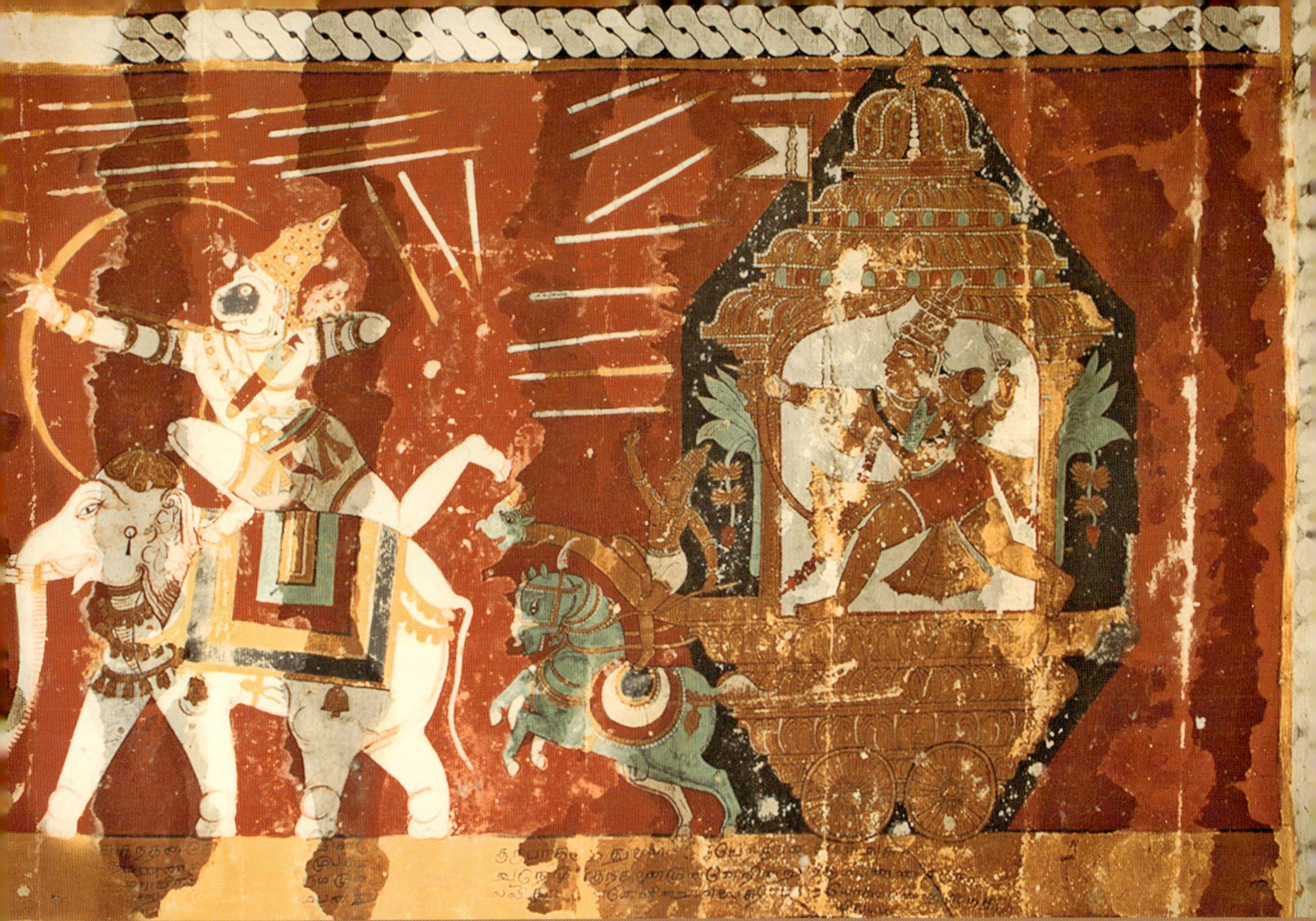

Panel 37-38, from right to left:

- *The war with Valāsura: Mucukunda in the advance guard, Indra behind him.*
- *War of gods and demons. Indra slays Valāsura.*

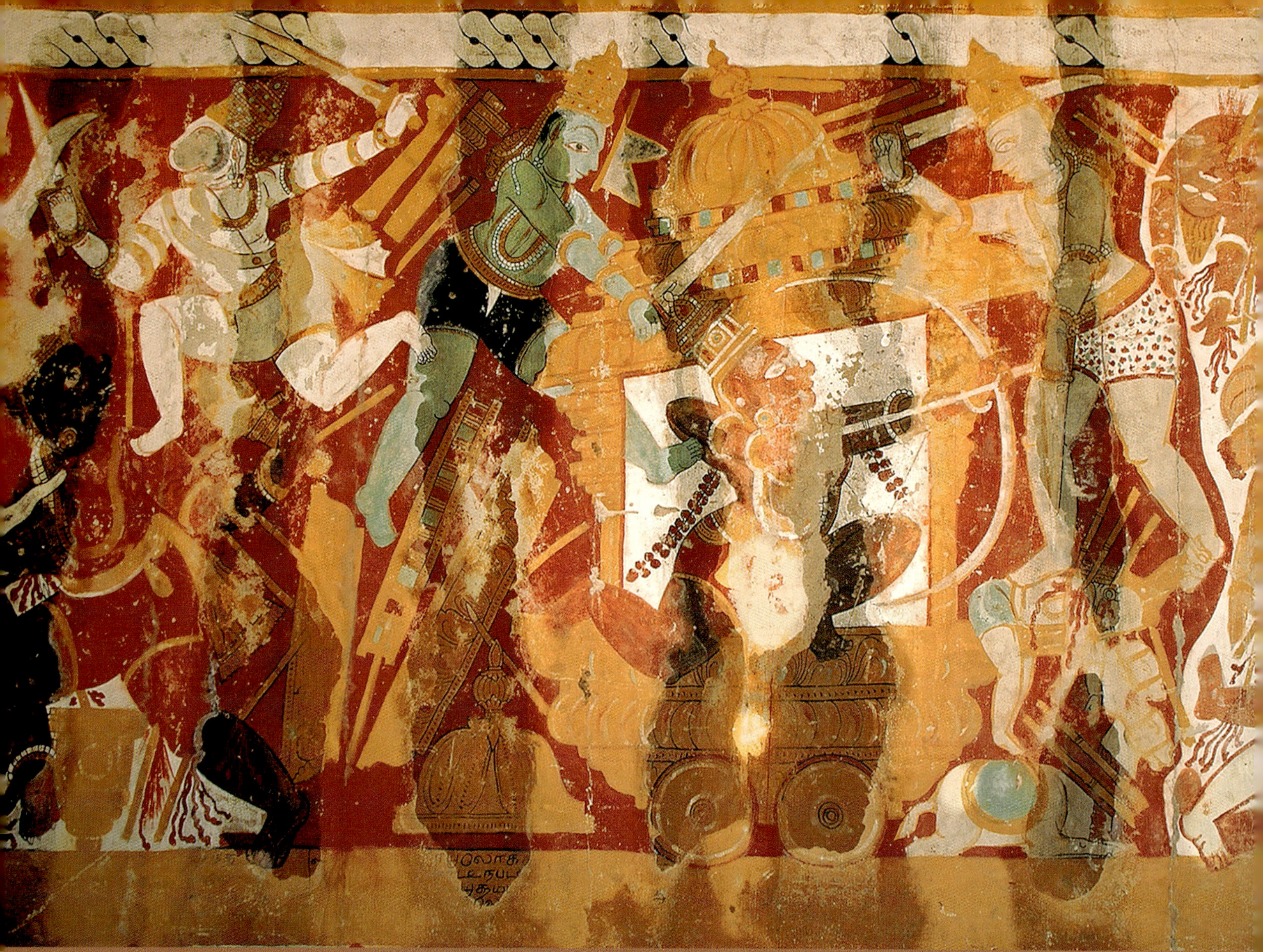

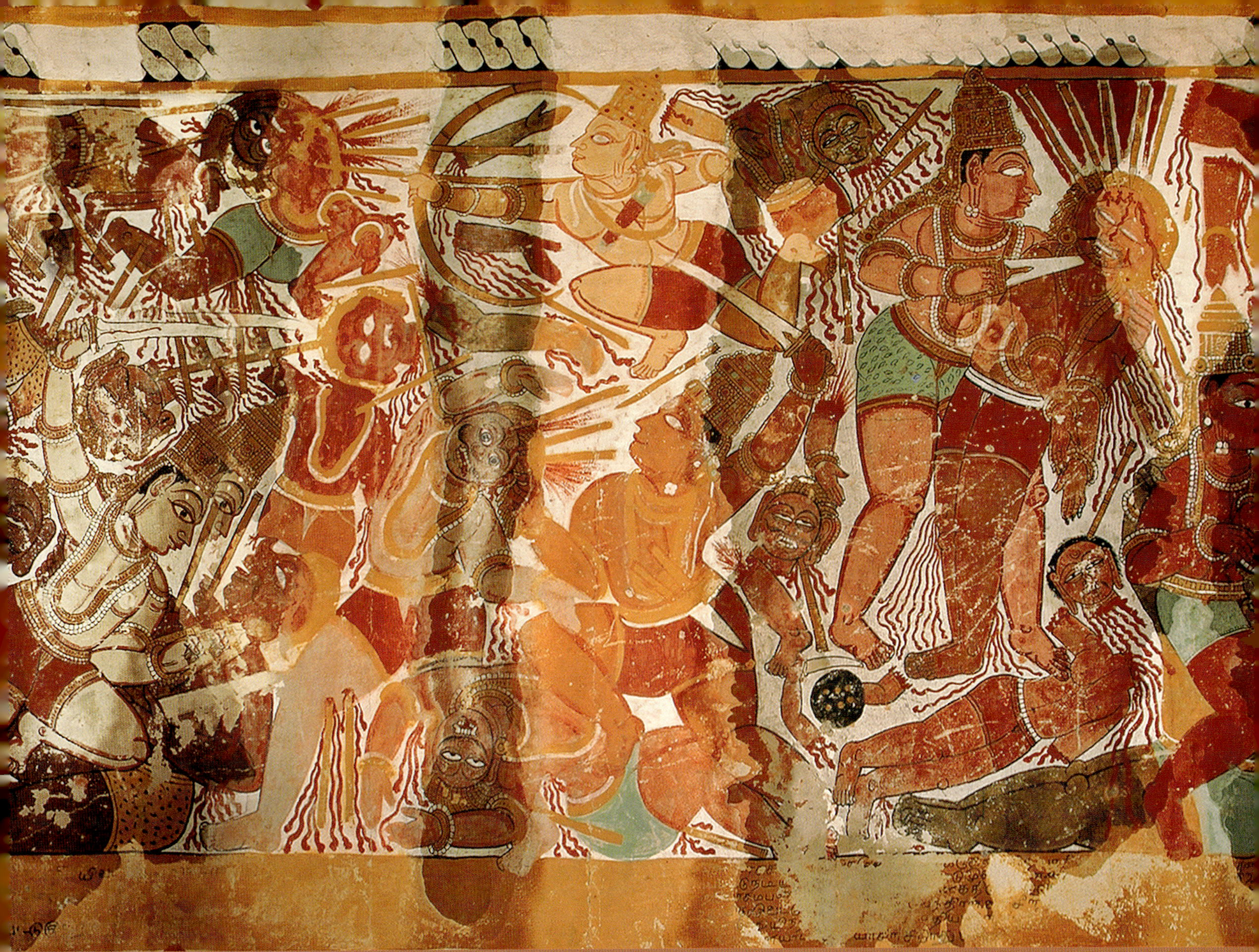

Panel 39-40, from right to left:

- *War of gods and demons*

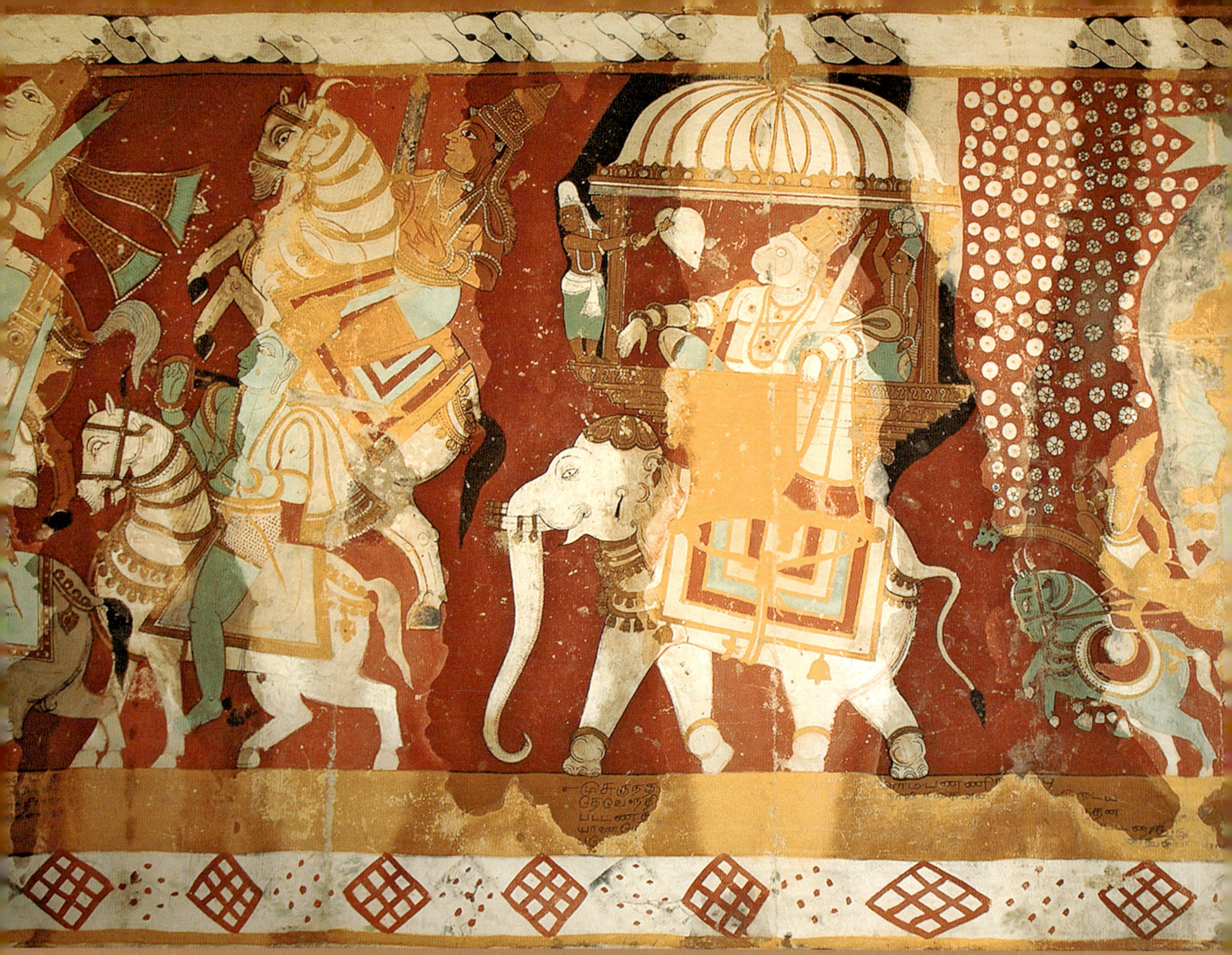

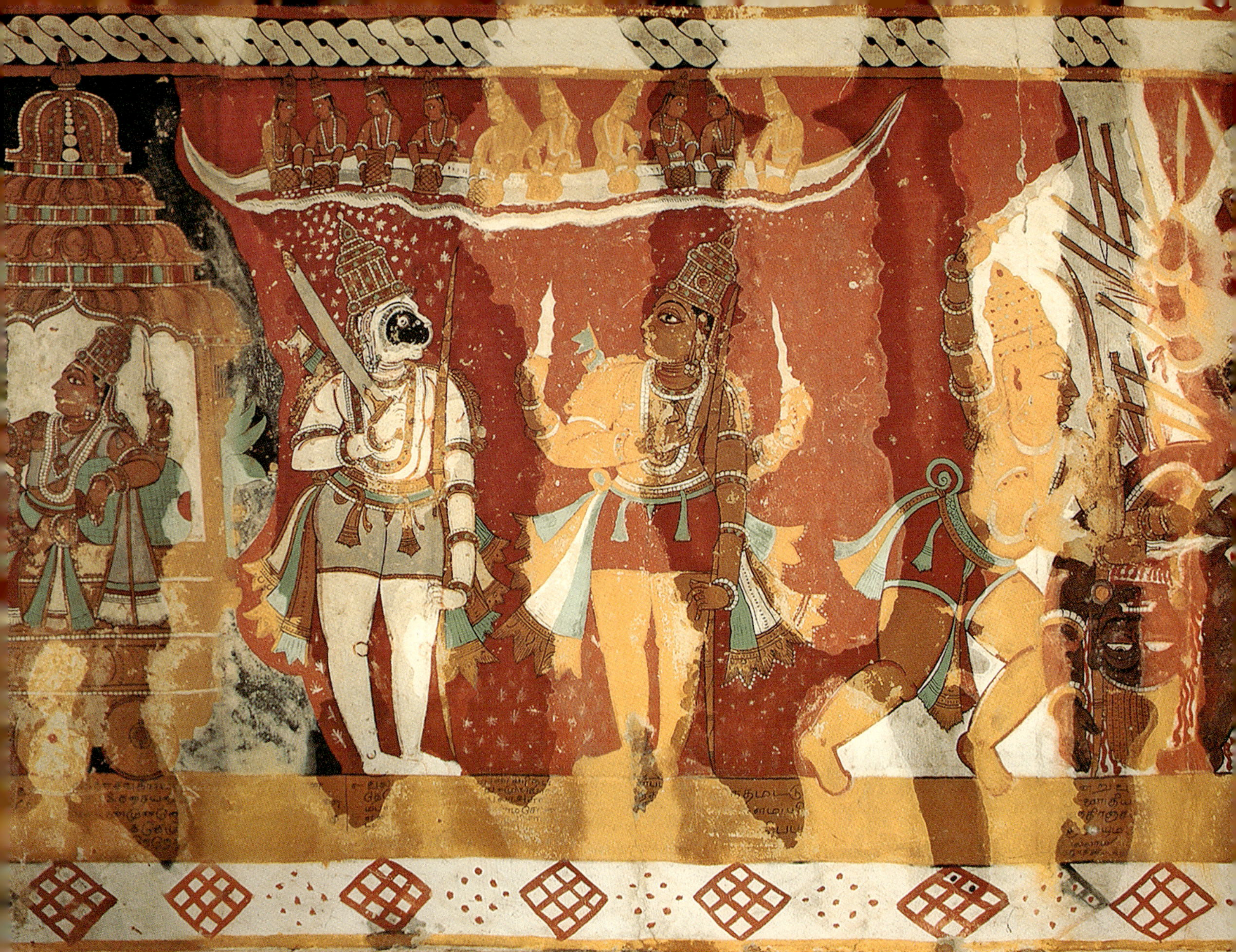

Panel 41-42, from right to left:

- *Indra thanks Mucukunda for his help. The gods rain down flowers.*
- *Indra and Mucukunda proceed to Indra's city.*

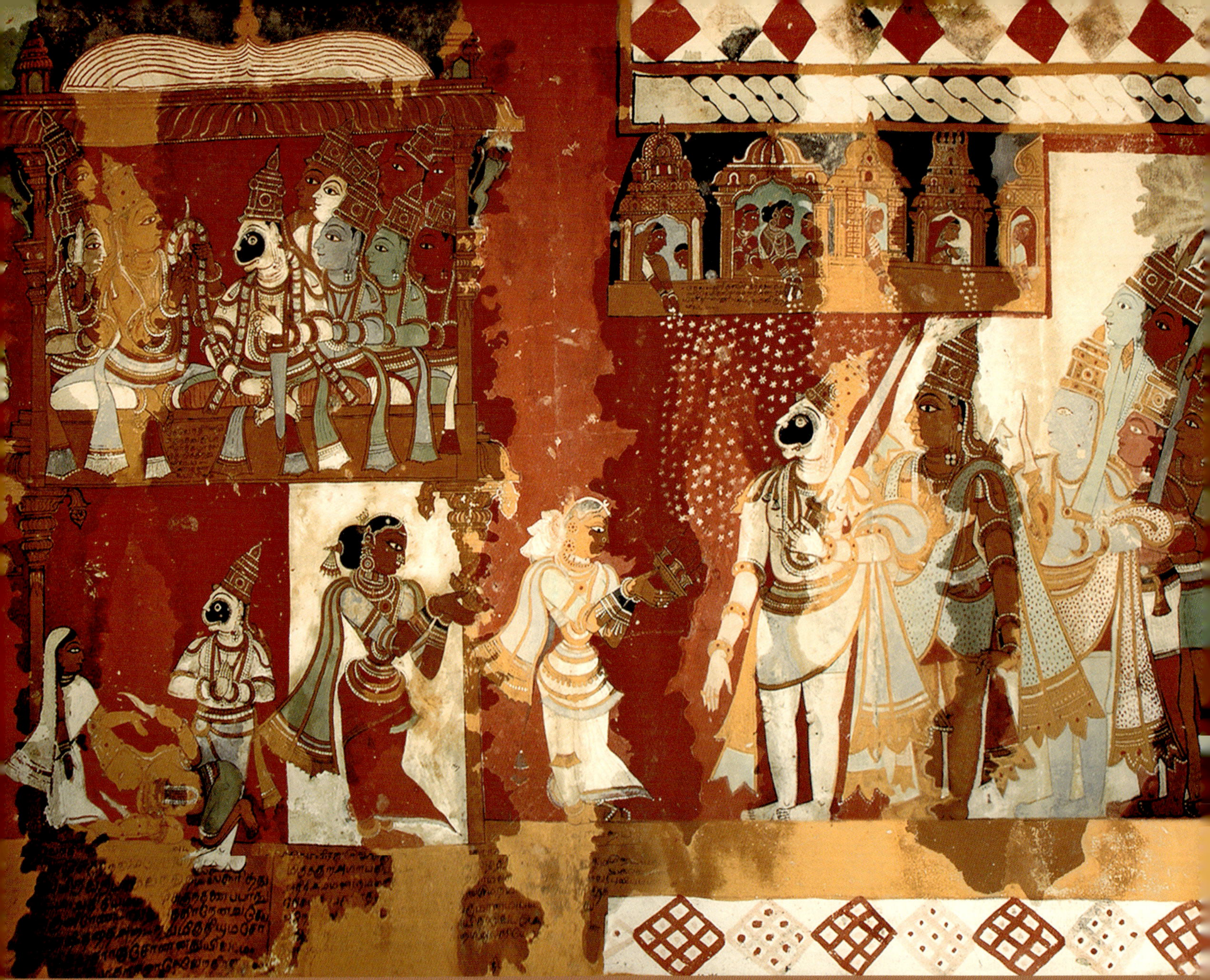

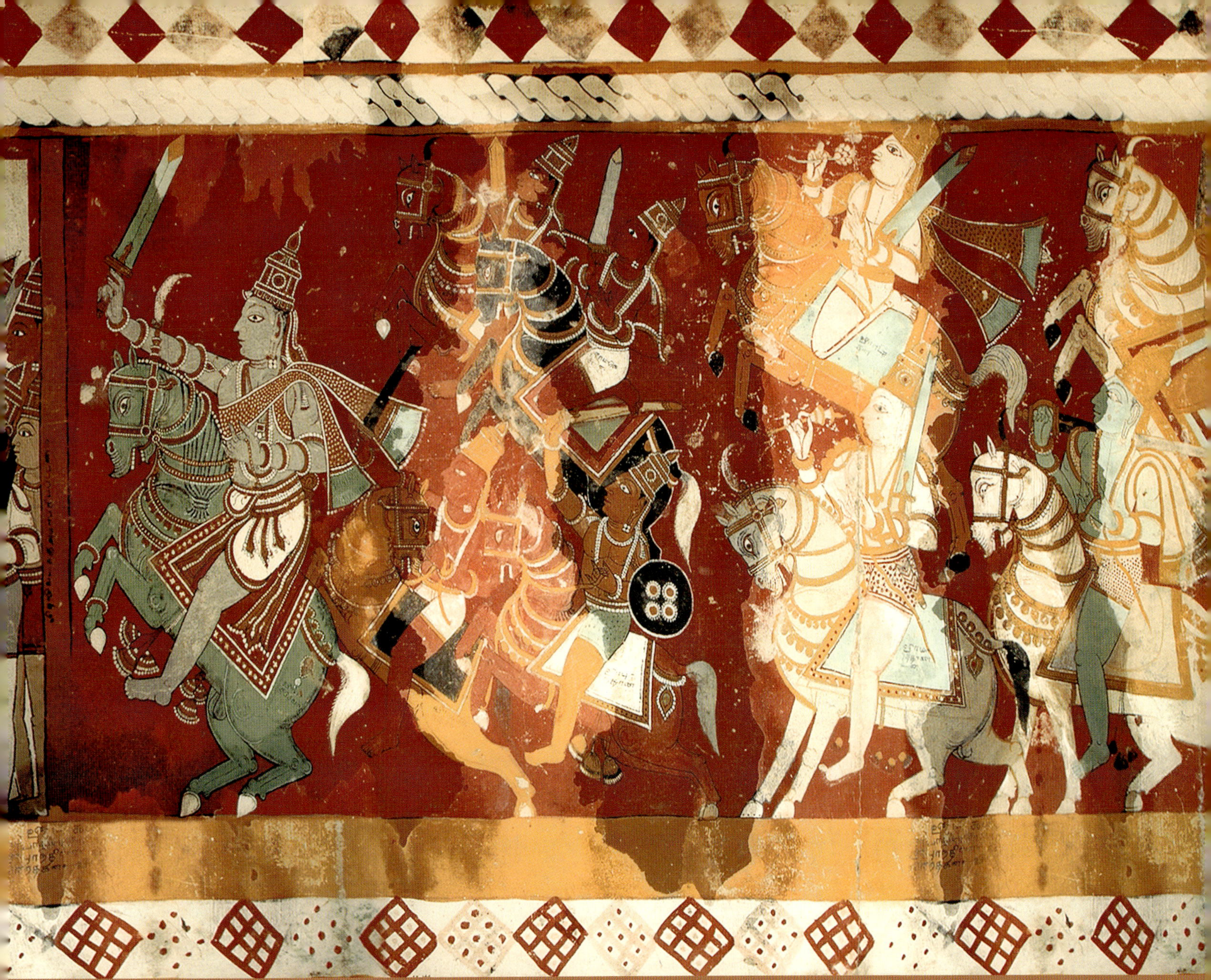

Panel 43-44, from right to left:

- *The nine heroes enter Indra's heaven.*
- *Mucukunda is welcomed into Indra's city. The women of the gods cast down flowers. Mucukunda is decorated with a garland of* parijāta *flowers in the upper story of the palace.*
- *Far left: Aditi, mother of Indra, welcomes Mucukunda and says, "You are a second son to me." [Note that this scene is not found in any of the Purāṇic sources from Tiruvarur.]*

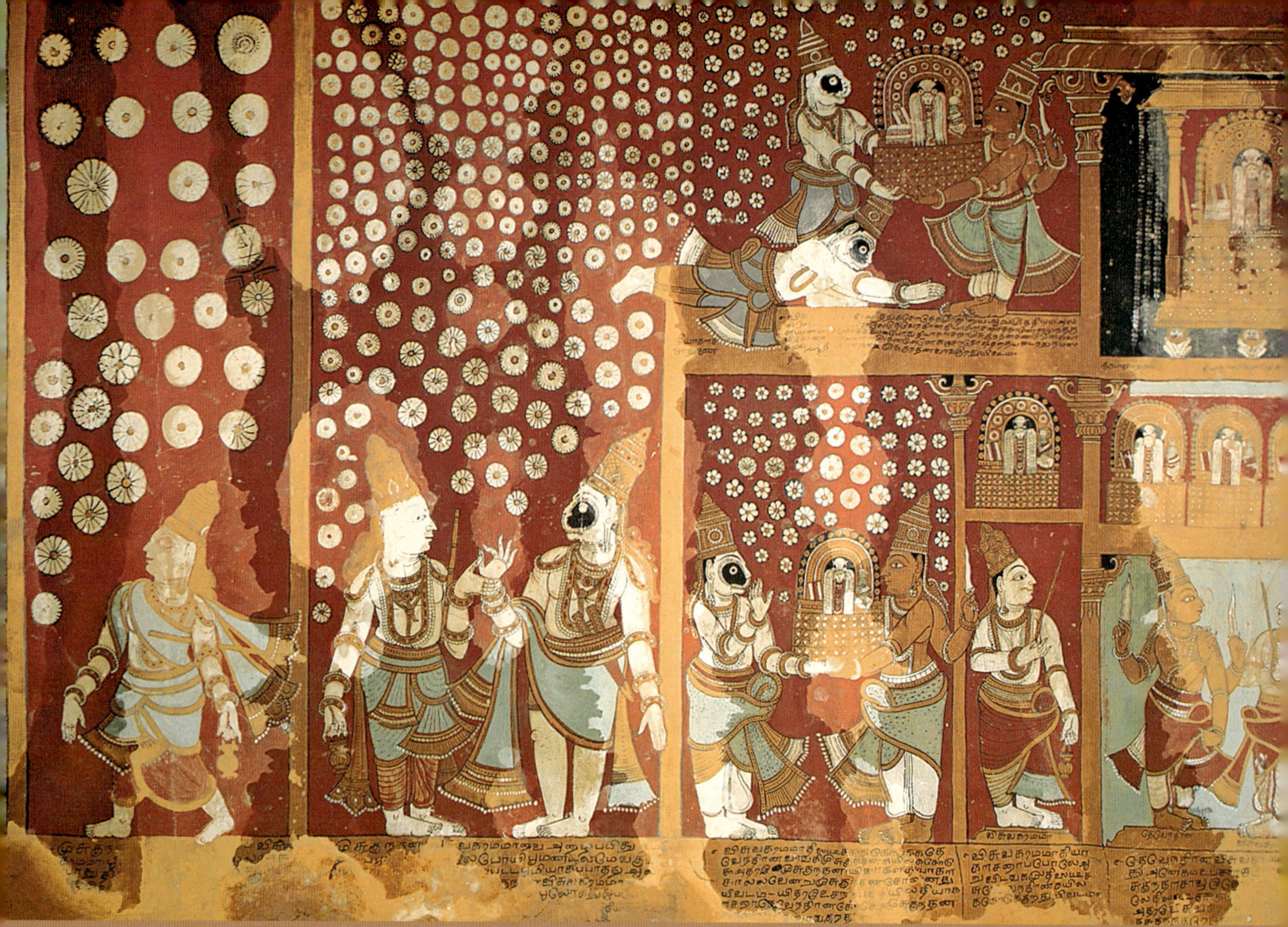

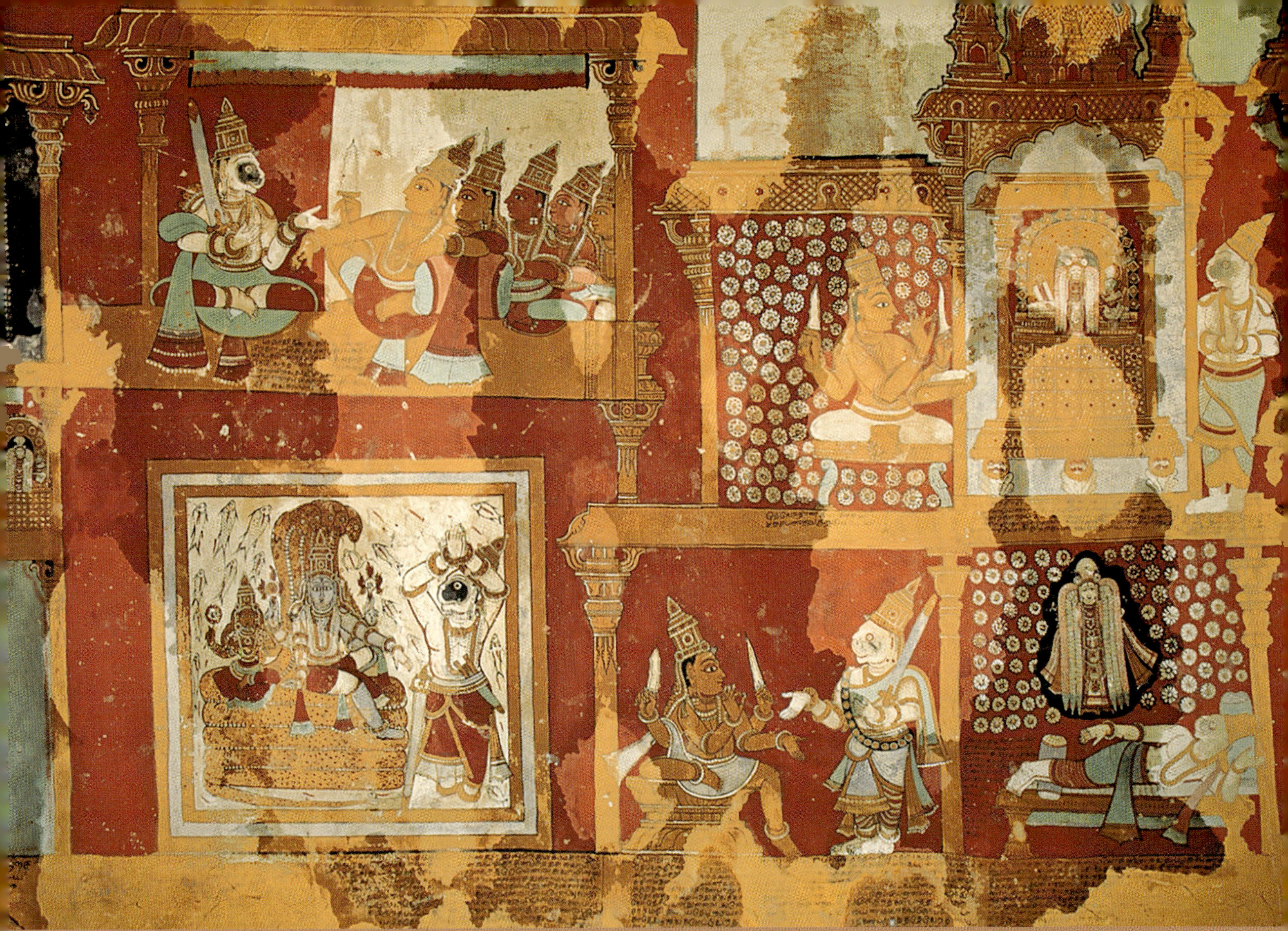

Panel 45-46, from right to left:

• Upper right to lower right to lower left to upper left: Mucukunda sees Indra's puja to Tyāgarāja. Tyāgarāja comes in a dream to Mucukunda and asks him to take him to Tiruvarur. Mucukunda asks Indra's permission. Indra sends him to the sea of milk to ask Viṣṇu. Mucukunda returns with Viṣṇu's reply. Indra summons Viśvakarmā.

• Indra asks Viśvakarmā to make six identical images of Tyāgarāja. Viśvakarmā presents them to Indra, who gives them to Mucukunda. Mucukunda rejects them one by one: "These are not Tyāgarāja." Indra gives the real Tyāgarāja to Mucukunda, who worships it [upper center].

Lower left: Mucukunda sends Viśvakarmā to earth to find the right home for Tyāgarāja.

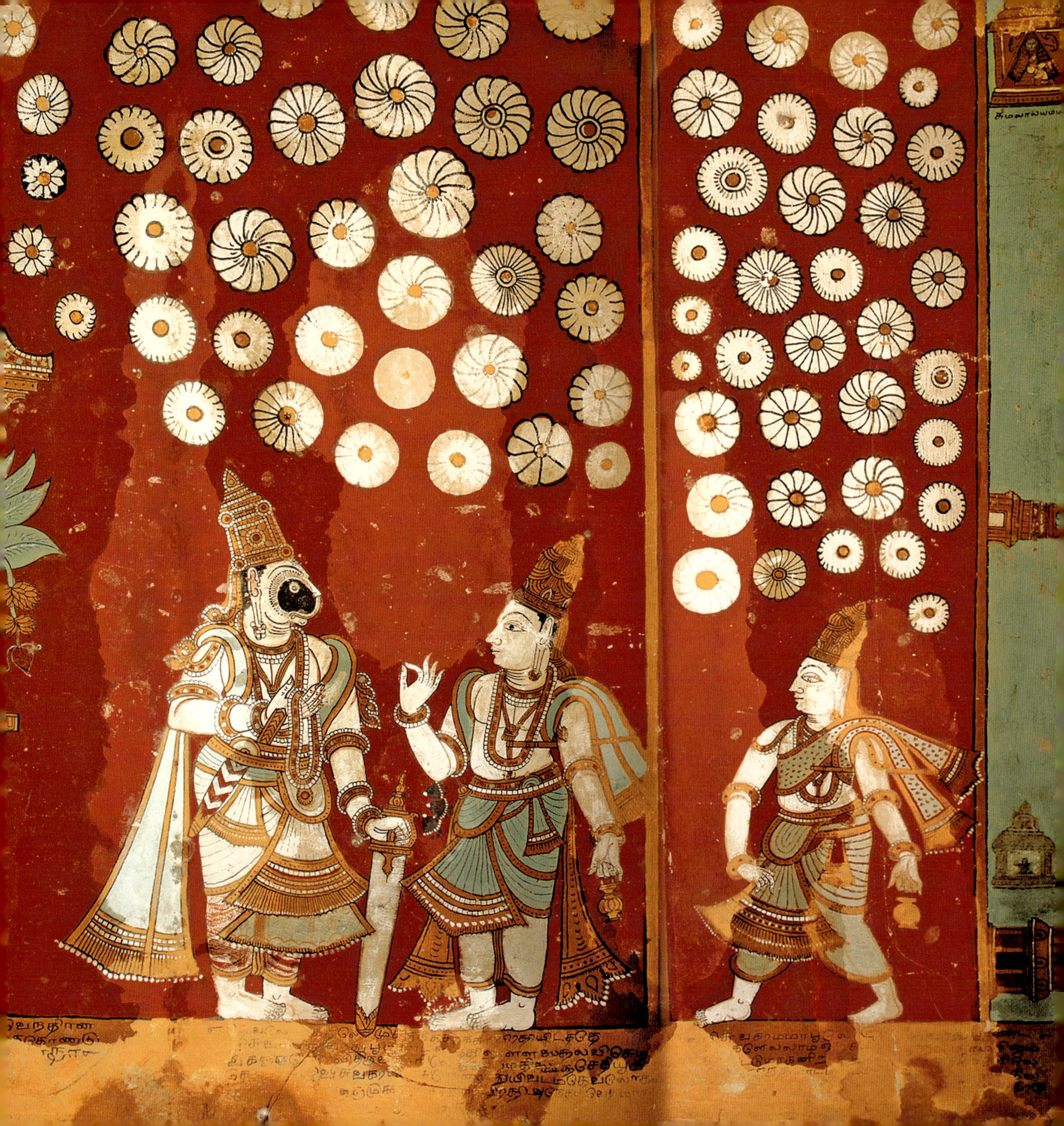

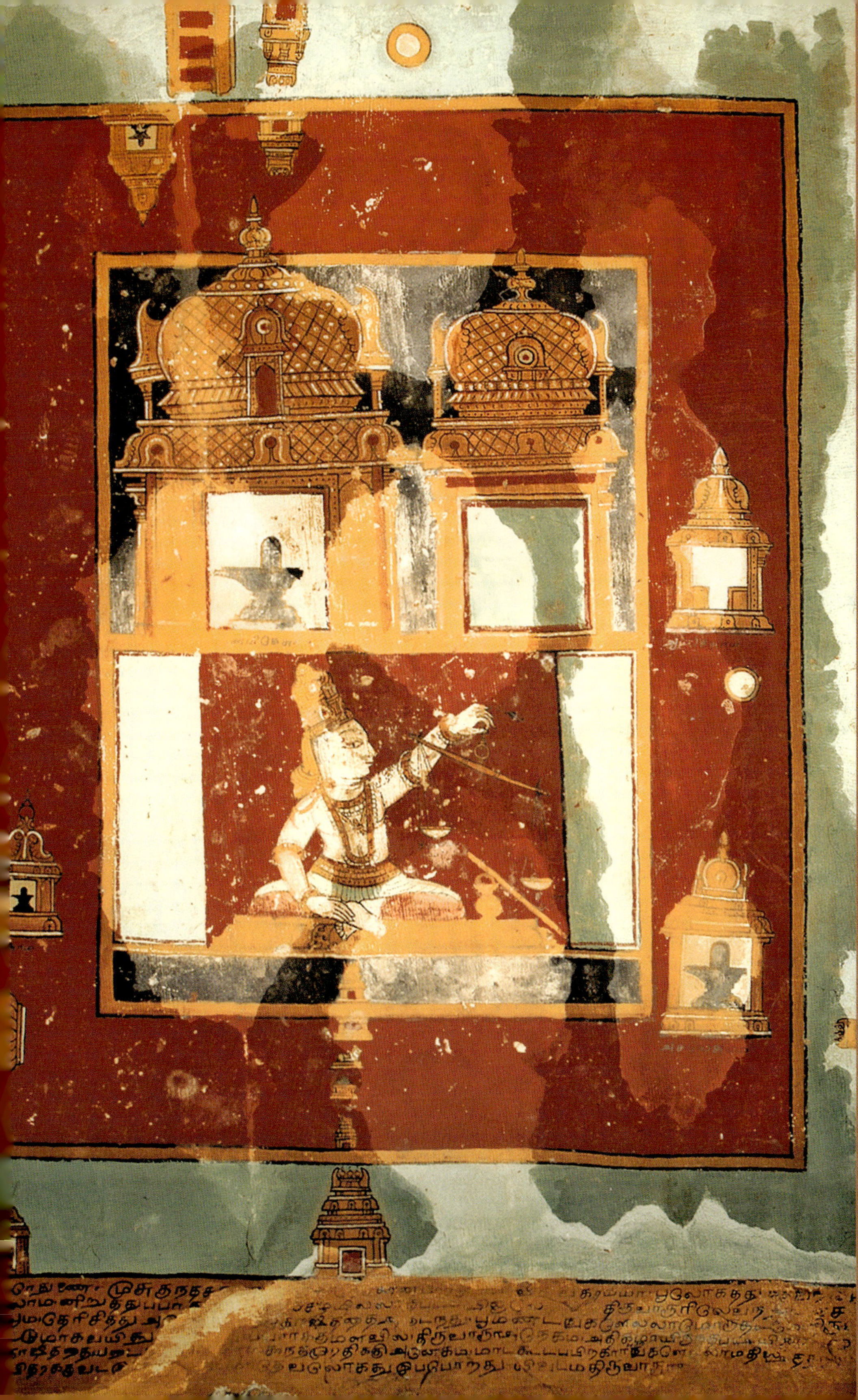

Panel 47-48, from right to left:

- *Viśvakarmā weighs Tiruvarur against all the other sites in the world.*
- *Viśvakarmā returns to tell Mucukunda that Tiruvarur is the right place.*

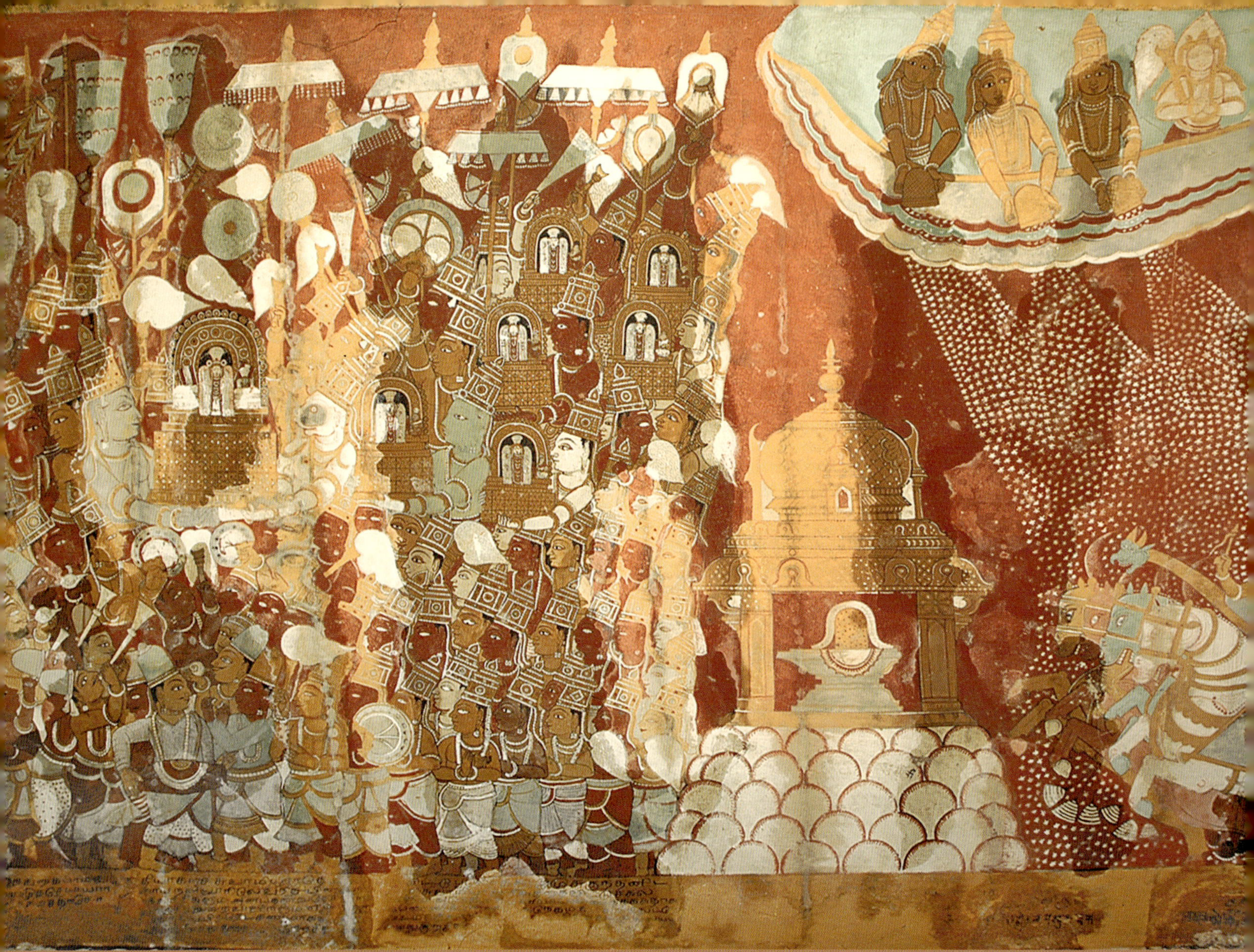

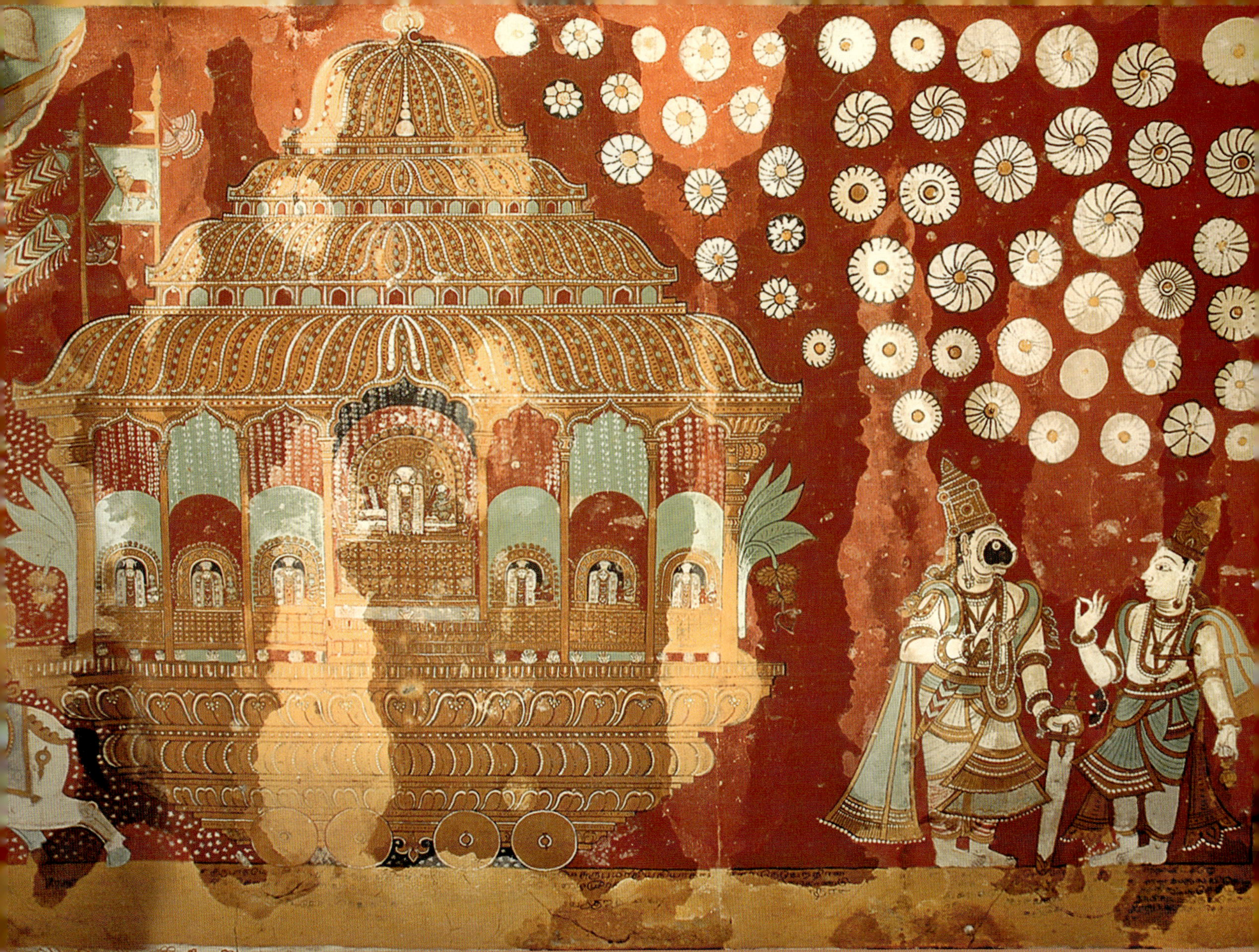

Panel 49-50, from right to left:

- *Tyāgarāja and the other six viṭaṅka images are taken to earth.*
- *Mucukunda carries Tyāgarāja to Tiruvarur. The nine heroes carry the other six images.*

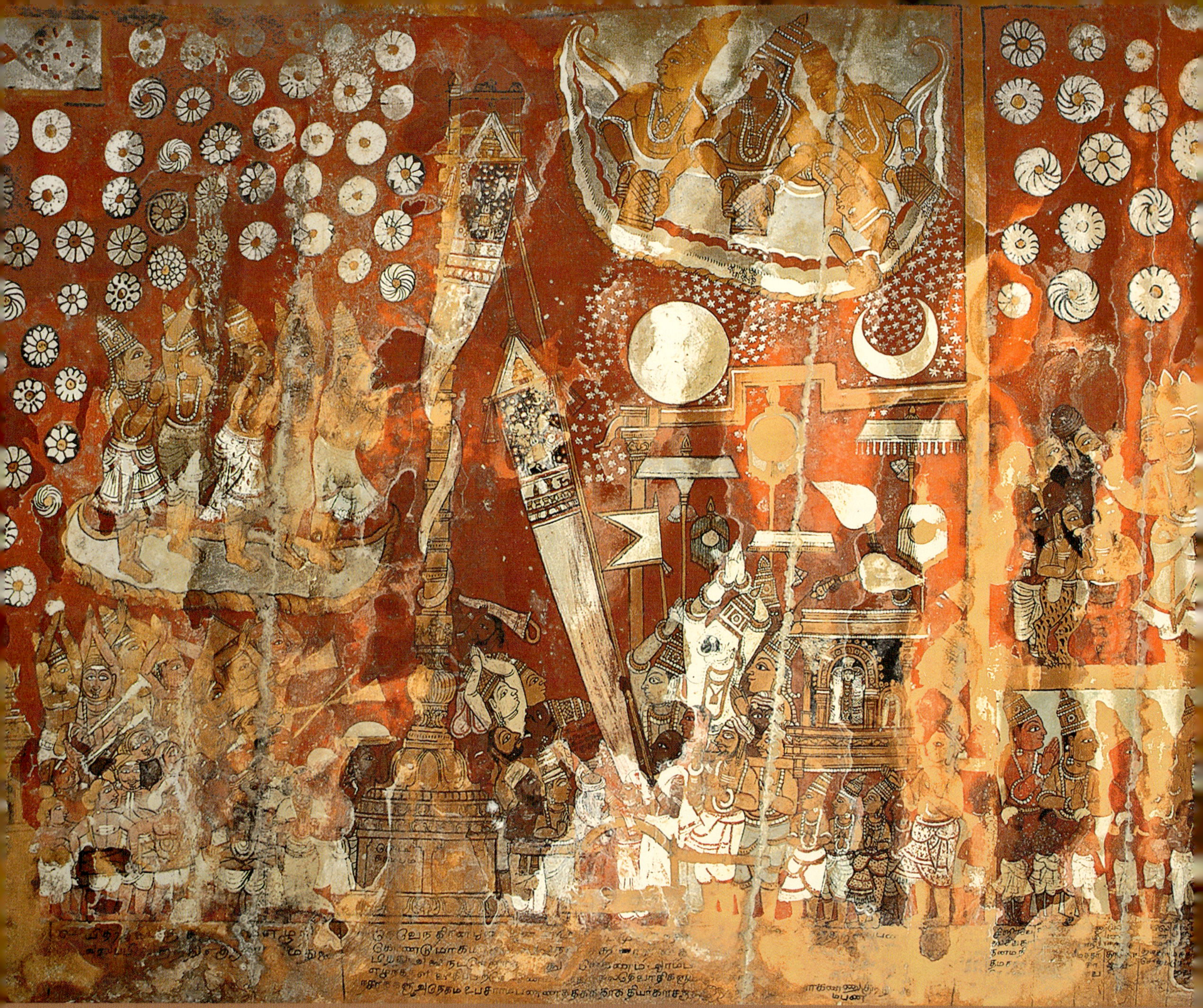

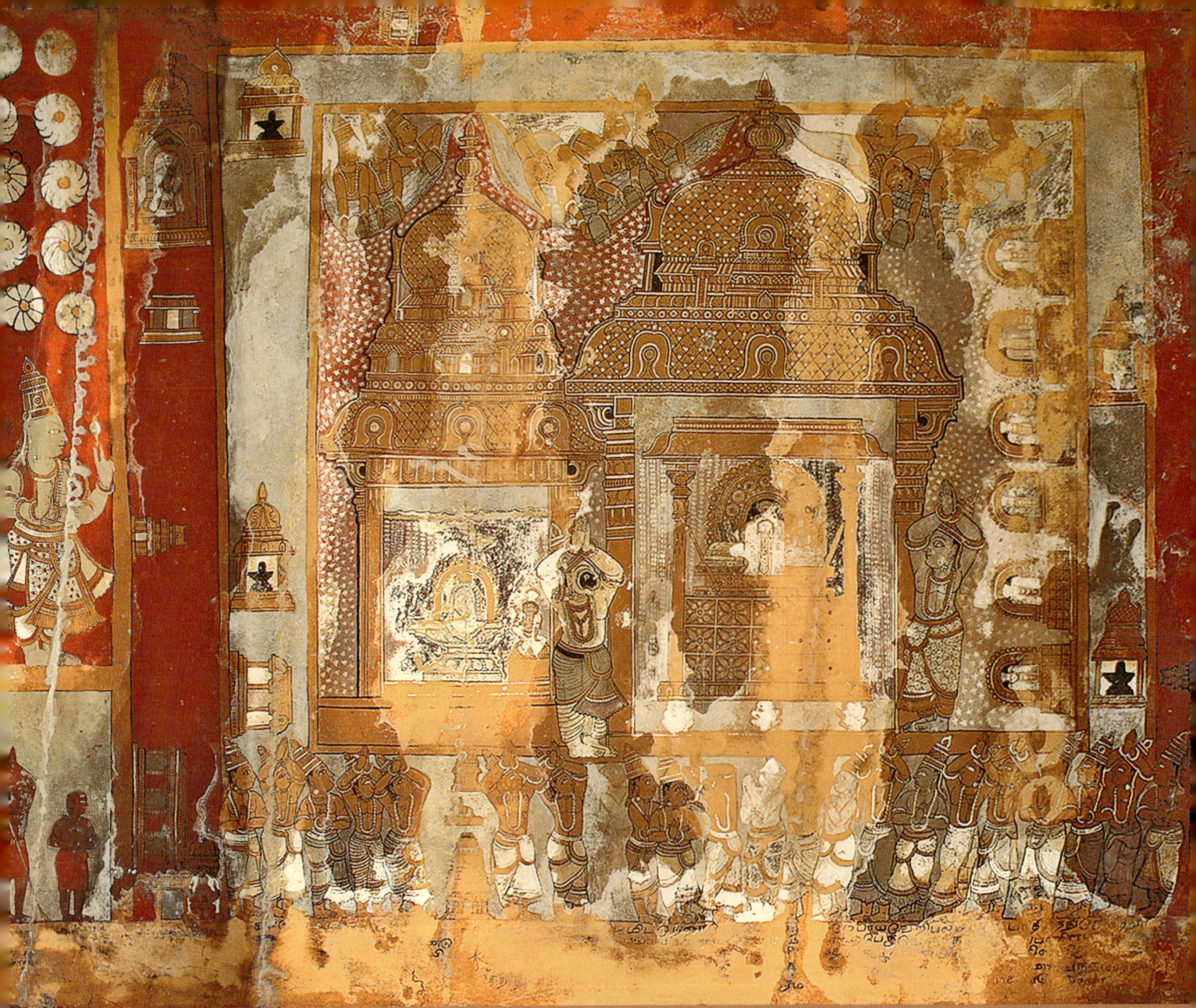

Panel 51-52, from right to left:

- *Mucukunda installs Tyāgarāja in his shrine to the south of Valmīkanātha.*
- *Viṣṇu, Brahmā, and the sages come to Tiruvarur for the Paṅkuṇi Uttaram festival. The flag is raised at the onset of the festival.*

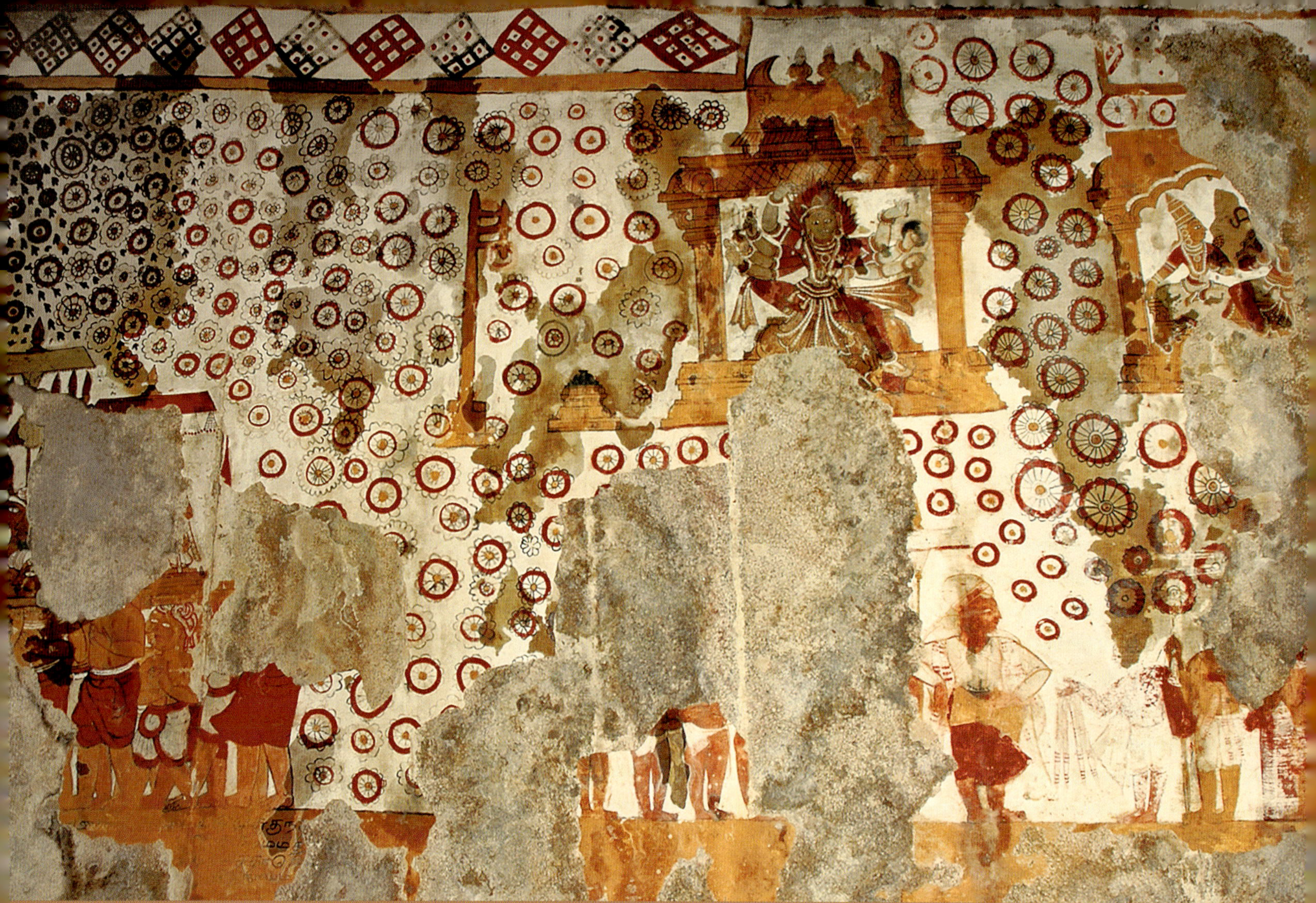

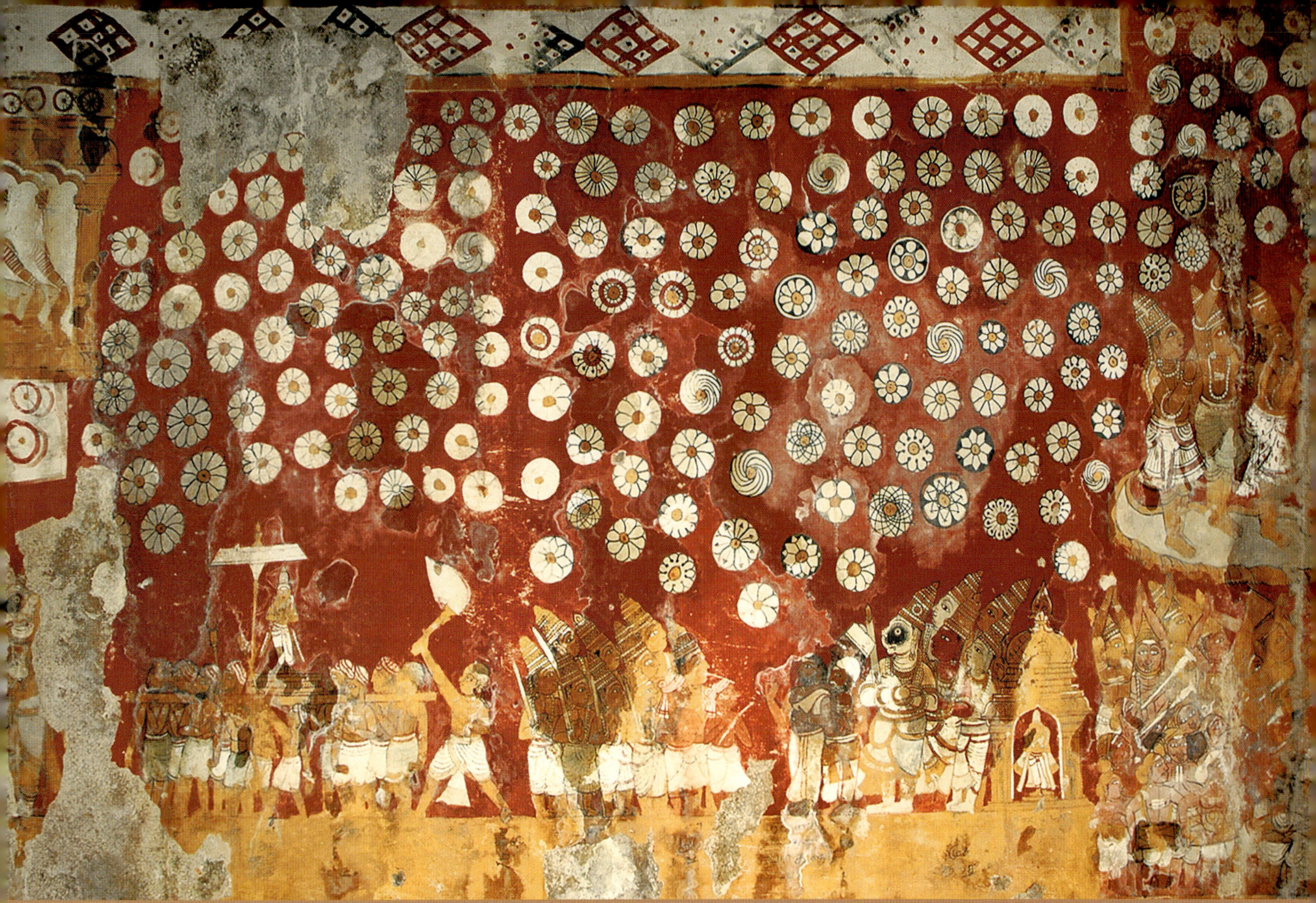

Panel 53-54, from right to left:

- *Processional.*
- *Bhadrakāḷi is carried in procession.*

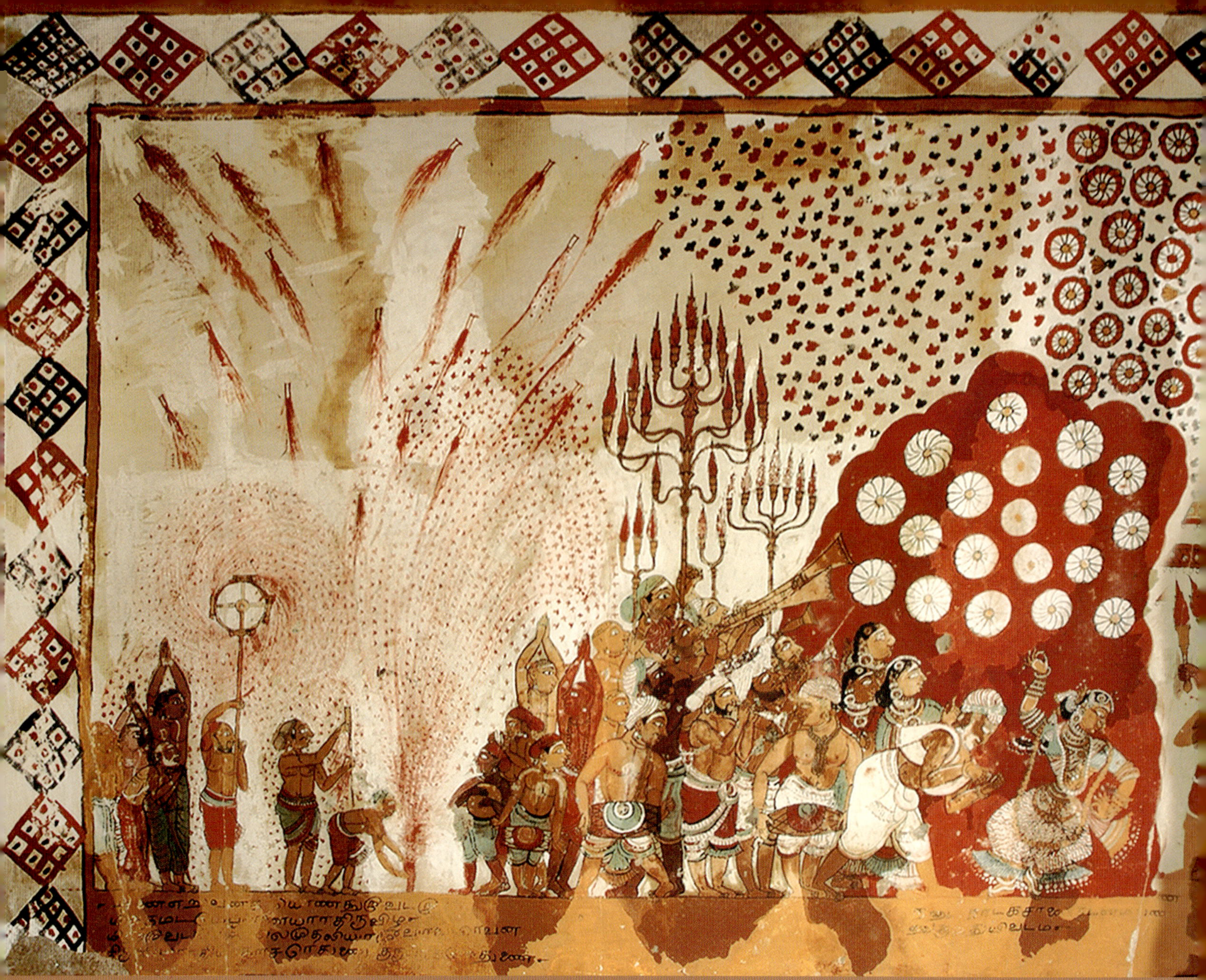

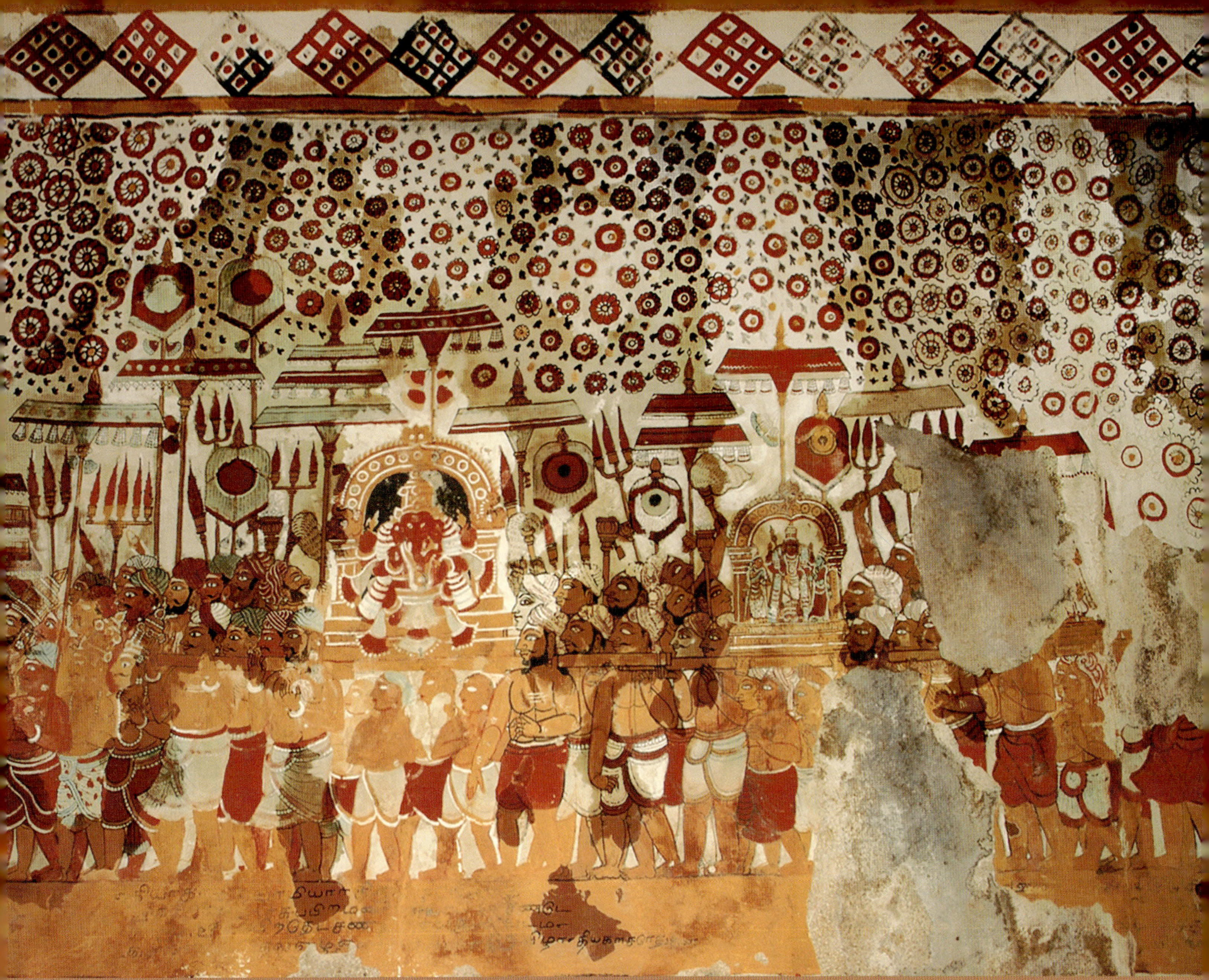

Panel 55-56, from right to left:

- *Gaṇapati and Subrahmaṇyasvāmi are carried in procession.*
- *Far left: Dance on the moveable stage.*

Panel 56

• *Bhairava, the three* Tevāram *poets and Māṇikkavācakar in procession*

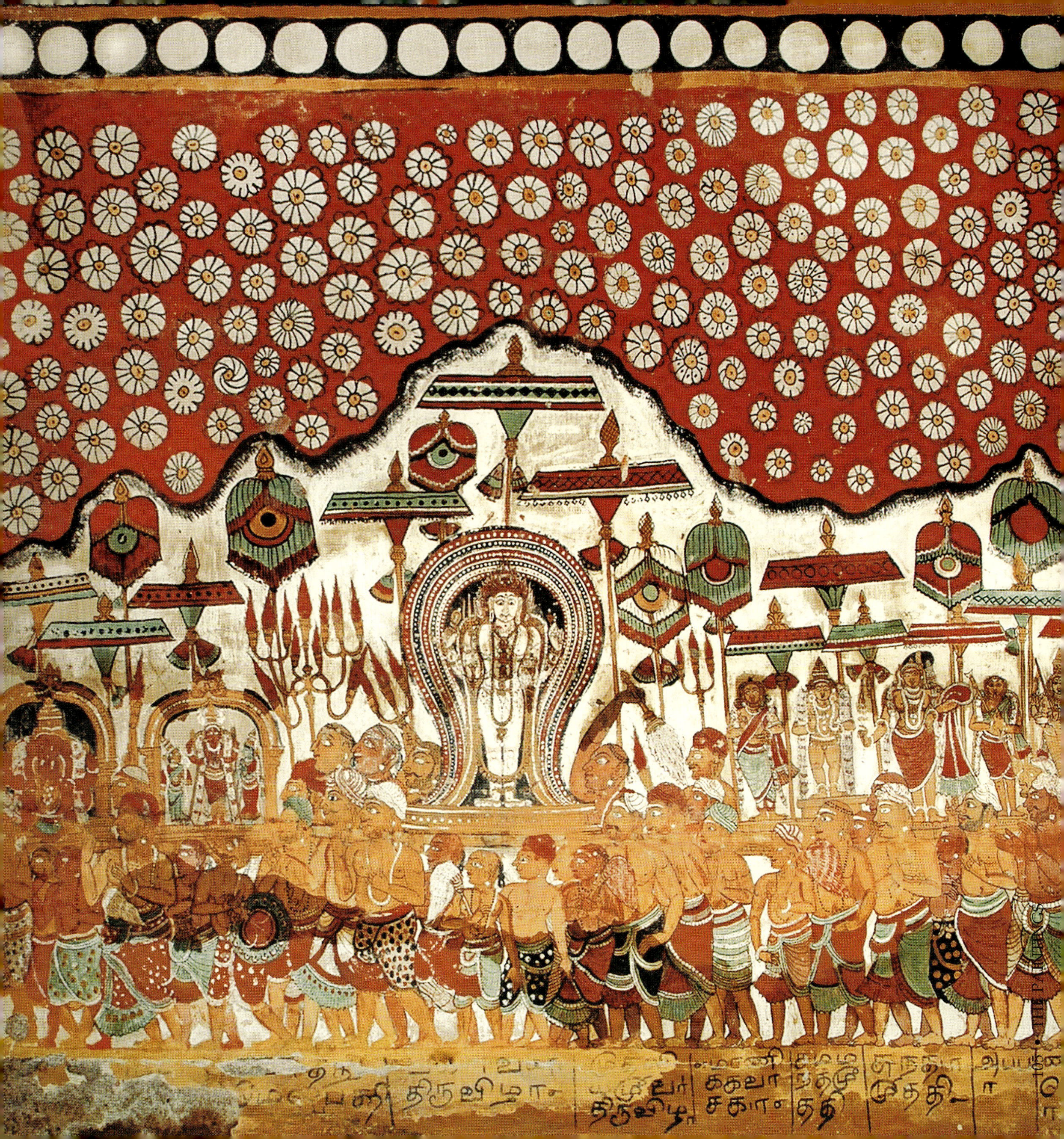
திருவிழா

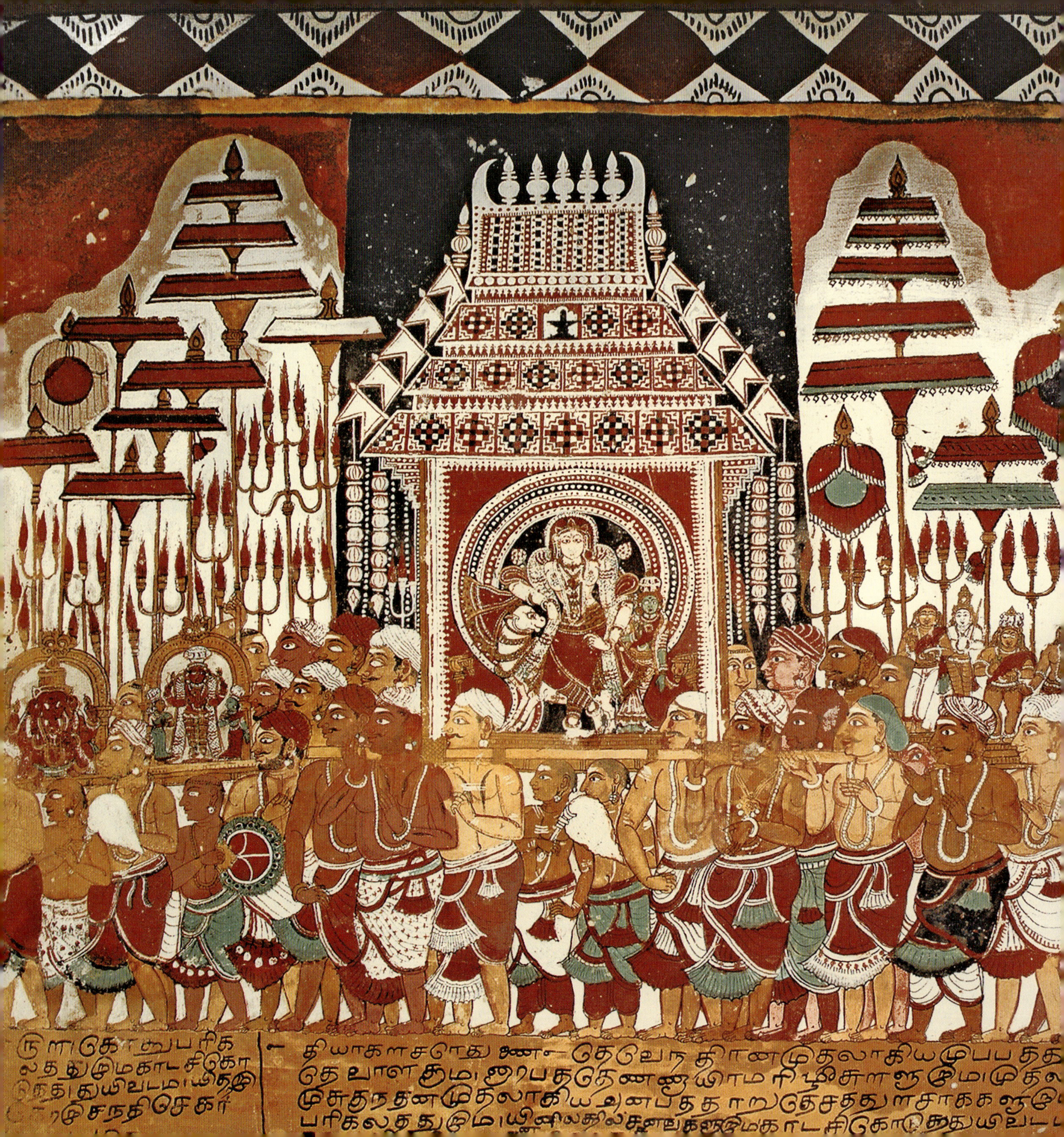

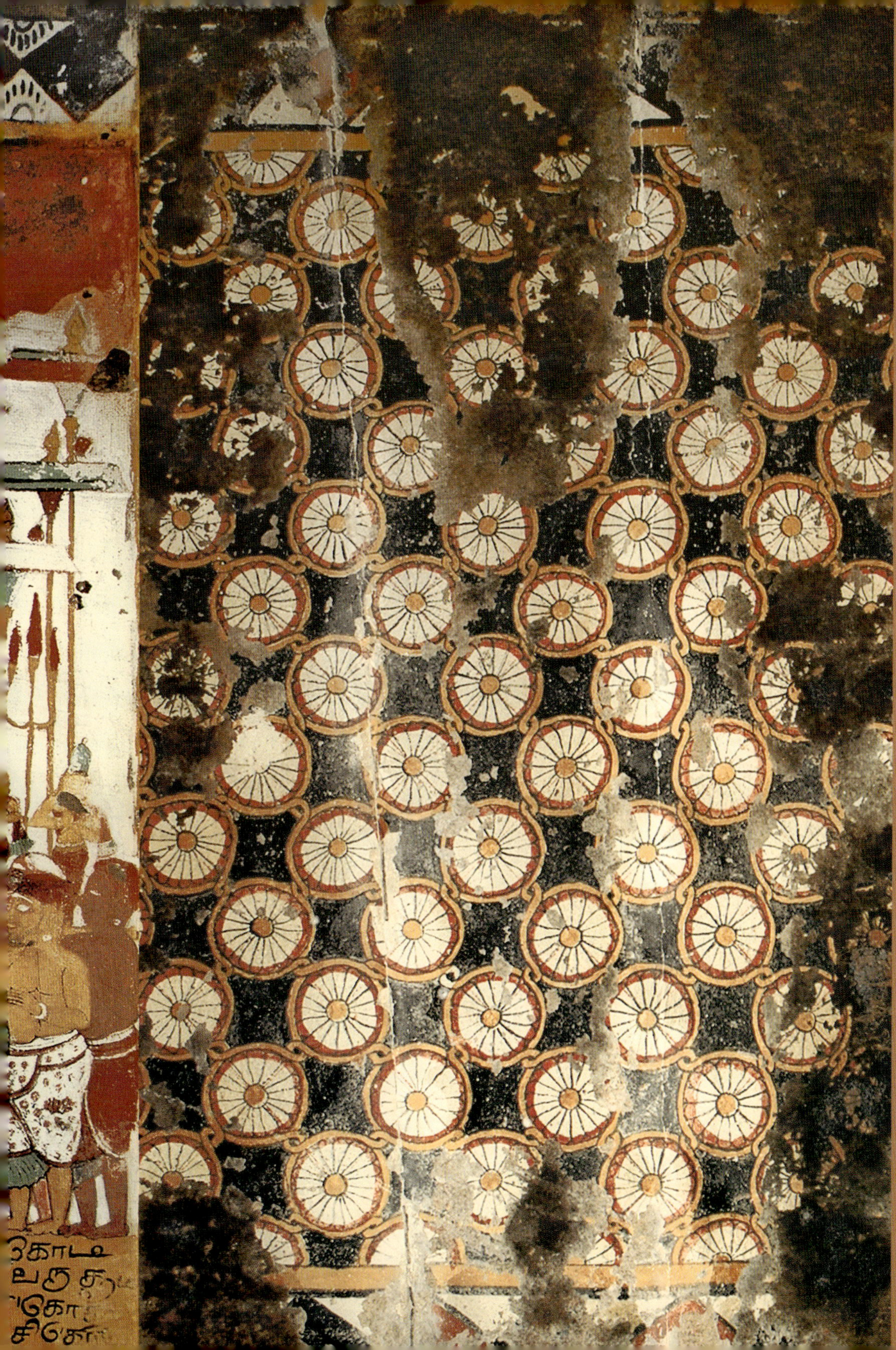

Panel 57-58, from right to left:

- *Stars in the night sky(?) (possibly firecrackers, atishbaji, with the procession?)*
- *Tyāgarāja/ Kāṭci kŏṭuttavar in procession together with all the gods, sages, kings of this world, and the people of Tiruvarur*

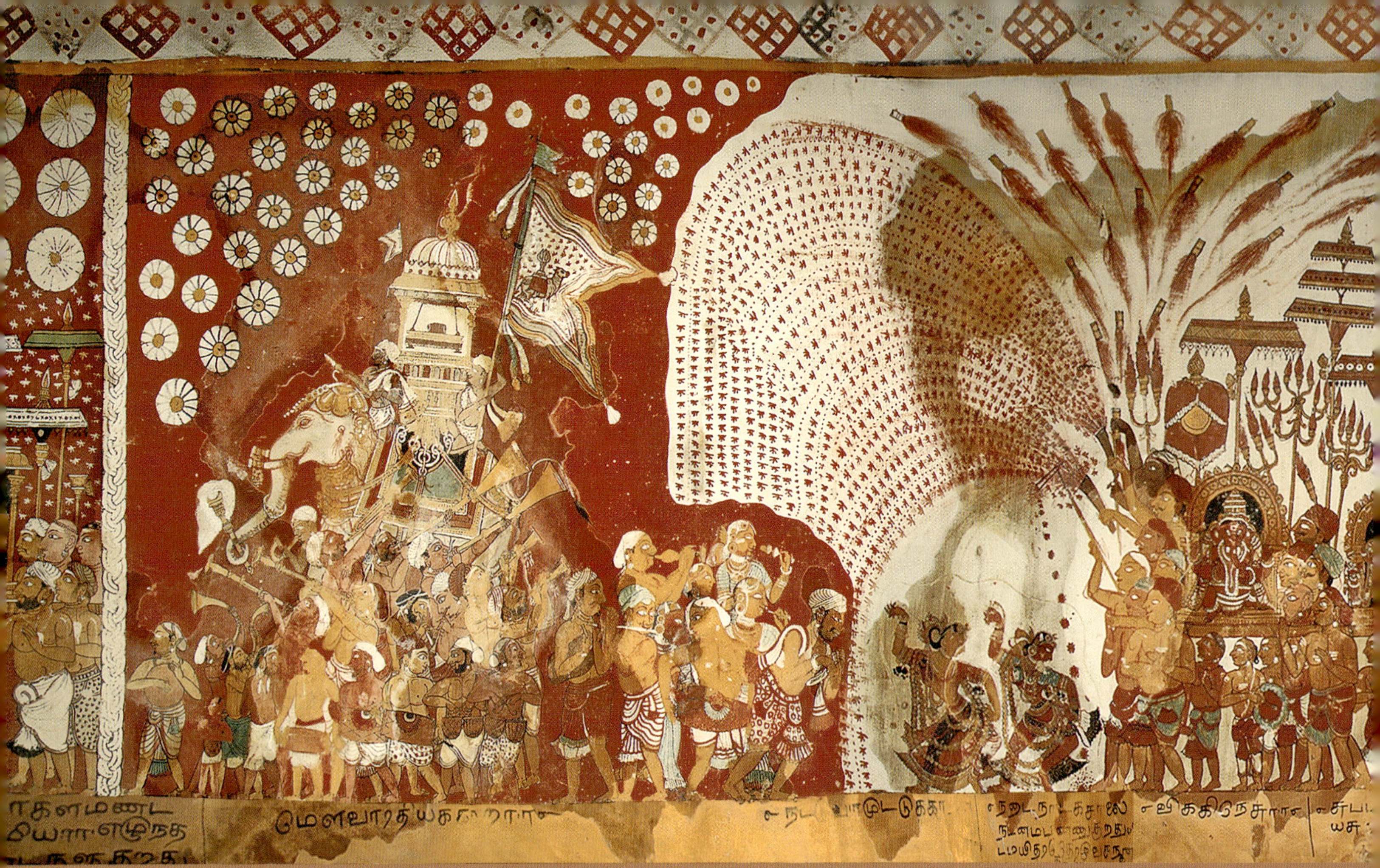

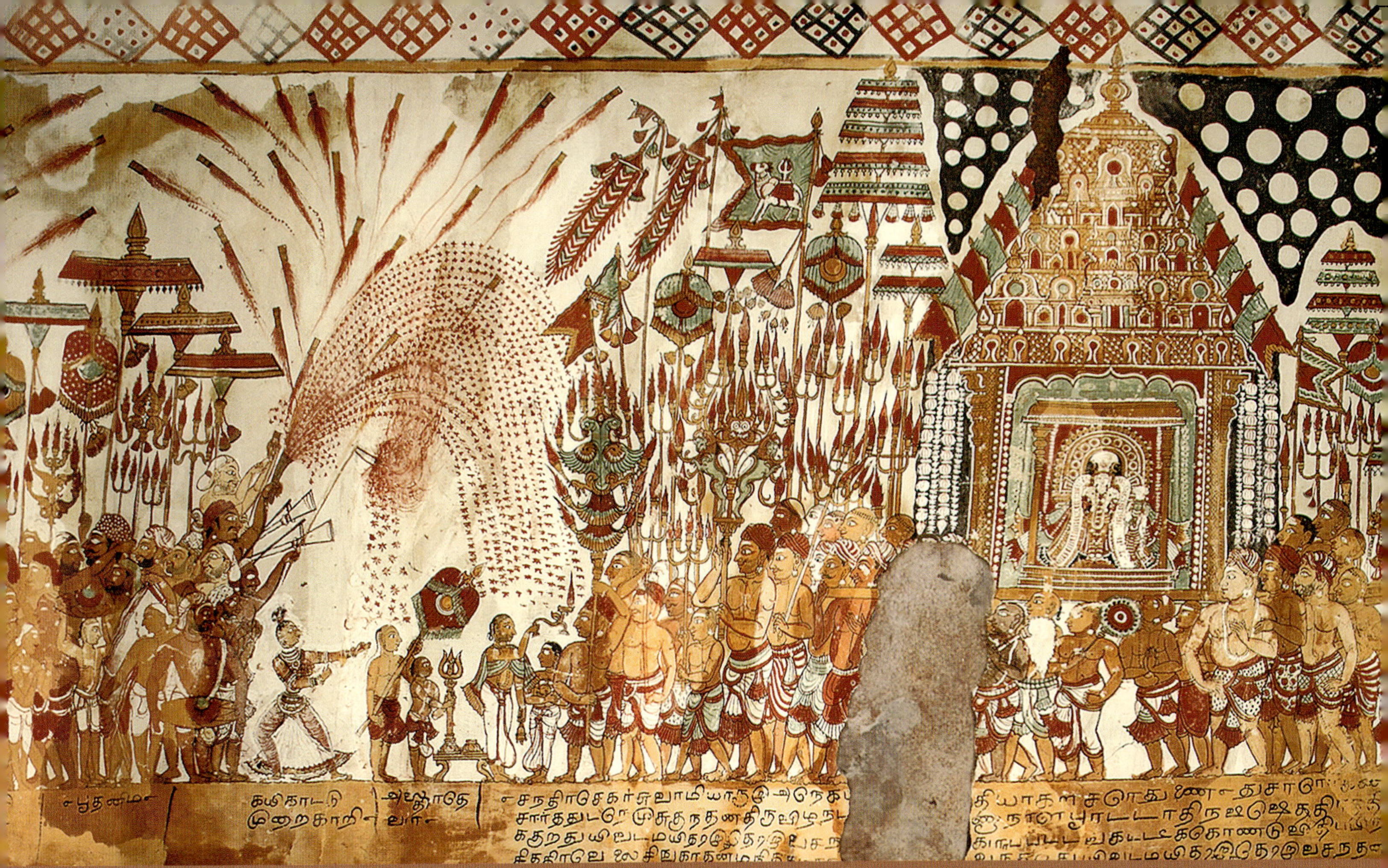

Panel 59, from right to left:

- *Vighneśvara, Subrahmaṇya-svâmi, and Candraśekhara in the Spring Festival*

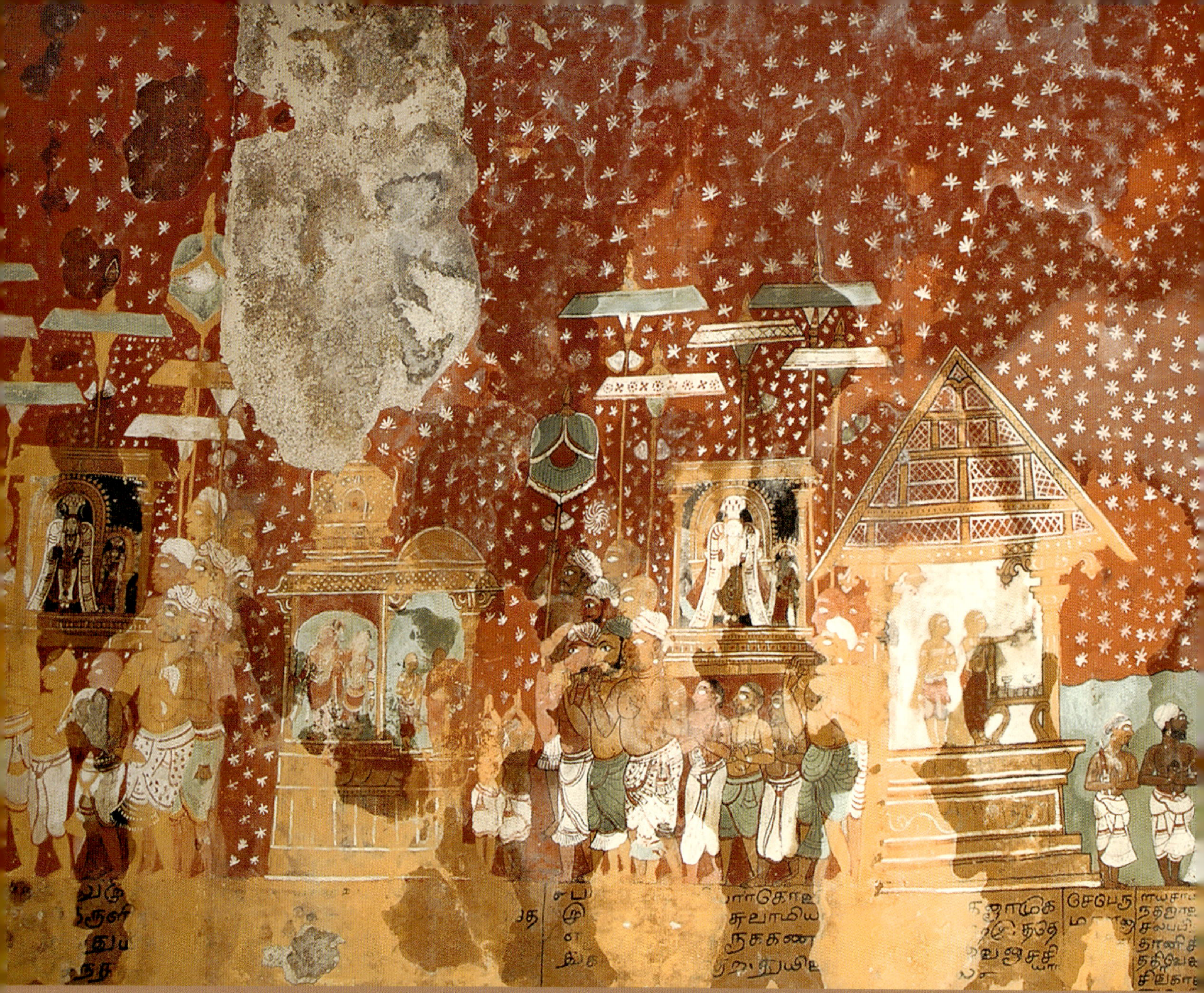

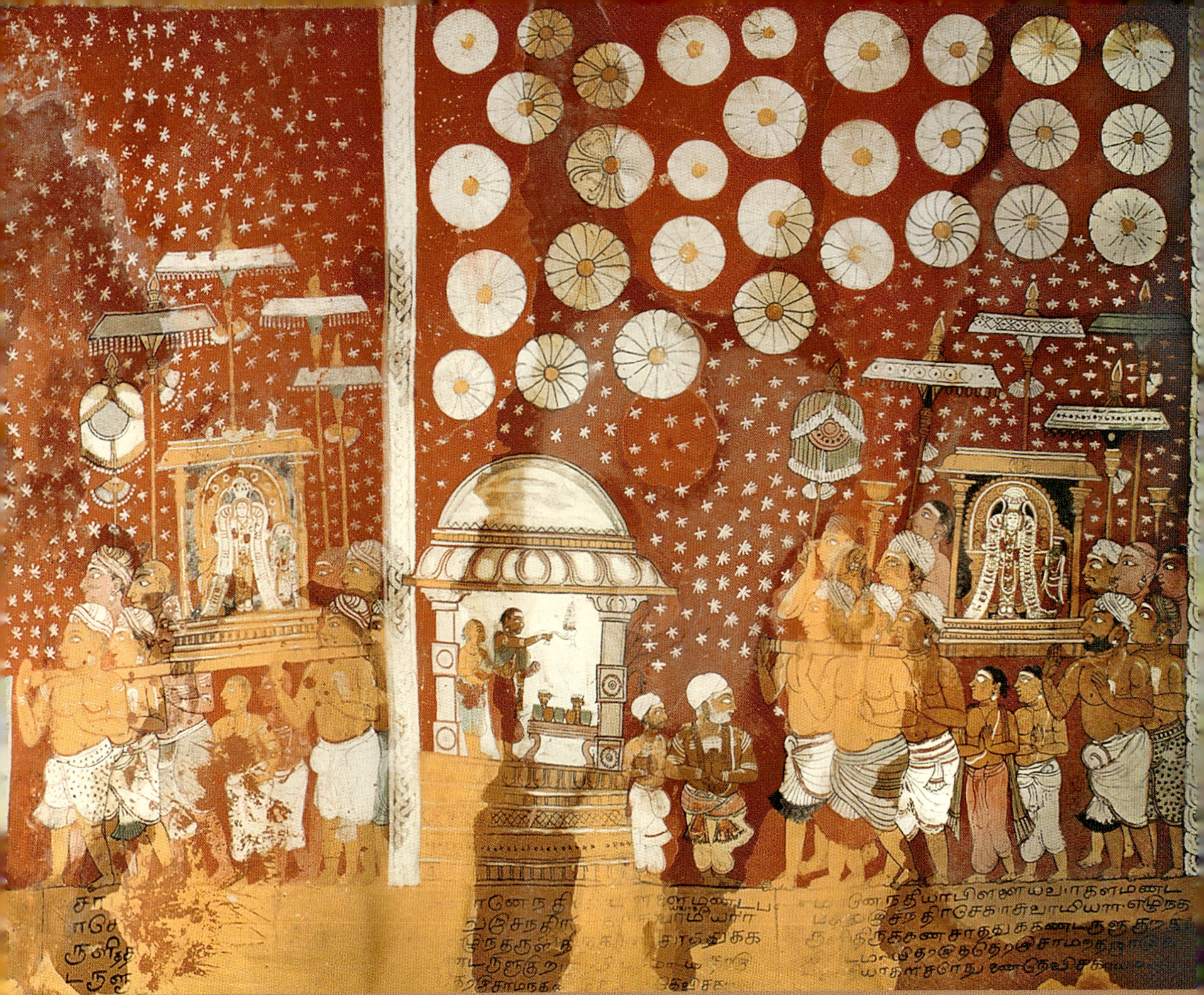

Panel 60-61, from right to left:

- *Candraśekhara halts at a* maṇḍapam *during his procession*
- *Spring Festival. Note self-portrait of the painter, together with his patron and a royal minister, in middle right of the panel.*

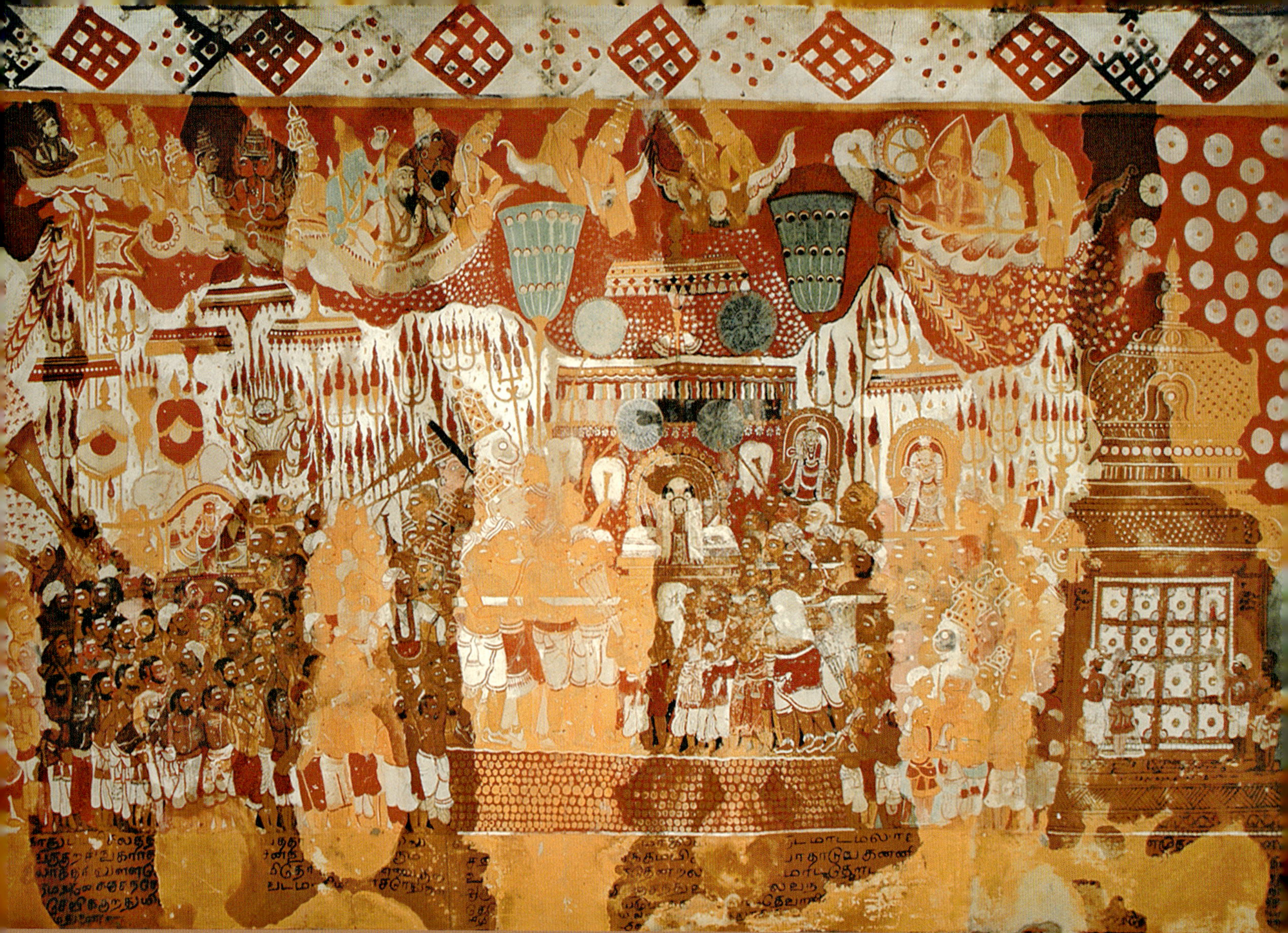

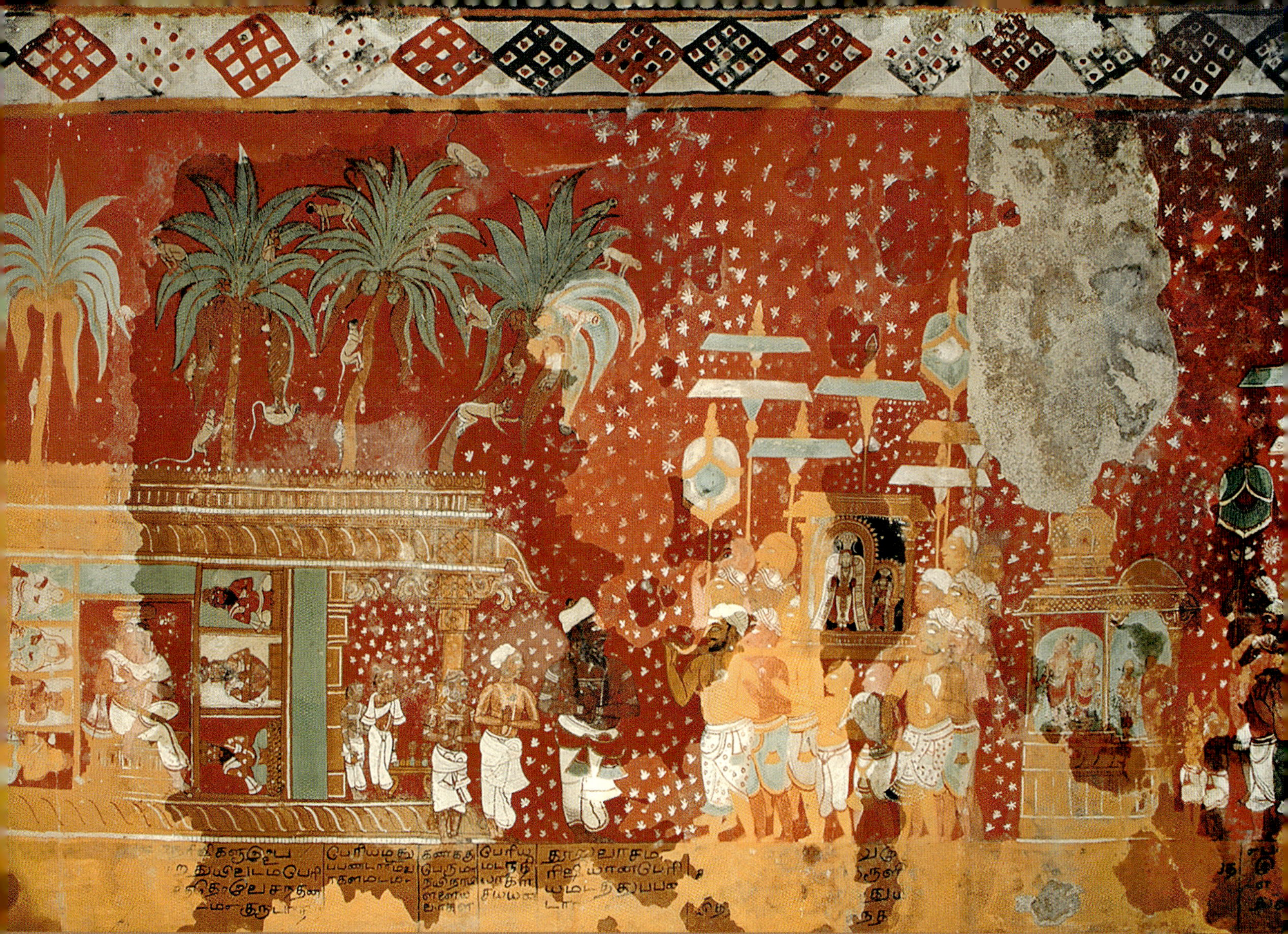

Panel 62-63, from right to left:

• *The procession halts at the Pĕriya Maṭam of Durvāsa-maharṣi, the Paṇḍāram, who welcomes the deity together with an accountant, Kaṇakku Pĕrumānayanāppiḷḷai, and Pĕriyamaṭattiyākarācayyaṉ.*

• Vasantotsava: *Fireworks. Women, gods and sages line the streets of Tiruvarur.*

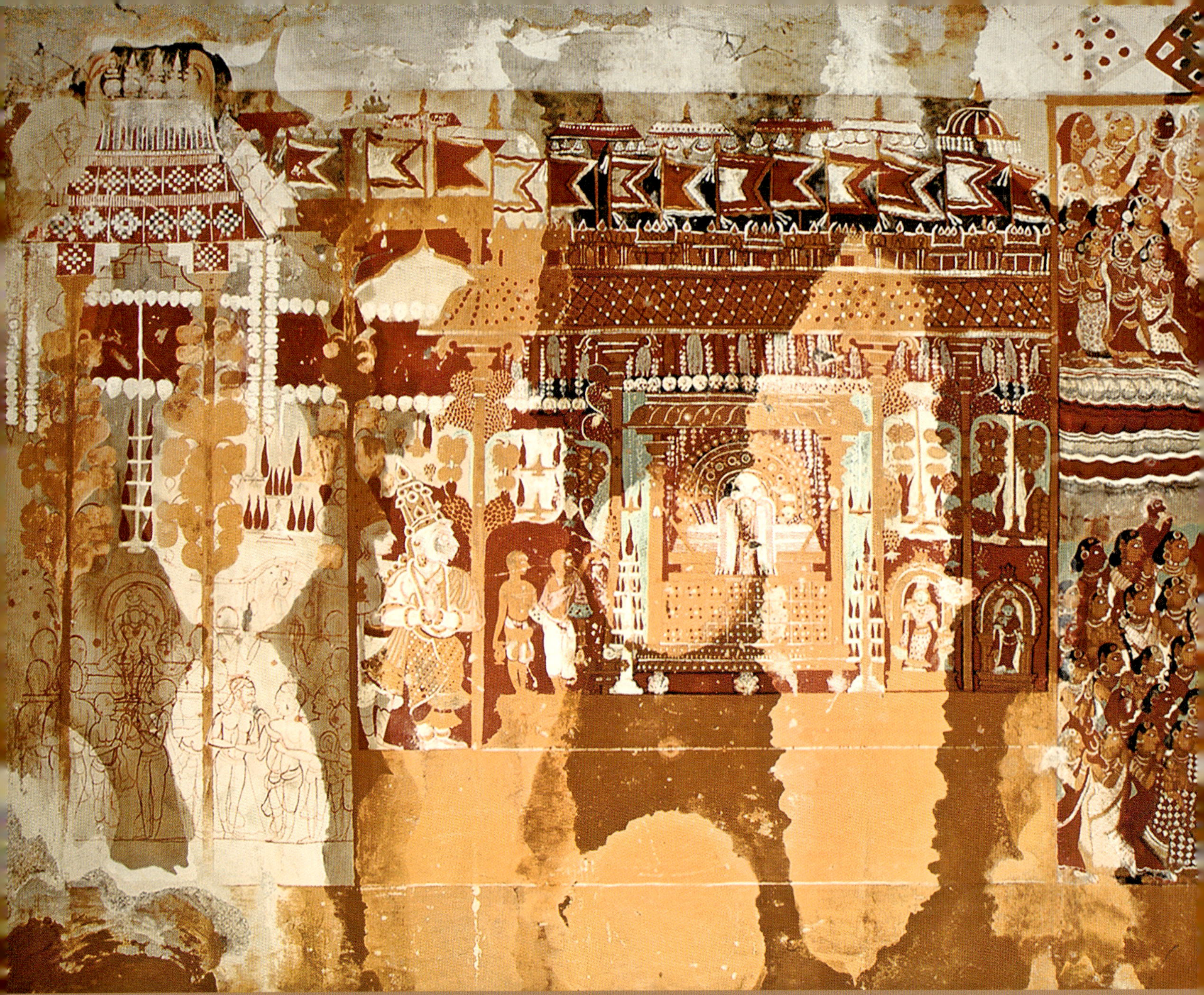

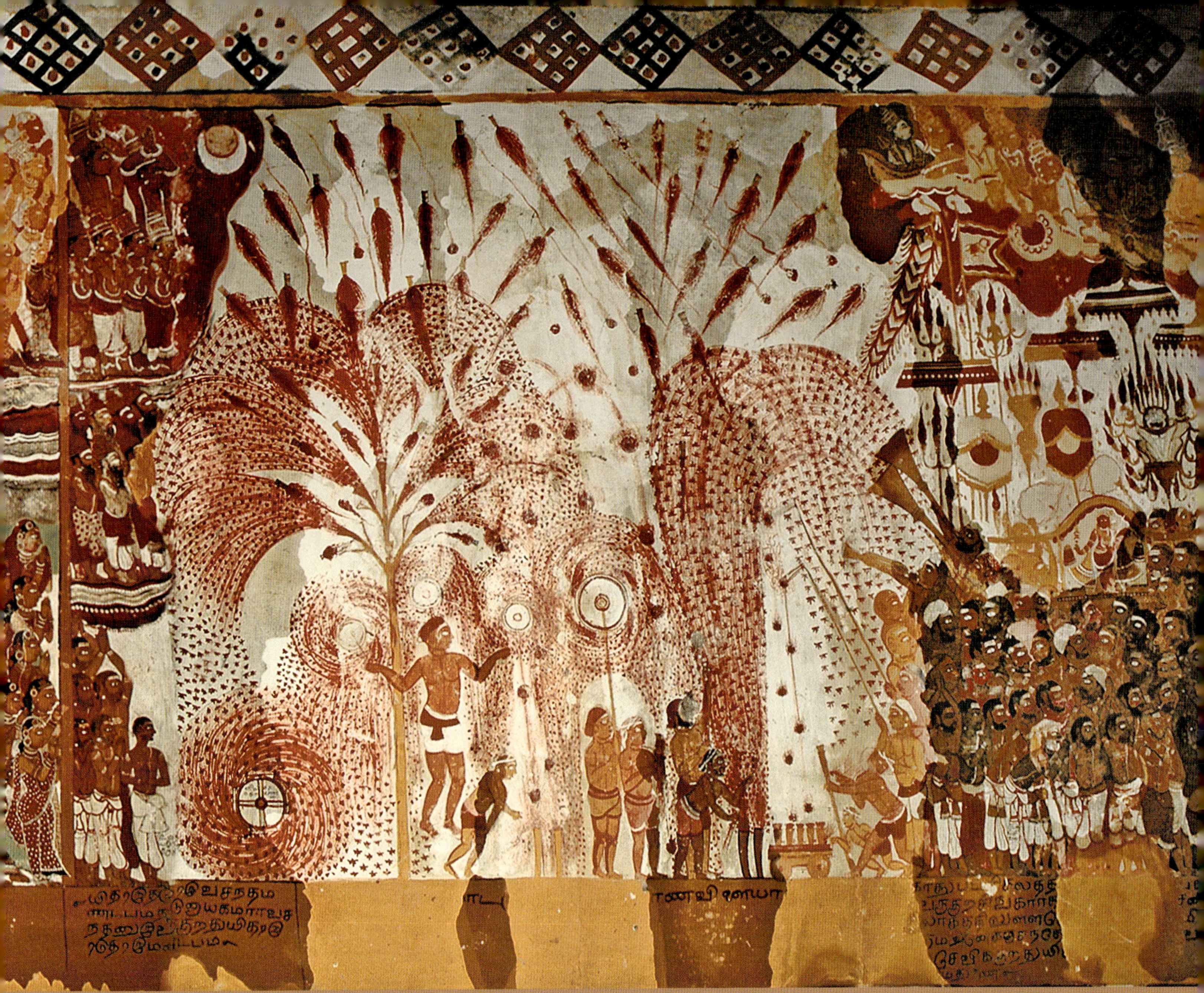

Panel 64, from right to left:

• Vasantotsava *(unfinished). The god arrives at the Vasanta-maṇḍapam.*

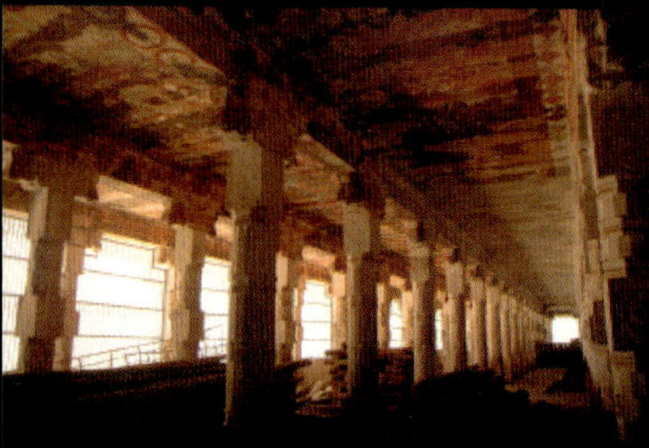

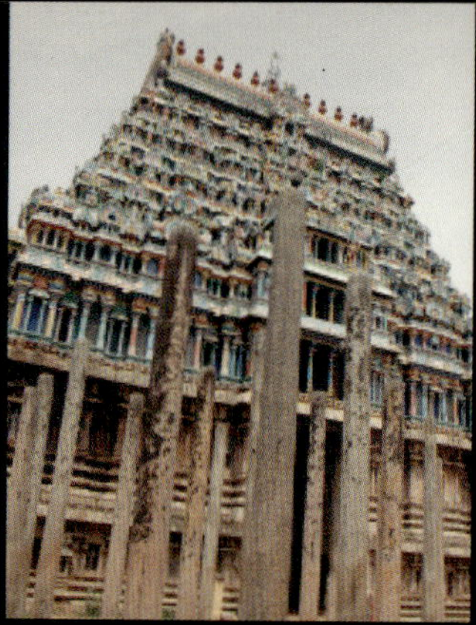

Listening to the Silent Echo of the Murals at Tiruvarur

Maya Tevet Dayan

1 Magic lies under the low ceilings in the Devasiriya Mandapam at the Tyāgarājaswāmy temple in Tiruvarur. The *maṇḍapam* is dark; weak rays of light penetrate inward and blanket the pillars with white dust. Then a new sense of colour comes to life. At first, it is only felt, unseen. As you go deeper inside, something pulls your glance upward. There, on the ceiling, in row upon row, organized in sequential oblongs, hundreds of eyes are looking down at you. It seems like real people live up there, very small people, with amazingly precise features. As they emerge from the dark, their golden bodies seem to drive out the darkness below. The red background behind them, glittering with small dots of white, replaces the white dust of light. Space slowly dissolves. Time, as well, loses its familiar meaning, for once you've noticed those eyes, they seem to have been there forever.

In the innermost *prākāra* of the temple, a dark stone corridor leads to the shrine of Tyāgarāja. At the end of the corridor, there is light, white against the black space that envelops the pilgrim. As one goes deeper in, new colours emerge, the yellow-red lights of the inner shrine, produced by dozens of candles. Many devotees tend to sit on the ground in front of the shrine during the *ārati*, raising their eyes upwards in the direction of the *mūrti*. The accumulation of compressed heat,

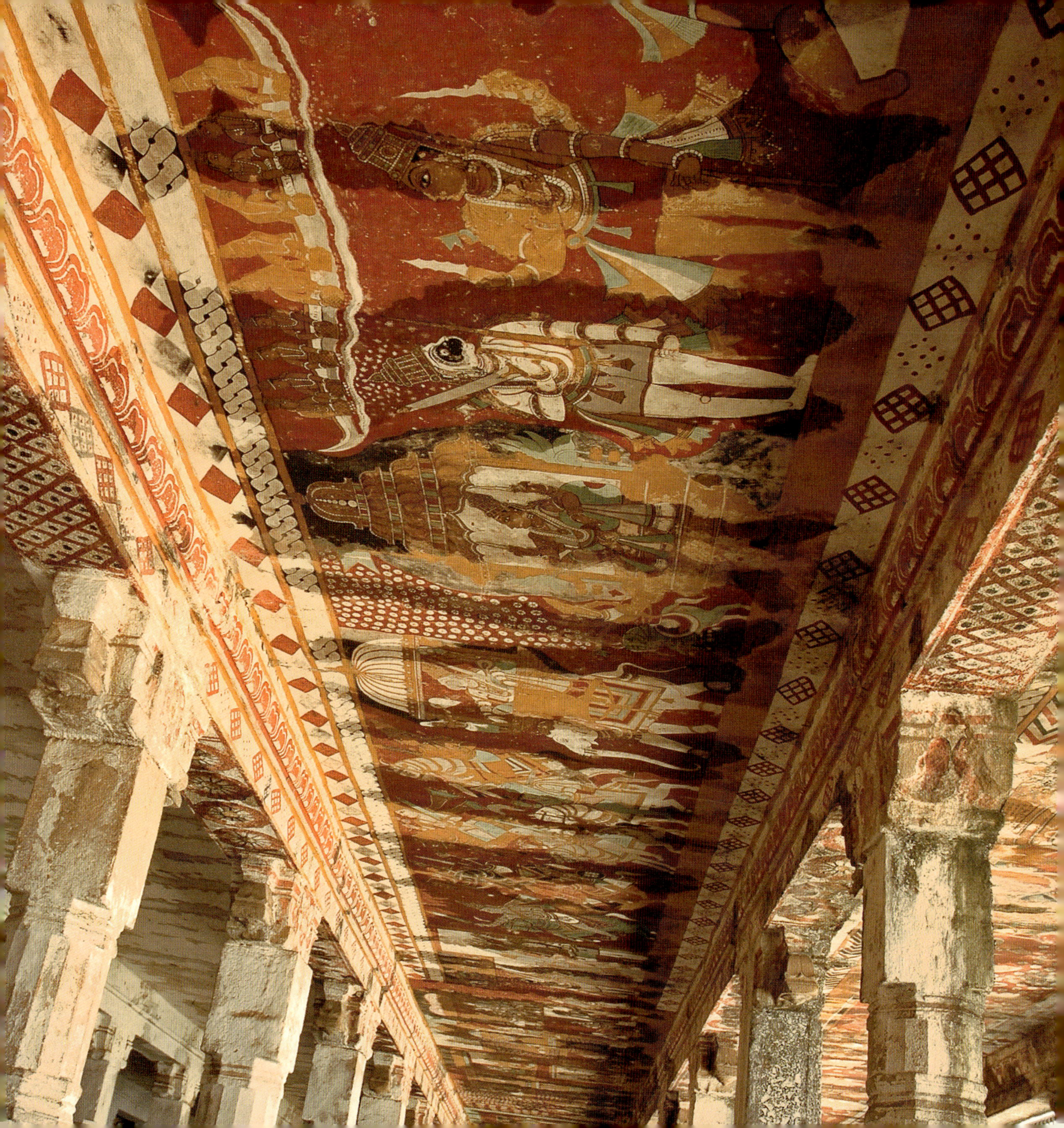

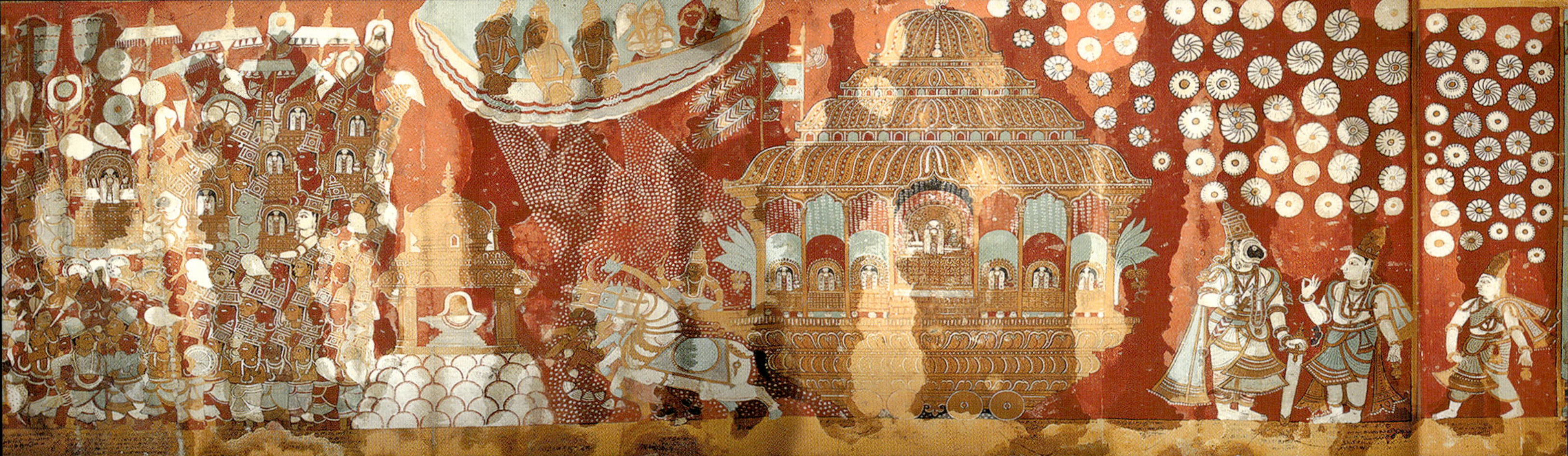

darkness, candlelight and concentrated glances creates a new reality. Along with the eternal deity at home in the stony womb of the *garbha-griha*, time itself stops, loses sequence and meaning.

Now the pilgrim, today, or three hundred years ago, moves to the Devasiriya Mandapam, where his or her experience repeats itself. The hundreds of eyes glancing at him from above echo the eyes of the *mūrti*, suddenly emerging at the end of the darkened corridor. One lifts up one's own eyes to the ceiling, just as one lifted them toward the *mūrti* from the floor in front of the *garbha-griha*. The red background of the murals echoes the yellow-red light of the *dīpaka*-lamps around the *mūrti*. Space dissolves. Time has become irrelevant.

In between time, outside space

2 We need to listen carefully to these murals. Three primary modes have to be considered in terms of their effect upon the observer's sensual perceptions and cognitive understanding. There are issues of spatial location, which determines how we see the paintings. There are issues of design, including matters of colour, style, narrative sequence, placement, repetitions, intertextual echoes, all of which affect the observer. In addition, very crucially, there are problems of content.

Of the surviving murals, two scenes show us the Tiruvarur temple itself.[1] Both scenes are situated in the middle of a long panel. The first one comes right after a major climax in the narrative: Indra gives Mucukunda the Tyāgarāja icon. As in any good story, just as the hero is about to get what he wanted, one last obstacle suddenly blocks his way. The sensitive Tiruvarur painter expresses that tension in the narrative with an

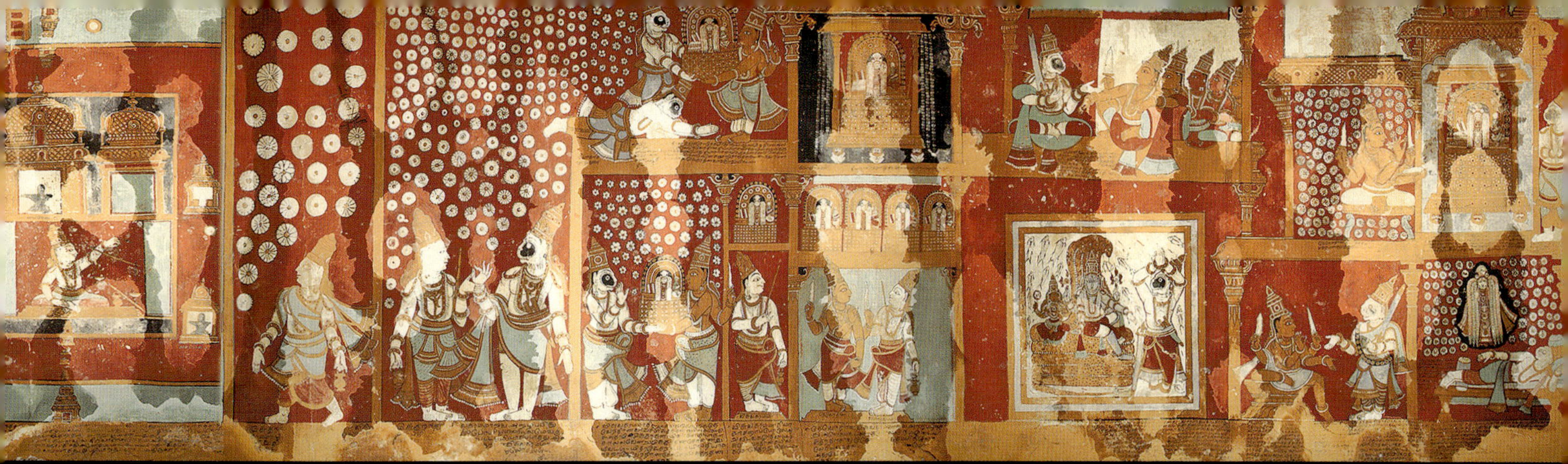

finally Mucukunda's farewell to Indra and Indra's departure. These two panels contain a total of six different scenes, two contrasting states of consciousness (dreaming and waking), two cognitive states (false and true perceptions, in the process of choosing the true Tyāgarāja image), twenty-three active characters, eleven appearances of Tyāgarāja (one of them as "real," one of them in a dream, twice as the original *murti* and all the rest as the replicas). These are a lot of details to take in, and the spectator must delay his or her progress through the *maṇḍapa* and focus his or her mind. Suddenly, after all this visual luxuriance, there is a moment of relative simplicity. A wide, light frame delimits a broad red square, the contour of the Tiruvarur temple as seen from some point far above. The main entrance is to the left, and outside the main building are five small shrines. In three of them we see a *lingam*. Inside the temple there are two registers. A large figure is seated cross-legged in the lower register, working with scales. He is Viśvakarmā, whose body expands to fill the entire space as he weighs Tiruvārūr against all the other shrines on earth. In the upper register two shrines are silently present. One of them contains a *lingam*. The other one is empty, waiting for the Tyāgarāja *mūrti* to arrive and take up residence within its walls.

There is a great silence in this scene. No figures, no *mūrtis*, no glittering candlelight. Rather, there are blank areas, clear squares and minimal colors. Most of the panel is empty, and the empty *garbha-griha* at the center of that emptiness assumes the form of an empty womb waiting to conceive. A new life is about to begin. The Kamalayalam, the great tank outside the temple, marks it off from the outside world. Its quiet, serene colours and squares also serve to distinguish it from the noisy reality of the preceding two panels. Here, once again, outside reality suddenly dissolves. And where the innermost space is still empty, the spectator finds himself or herself in a temporal limbo, right after the end, right before the beginning. And time, once again, loses its familiar meaning. The content of the painting reflects the cognitive experience of the encounter with Tyāgarāja during his evening *pūjā*.

Later on, when the shrine of Tyāgarāja is depicted [p. 97], the *mūrti* is already at home in it; outside, human beings and celestial creatures are paying homage to him. This painting of the shrine echoes the sensual experience of encountering the temple: the long corridor leading to the *garbha-griha*, the slow movement, the raising of one's eyes toward the bright deity at the farthest end, rising out of darkness.

The powers of the *maṇḍapa*

3 This sensitive delicacy of painting and observance is ascribed to the artist Cinkâtaṉaṉ, who worked under the patronage of the Maratha King Sahaji of Tanjore, in the late seventeenth century. In painting the murals of a *maṇḍapa* in a temple built during the rule of Raghunātha Nāyaka (1612-1634), Cinkâtaṉaṉ was carrying on a great artistic tradition, one distinctively Nāyaka, with a set of characteristic diagnostic features.

Most prominent among these is the initial decision to paint murals here, on the *maṇḍapa* ceiling. For the Nāyaka kings, the *maṇḍapa* seems to have played a special role. First and foremost it served as a special space inside the temple where these kings deliberately chose to display their regal splendour. The Nāyakas were military generals appointed by the Vijayanagar kings. Their capitals were located in Madurai, Vellore, Senji and Tanjavur. When the Vijayanagar centre was decimated in the battle of Talikota in 1565, these generals became powerful and virtually autonomous monarchs. They ruled their kingdoms till the end of the eighteenth century, by which time they had made a rich contribution to the art and architecture of Tamil Nadu. The *maṇḍapas* they built, along with the very tall *gopurams*, are the most significant architectural expressions of their strength.

Among these *maṇḍapas* are the Pudu Maṇḍapa in the Mīnâkṣī-Sundareśvara temple at Madurai, the front *maṇḍapa* in the temple at Krishnapuram, the Kalyāṇa Maṇḍapa of the Jalakaṇṭheśvara temple at Vellore and the *maṇḍapa* in the eastern *prākāra* of Raṅganātha's shrine at Srirangam.[2] All of them are characterized by massive pillars that carry life-size portraits of rulers, consorts and their retinue, or donor-chiefs. Other sculptures are also to be found on the pillars: these are of gods, women in graceful poses and semi-tribal figures like the Kuṟava and Kuṟatti hunter and huntress. We also find a rich collection of sculpted warriors and horses. In all these respects, Tiruvarur's *maṇḍapa* is a clear expression of Nāyaka architectural innovation: the thousand-pillared *maṇḍapa*, along with the high raised *gopuram*s.

When you enter a Nāyaka *maṇḍapa*, you become a witness to a parade of power, not only that of the Nāyakas, but also of the carved stones. The monoliths in it, as well as the large figurative sculptures, express the Nāyaka recognition of the power embedded within stone forms. If the great stone *gopurams* were an ambitious attempt to bring men closer to god, the multi-pillared *mandapas* may have been an attempt to widen

[2] The list comes from: K. R. Srinivasan, *Temples of India* (New Delhi: National Book Trust, 1972).

a space, architecturally as well as mentally, in order to bring god closer to men. For the Nāyakas, the *maṇḍapa* was no longer a mere architectural unity but rather an arena for a new cosmological unity, one that carried new meanings and possibilities. No wonder, then, that the *maṇḍapa* was chosen as most suitable not only for the ostentatious depiction of royal glory but also for descriptions of supernatural, though locally enacted, stories like that of Tiruvarur, stories about how god eventually found himself so close to man.

Mighty stones and delicate paintings

4

The word "mural" takes its meaning from the Latin root *murus*, which means wall and refers to any of the traditional Indian three-fold classification, *bhūmika*, *bhitti* and *prastara*, floor, wall and ceiling, respectively. It seems there are hundreds of murals spread through temple sites in Tamil Nadu.[3] Well-known among them are Srirangam, Chidambaram and Kanchipuram. But there are also many lesser-known places like Tittakudi, Thirupudaimaruthur and Natham.

Murals in South India are not "true fresco," where colours mixed with water are painted directly on to wet plaster, eventually creating a painting that is an integral part of the wall. Rather, they are "dry fresco," made as a separate layer on a dry, plastered surface, hence not as permanent as "true fresco."

Like most Indian murals, including those at Ajanta, the Nāyaka murals were painted on finely plastered lime walls. The surface of brick or stone was plastered in two layers. The top-most layer was given a fine finish, and paint was applied after the plaster had dried. Vegetable and mineral colors were used along with vegetable gum

[3] An assumption made by Prof. Balusami, who is currently involved in the documentation and analysis of Nayak paintings

for binding. The brushes are presumed to have been bristles made from banyan roots.

The themes vary. Some Nāyaka murals illustrate the main temple festival, with its processional *vāhanas*; others depict stories from the *Purāṇas* or hagiographical accounts of saints. In temples like Srirangam and Chidambaram, the origins and the plan of the temple are shown.

In style, Nāyaka paintings have a popular or folk quality. In contrast to the greater depth in volume of the Chola painting tradition, the Nāyakas adopted a more realistic and people-friendly technique. The human figures do not seem to follow classical proportions; they are characterized by pointed noses, fierce eyes, angular contours and limbs, and peculiar arrangements of garments on the body, with patterns characteristic of the period. In a few paintings, the figures have their eyes extended in a special way, jutting out of the profile. Men appear with pot-bellies and are almost realistic. They are also conspicuously decked with ornaments, while the background remains minimal with simple, linear houses, trees and foliage. The layout of the panels looks like filmstrips or a page from a modern comic; the narrative develops along rows of panels, separated from each other but set in sequence. Most of the paintings carry either Tamil or Telugu labels.

But Ciṅkâtaṉan of Tiruvarur worked somewhat differently. On the mighty pillars he created figures that are both delicate and accurate. Though tribal in design and not answering the Indian proportions, they are realistic in expression and style. One can sense their genuine excitement during the *abhiṣeka* at the episode depicted on p. 106. That excitement is clearly observed by the diagonal design of the group of devotees, musicians, dancers and animals. The elephant in the middle actually stands on top of the people. Below him, people are marching in three terraces. Along with the shrine carried on top of the elephant, the whole happy group assumes the structure of a *gopuram*. Diagonals are also in evidence in the small details of that festival procession; swords and trumpets, arms and legs, flags and ribbons, are all diagonal to each other, thus creating a sense of joyful disorder in the scene. That disorder contrasts clearly with other multi-figured scenes, such as the organized and frozen soldiers, facing a coming battle [pp. 80-81], or the silent, reverent crowd attending the auspicious moment of distributing the seven Tyāgarāja *mūrtis* among the seven *viṭaṅka* shrines [p 94].

The design of the figures is another expression of the psychological subtlety in the artist's work. Each figure in the *utsava* is different; their colours differ from one another; their garments are variegated; their eyes turn in different directions. Their expressions are never the

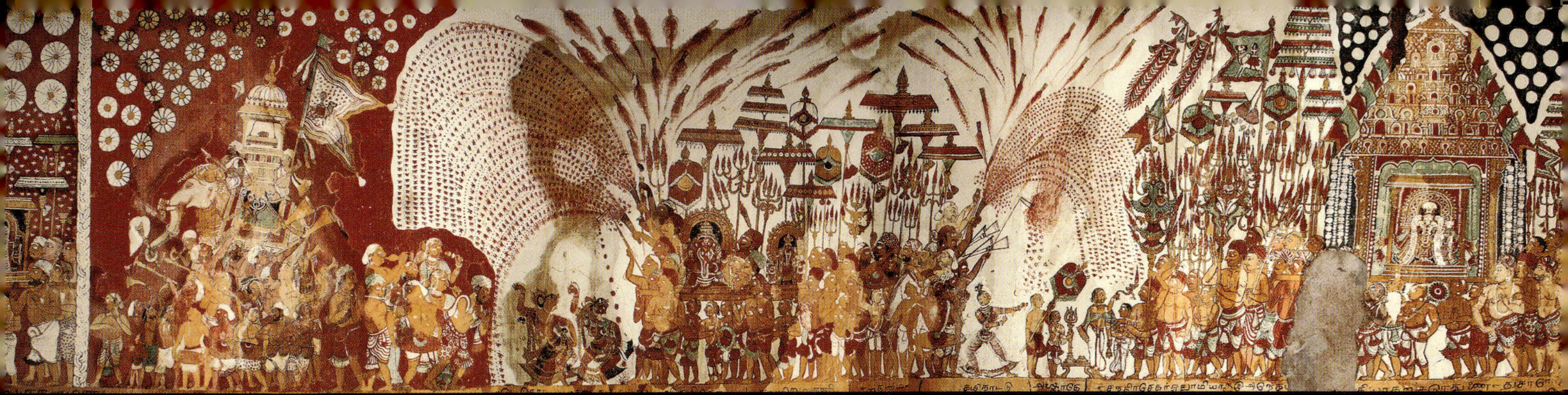

ame. While most of the musicians are deeply involved n their music, a flautist on the right side is exchanging ooks with a man next to him. In the right corner a nan is leaning towards the dancer with an ambiguous smile. A child is lost in the crowd and stands frozen. f we look at other Nāyaka murals, such as those rom Srirangam that are ascribed to the same style, ve find similar figures, in conversation, arranged in a ribal design.[4] But the figures at Srirangam are highly lecorative in style and schematic in motion, while hose at Tiruvarur naturally move through space. Most enchanting are the monkeys hanging on the trees above he procession. Not less than fifteen monkeys appear, none of them copying the others, and all of them full of ife.

Ciṅkâtaṉaṉ holds to the visual tradition; he unfolds he narrative by repeating the figures and attending to the consistency of the scenes; still, his figures seem almost to burst out of the stone.[5] They are so alive that one might think that although the Tiruvarur artist was painting under the influence of well-known artistic codes, he was, in fact, striving to create more than just a mural. The contrast between the vital figures and the stony surface is so marked that one could speak of a colourful meditation on the impossible connection between art and reality, between stone and life. Can a stone come to life? Can art truly enliven stone and, if so, under what conditions? Or perhaps it is all a matter of

[4] See panels from Srirangam – Vishṇu lying on Śesha and man and woman conversing.

[5] In fact, several of them actually step out of their frames. Most striking is the foot of the defeated demon escaping on p. 61; but look, also, at the feet of the crowd in pp. 106 and 107.

perceiving things with a certain attention? A different metaphysics of space and of time, or different modes of perceiving space and time, are being exemplified. Thus the painter achieves two goals in one artistic act: first he turns his art into a performance of the story it illustrates, iconically embodying the transitions among disparate domains; secondly, he creates the artistic conditions for transformation. The onlooker moves from everyday, commonsense reality to a different universe, one that makes a different kind of sense. His or her reaction is cognitive as well as sensual. Once again, there is an echo of the transformative reaction by the pilgrim to the stony, yet fluid, *garbha-griha*.

Pirouetting with murals

5 An awkward feeling slowly penetrates one's consciousness soon after one starts following the murals of the Mucukunda story. As in most Nāyaka murals, these paintings are accompanied by labels in Tamil, telling the story that is being illustrated and, apparently, offering instructions to the painters. Written labels are perhaps the most prominent, unique attribute of Nāyaka painting and are considered by scholars to be a direct continuation of the conversational quality in art that began during the Vijayanagara era.[6] That attempt to converse alongside and through the paintings is a substantial element of the Tiruvarur paintings. Its importance lies in the persistent, indeed unavoidable resistance that it generates. Interestingly, while Tamil itself runs from left to right, the painted sequences consistently proceed from right to left. Reading the paintings is at odds with reading the written text.

Upon entering the *maṇḍapa* the spectator has to turn right and continue walking until he or she reaches the far eastern wall, then turn left and proceed north. On the far northern corner is the first mural: the

---

[6] C. Sivaramamurti, *Indian Painting* (New Delhi: National Book Trust, 1970).

Mucukunda story begins. To follow it correctly, the spectator has to proceed with his or her right shoulder turned toward the paintings, while his or her eyes are turned upward. At times, the end of one panel feeds into the start of the next through a 180-degree turn, so that to see the new panel clearly, the spectator must face in the opposite direction. One feels as if one were following a twisting snake. To put it differently: the heads of the figures in one panel "touch" the heads of the figures in the following panel, whose legs "touch" the legs of the figures in a third panel, and so on. Moreover, the initial series, *running north-south* along the length of the window, takes a left-angle turn into the second series (running east-west); the third series runs exactly parallel to the second before feeding back into the longer (north-south) segment of the ceiling, where the fourth series flows *from south to north*. When the narrative reaches the far (northern wall), it again turns 180 degrees and proceeds, as the fifth series, halfway back toward the southern end of the *maṇḍapa*. You begin with your back to the window, turn to face the window as you follow the central panel (the climax of the narrative), and end with the window behind you again. It is a dizzying, disorienting experience; and this manner of telling a story cannot have evolved by chance.

There is no easy way to explain this arrangement of the composition, just as there is no easy way to follow it while studying the murals. In fact, as a spectator one has to choose between taking a detailed look at the paintings or somehow "keeping grounded." One sometimes feels deliberately confused: while the labels along the paintings are trying to converse with you, the paintings act differently. They direct the spectator back and forth along the rows of pillars, until any feeling of familiarity with the space around one is lost. This slightly twisted mode of walking and seeing, guided by the murals from above, has an immediate effect on the observer. To begin with, he or she somehow splits into two: one part converses fluently with the murals, while the other strives to keep track of directions. Is that a fair thing to ask? One could, of course, give up, for a little while, a sense of direction, thus renouncing one's familiar, commonsense orientation in space. Is this a necessary part of the visual experience triggered by the paintings? We have already discussed the dissolution of space in the *maṇḍapa*, but now a new factor is added; the spectator, walking naturally along the length of the panels, always turns to the right in order to see the paintings clearly. When one reaches the end of a given series of panels, one again turns right to order to begin viewing the next. As if there were not enough rotations and twists, there are also a few vertical compositions within the horizontal sequence. These demand that the spectator turn again, on the spot, to capture them fully. That rotation around the murals re-enacts a rotation inside the temple. The devotee in Tiruvarur reaches the *mūrti* only after making three full *pradakṣiṇas* in the three wide *prākāras* surrounding the inner shrine. After receiving darshan, he or she turns back, again with his right shoulder in, and goes straight outside. For the spectator of the murals, the *pradakṣiṇa* motion is clear from the start. Recall the vertical sequences mentioned above: these are all depictions of gods to whom, as the artist discovered, it is necessary to pay homage with a *pradakṣiṇa*.[7] Of course, once the *pradakṣiṇa* is accomplished, these are no longer merely paintings. They become real temples inside the murals. The gods depicted in pigments and water have become real *mūrtis*. The echo is no more an echo. The painted images are a comprehensive creation of the imagination, activated by any observer of the murals. In that imaginative act, real things are created: real temples, real *mūrtis* and real time. So when the spectator walks around the murals, in a *pradakṣina* direction, losing track of commonsense and of outside reality, his experience of the god is also real.

[7] See pp. 56-57 and 63.

6

The creative imagination awakened by the murals is an expression of a wider imagination, internal to the temple of Tiruvarur, a game of concepts, forms and associations played by the different components of this temple. Those who enter into the game are carried along by its inherent logic. As a result, though emerging from a long architectural and artistic tradition, the Tiruvarur murals are revealed as a subtle interplay of inner language and of local event. That event happens every night and has gone on for centuries, but it also happened only once, an irreplaceable cosmic moment: the arrival of Tyāgarāja on earth, preceded by the Mucukunda story.

Echoes are a crucial part of this narrative. The face of the monkey from Indra's heaven is echoed in the face of the great warrior king he has become. The genuine Tyāgarāja *mūrti* is echoed no less than six times, so as to cause both a crisis and a climax in the narrative. Layers of reality are echoed again and again: the *mūrti* installed on Vishṇu's heart is the *mūrti* appearing in Mucukunda's dream, the *mūrti* appearing seven times, the *mūrti* crossing worlds and hands. Within a unique local metaphysics, it is only logical that the murals that re-enact the experience of the *garbha-griha* turn the *maṇḍapa* they inhabit into an echo of the *tīrtha* as a whole and of the divine world that it condenses and makes present.

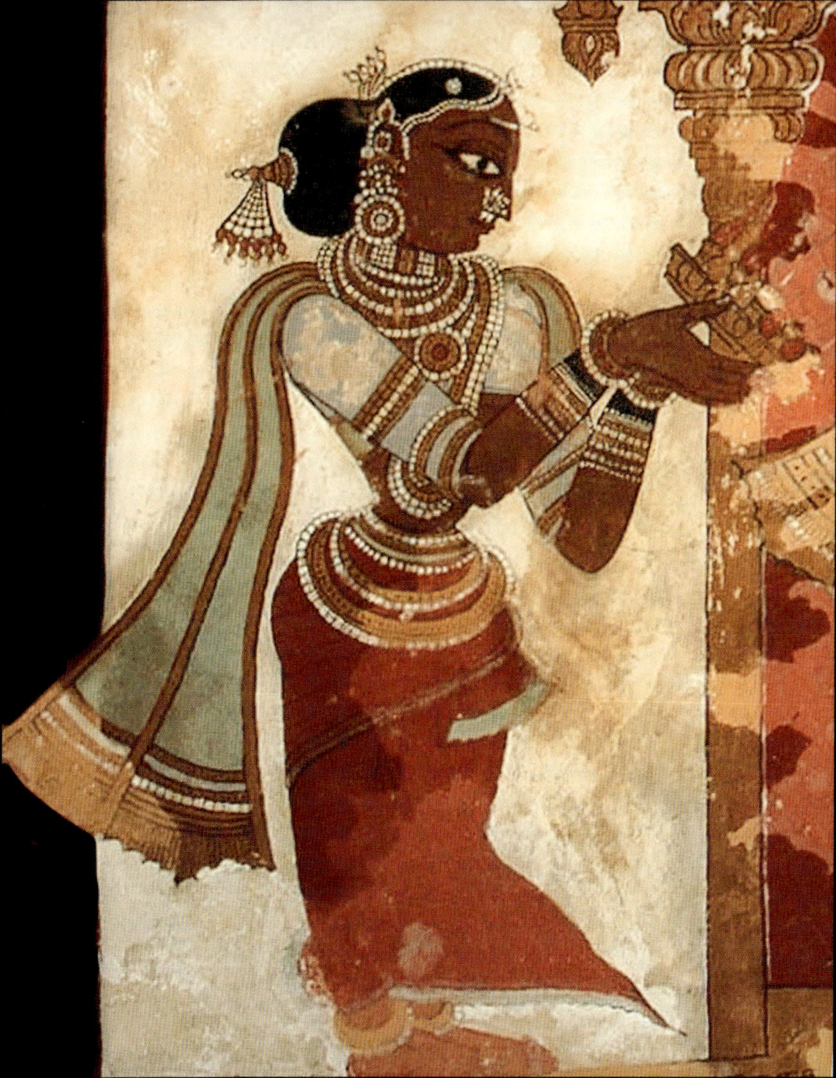

Notes to the panels and accompanying inscriptions

The Tamil inscriptions painted beneath and to the sides of the ceiling panels give us a coherent version of the Mucukunda narrative which differs, in certain interesting respects, from the canonical versions of Maṟaiñāṉacampantar and Campantamuṉivar. Here Indra goes to Cidambaram to ask Viṣṇu/Govindarāja – who has just defeated Vārkali – for the Tyāgarāja icon (panels 15 and 16). Mucukunda reigns in Ayodhya (panels 30, 31). Aditi, Indra's mother, welcomes the conquering Mucukunda into heaven (panel 44). Tyāgarāja comes to Mucukunda in a dream to ask him to bring him down to earth (to an unspecified location: panel 40). Mucukunda then sends Viśvakarmā to earth to locate the proper site for the god, and Viśvakarmā weighs the sacred places of the world against Tiruvarur – which outweighs them all (panel 47). Studying the paintings together with the inscriptions, we cannot avoid the impression that they record a more consistent, fuller, and possibly more archaic version than the ones available to us in the literary sources. We assume that these paintings faithfully reflect the living oral tradition of Tiruvarur in the mid- to late seventeenth century.

The language of the inscriptions is a semi-formal Tamil heavily influenced by colloquial forms – and thus provides remarkable evidence for the late seventeenth-century dialect spoken in the Kaveri Delta. In lieu of a complete grammatical description, a few observations may be in order. *Sandhi* usually follows colloquial pronunciation. Note the prevalence of the *paṇṇu* verbalizer (as in modern speech); the shortened deictic *i*; general orthographic instability (including loss of vowel length in borrowed lexemes: *kĕruṭavākaṉaruṭarāyi*, 16); extensive Sanskrit borrowings; initial on-glides; present *pĕyar ĕccam* and verbal nouns in *[*k*]*kuṟa*[*tu*]; and common collapsed morphemes (*e.g.*, elided *r*, *etuttu* < *etirttu*, *pāttu* < *pārttu*, etc.). Medial geminate – *tt* – , as in the *viṉaiyĕccam*, is often palatalized (*kŏṭuccu*, *cuṭṭiccu*). Among unusual lexical items, we note: *kaṭṭiyakkāraṉ*, "messenger"; *muṭṭukkārar*, "*mattaḷam* drummers." Standard features of seventeenth-century Tamil epigraphy – the absence of *puḷḷi*, unmarked long *e* and *o* – are, of course, in evidence throughout. (In transcription I have followed the modern conventions, marking the *puḷḷi* and the short *ĕ* and *ŏ*.)

The inscriptions cannot, for the most part, be read with the naked eye by spectators looking up from the *maṇḍapam* floor. In many cases, they appear to embody instructions to the painters or to serve as markers of continuity in the painted text: once the panels were boxed off in outline, their narrative content was explicated before sketching itself began. Hence the frequent directional pointers, meant also to maintain the narrative sequence: "to the north of this panel [paint the Ocean of Milk]," and so on. Hence, also, the frequent redundancy and repetitions in these directions, as if the thematic and narrative arrangement of individual panels were only tentatively determined in advance. But Nāyaka-period paintings usually include verbal texts as integral parts of the artistic enterprise. Thus the Tiruvarur panels seem to have served a double purpose – at once defining the sequence and spatial organization of the planned panels and identifying and labeling the narrative components one by one.

Sadly, perhaps 50% of the original inscriptions have been damaged beyond legibility. I offer below tentative readings of those portions of the texts that can still be deciphered. The many lacunae are signaled by dots. Conjectured restoration is signaled by square brackets. Rounded brackets { } mark scribal errors. Passages which allow for the decipherment of only one or two graphemes or lexemes from a longer text are not referenced here. It is to be hoped that at some point infra-red photography or other technical means will allow for the restoration of the damaged portions of these captions.

The Inscriptions

PANEL

1 [yi viṭam viṣṇu tevatāruvaṉatti[le]…puttiraṉ[ukkāka]…civatyāṉamāka yirukkiṟatu….

Left: makāviṣṇu tevatāruvaṉattile makāliṅka aṟciṉai p[aṇṇukiṟatu]

---

3 Left: comā[skanta]…..

---

5 cuvāmi anukkirakam paṇṇi…[pālka]ṭalile vantu paḷḷi[kŏṇṭu]…arccuṉai paṇṇukiṟatu…tirupārkaṭa[l]….
paccai yet′ ĕṉṟal…

---

6 teventiraṉ caturaṅkapĕlatto[ṭu]…kūṭa vārkaliyuṭaṉe yuttattukku poṟa[kkiṟatu]/ yitarku tĕrku

Right: teventiraṉ kŏluyi...yuttam paṇṇi tevaloka[ttukku?...a]nta cetikki kaṭṭiyakkārar…

7

teventiraṉum vārkaliyum ivarkaḷ rĕṇṭu perum yuttam paṇṇukiṛatu i viṭam

Far right: teventiraṉ

Lower middle: yuttakaḷam

Left: vārkkali acuraṉ

Far left: [teventiraṉai vā]rkali turattukiṟatu

---

8 teventiraṉum vārkaliyum yuttam paṇṇi…varukiṟāṉ avacĕyappaṭṭu tirupārkaṭalile viṣṇuviṉ[iṭattil] aṟikkai
paṇṇuvom ĕ[ṉṟu]

---

9 makāviṣṇuviṉiṭattile teve[ntiraṉ] vārkaliyuṭane yuttam paṇṇi avacĕyappaṭṭu…yuṭane aṟikkai paṇṇi….[te]
ventiraṉaip pā[ttu]…ṉīr citamparattile….paṇṇum

Left margin, vertical: yitarku vaṭakkup pakka (?) tirupārkaṭal. Note: Directions to the painters, or to mark the continuity of reading ("to the north, the Ocean of Milk")

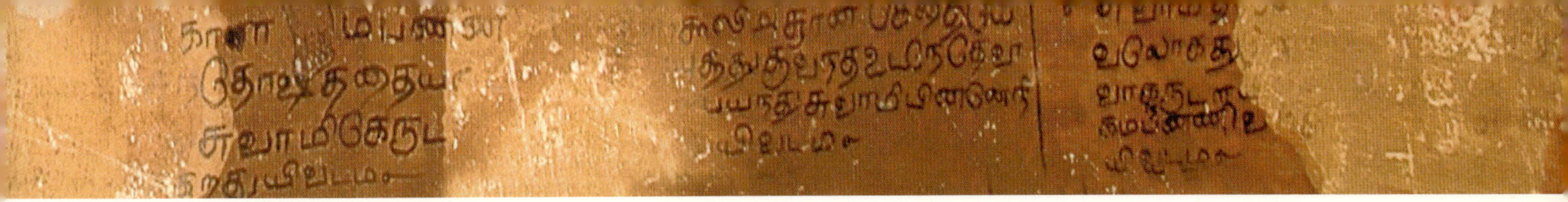

PANEL
10 10. viṣṇu cŏṉṉapiṟakāram teventiraṉ tirupārkaṭal viṭṭu [cita]mparattile vantu capāpati tĕri[ca]ṉam paṇṇi viṣṇuvai…paṇṇukiṟatu i viṭam….

12 Center: makāviṣṇuvum vārkali[yum] ivarkaḷ rĕṇṭu perum [yuttam] paṇṇukiṟatu i viṭam
Left: vārkali acuraṉ viṣṇu uṭaṉe ĕtuttu [= etirttu] yuttam paṇṇukuṟatu i viṭam

13 vārkaliyuṭa ter cuvāmiyuṭa pāṇattiṉāle tĕriccu kiṭakuṟatu i viṭam

Left: [te]valokattukku…karuṭavākarūṭa…[sic]

16 Right: viṣṇu cita[m]parattukku [vantu? uṭa]ṉe teventiraṉ…kŏṇṭu vantu câṣṭâṅkamāy [namaskarikkuṟatu/] i viṭam / citamparam

Middle: itarku tĕrku cuvāmi tirupārkaṭalukku poṟatu [See note to panel 9. "To the south…."]. cuvāmi kĕruṭavākaṉaruṭarāyi nāṭakacālai pārkkiṟatukku / tĕrku inta maṭṭum citamparamāy / itarku tĕrku tiruppārkaṭal

Left: [te]ventiraṉ cu…yuṭaṉe tiruppār[kaṭalukku] varukiṟatu / tĕrku tiruppārkaṭal

17 Right vertical: [tuṇai] intak kataiyĕllām tiyākarācacu[vāmi tevalo]kattukku varukkuṟatu…

Left: inta mūrttiyai vaittu pūcaip paṇṇiṉāl catrukuc cĕyam paṇṇalām? ĕṉṟu teventiraṉ cantoṣattai yaṭaintu na[ṭu]kkuṟatu i viṭam

Right: viṣṇu tiruppā[rkaṭal…] te[ventiraṉ]p pāttu…kup pom ĕṉṟu anta mūrttiyai ṉām pūcai pa[ṇṇiṉāl cattrukku caṅ]kāram paṇṇa….vaittuk kŏṇṭu tĕṇṭaṉ p[aṇṇi]…

18 Left: mu[ppatu] koṭi [tevar]….mūrti

Right: teventiraṉ inta…tiyāka[rācar]….cantoṣattai….tevalok[attukkup] poṟatu

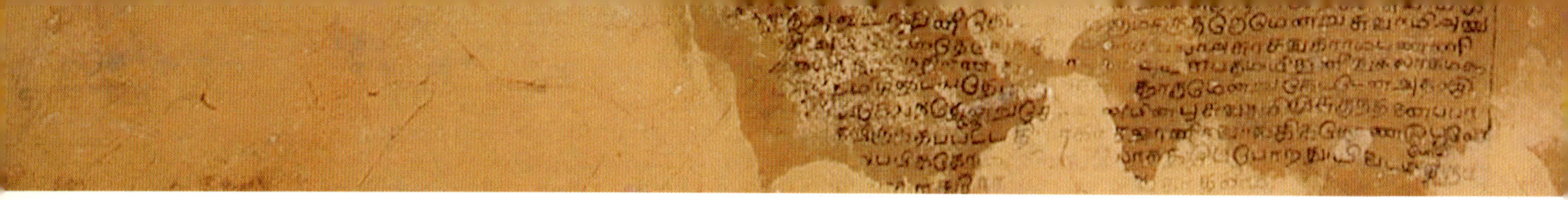

PANEL

19 Left to right: menakai / arampai

---

20 ….kuḻalkāraṉ…

Left:…vāttiya…cevi…

---

21 makāviṣṇu pūcai paṇṇaccŏ[ṉṉa?] mūrtiyai teventiraṉ va…kŏṇṭu…tevalokattukku vantu…pūcai paṇṇukkuṟatu

Far left: [te]ventiraṉ…arccuṉai

---

26 valā acuraṉ teventiraṉai pāttu vĕku ko[pam a]ṭaintu pa[ṭai?]…kūṭittu yuttam paṇṇu…muṉ yu[ttam paṇṇiṉa] vārkali acuraṉai kaṇṭu teventiraṉ…uṭaṉe ĕtuttu yuttam paṇṇu[kiṟatu]….kuntamūrtti…kattinṉāle yĕtuttu yuttam….

---

27 Left: yitarku….teventiraṉ….kiḻaku [va]ntu….mucukuntacakkaravartiyai [a]ḻaittu vara tūtar(?)…yitarku merku

---

28 acurappaṭaiyĕllām…kūṭṭik kŏṇṭu nikkuṟa[tu]….itarku merku tevappaṭai nikuṟa[tu]…atarku merku teventiraṉ…mukamāka yiruntu kŏṇṭu kaṭṭiyakārarai aḻaittu namakku pĕl[…pū]lokattile yirukkuṟa mucukuntaṉai aḻai….kaṭṭiyakkāraṉai…anuppuvikka…

---

29 Far right, bottom: [ayo]ttiyā paṭṭaṇam

---

30 Far left (note missing vertical dividers): mucukunta cakkaravartiyai teventiraṉ aḻaittu varac cŏnn… kaṭṭiyakkāraṉ pūlokattukku mucukunta cakkaravartiyai aḻaikkuṟatu i viṭam / kurupātame tuṇai

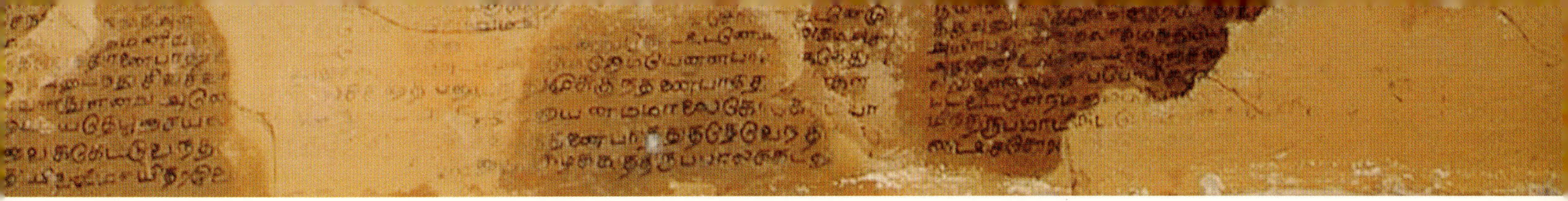

PANEL

30 Middle: …yam kocalainā̱ṭu ayotiyyāpuripaṭṭaṇattile mucukunta[ṉai] teventiraṉ aḻaittu vara…navavīrar[ka]ḷ ŏṉpatu perum cuppiṟamaṇiya cuvāmi anukkira[[ttiṉāl] mucukuntacakkiravartikku tampimār…kāy irukka yippaṭi ve[ku?] kālam...[pari]pālanam paṇṇikkŏṇṭu kŏluvāka yirukkaiyile teventiraṉ [valā acuraṉai] caṅkāram paṇṇukku[ṟa]tāka mucukuntaṉai aḻaittu vāruṅkoḷ ĕṉa cŏ…kaṭṭiyakkāraṉ vantu mucukunta cakkiravarttiyai aḻaikkuṟatu i viṭam

31 mucukunta cakkaravarttiyuṭaiya naṭṭuvar muṭṭukkāṟar ṉāṭakacālai ivarkaḷ yĕllārum… naṭaṉam paṇṇukuṟatu yi viṭam. yita[rku…mu]cukuntaṉ[ai]…teventiraṉ aḻaittu aṉuppina paṭi… mucukuntacakkaravartti [te]valokattukku poṟatu / yitarku

32 Far left: …ca-turaka-patātiyuṭane mucukunta cakkaravartti teventiraṉukkāka valā acuraṉai [caṅ]kāram paṇṇa[kku?]tāka tevalokattukkup poṟatu / yitarku kiḻaku teventiraṉum mucukuntaṉum cantippatu

Right: teventiraṉ mucukunta cakkaravarttiyai aḻaittu va[ra] cŏlli tūtar….[anup?]piviccapaṭiyiṉāle mucukunta cakkaravarttiyum navavīrarkaḷ….ĕllārum kūṭikkŏṇṭu tevalokattukku…vanta valācuraṉ caṅkāram paṇṇa poṟatu / yitarku kiḻaku teventiraṉum mucu[kuntaṉu]m cantippatu / kurupātame tuṇai

34 Bottom line: …mūrtti tiruviḷaiyāṭal…

37 kurupātame tuṇai/ teventiraṉ valā acuravuṭaṉe mucukuntaṉai muṉṉe niṉṟu yuttam paṇṇa…ṉiṉṟu alaitti [pi]ṟayokam paṇṇukkuṟatu yi viṭam

38 Far right: acurappaṭai…anta rĕṇṭu p[erum?]…

Far left: …taṉ astira…viṭṭu…

42 Far right: caṅkāram…[canto]ṣattai yaṭaintu….

Left: mucukunta…teventira[ṉ]…paṭṭaṇatt[ukku]…yāṉai me[l]…

PANEL

43 Note names on the figures: vīramakentiraṉ / vīrarāṭcakaṉ / vīraputtiraṉ / vīramārttāṇṭaṉ / vīrapākutevaṉ.

Top right: tevastrīkaḷ mucukuntaṉai kaṇṭu vĕku cantoṣattai yaṭaintu totiram paṇṇi puṣpappū varuṣikuṟatu i viṭam

Upper left: teventiraṉ mucukuntaṉukku pāricātakamālai kŏṭukkiṟatu i viṭam. aramaṉai uppirikai

Lower right: teventiraṉ mucukuntaṉai....paṭṭaṇattukku aḻaittu...mucukuntaṉaik kaṇṭu...vĕku cantoṣattai yaṭaintu mikuti...puṣpavaruṣam varṣittu....
vīrakeca[ri] vīramakentiram vīramakecan...vīrarāṭcakaṉ vīra...tevarkaḷ ivarkkaḷ yĕllārur[um...a] marāpatipaṭṭaṇattukku va[ntu[...

44

Middle: arampai

Lower left: ...irukkuṟa amarāpatipaṭṭaṇa[ttukku]....aḻaittu...tāyār atiti ammaṉai namaskarikka... pakumāṉam paṇṇukuṟatu
...itarku vaṭakku...

Far lower left: teventiraṉ...aḻai...mucukuntaṉ...iruvarumāka vantu namaskarittu...atitiyammaṉ mucukuntaṉai pāttu...ĕnakku ṉī rĕntāvatu puttiraṉ ĕnru vĕku cantoṣattai yaṭaintu mikutiyum cŏ... upacāraṣ cŏṉṉatu yi viṭam...tiyākarācarai teventiraṉ...
Note that this meeting with Aditi is unique to the version embodied in the murals.

Mid upper level: teventiraṉ tiyākarāja pūcai paṇṇukuṟatu

Lower right: tiyākarācarai mucukuntaṉ pūlokattile vaittu pūcai paṇṇa[...ve]ṇum ĕṉṟu anekam cantoṣattai yaṭaintu nittira paṇṇi...tiyākarācar mucukuntaṉiṭatte vantu...kku anumati kŏḷḷukuṟa potu...

45 Lower left: ...ṉī keṭṭa [varam?] ṉām tarukuṟom ĕṉṟu cuvāmi anu[kkirakam...] valācuracaṅkāram paṇṇi.... pinpu cuvāmi mucukuntaṉai pāttu....vāṅki kŏṇṭu pūloka...lokattukkup poṟatu

Upper right: makāviṣṇu uttaram paṇṇina piṟakāram mucukuntaṉ teventiraṉiṭatte vantu teventiraṉ.... cŏlliṟavatu vicuvakarmā...aḻaippikka

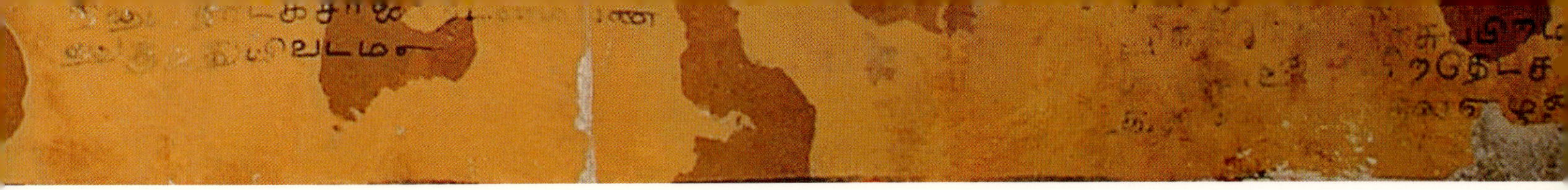

Lower right: teventiraṉ vicuvakarmmāvai antappi[ṟakāram?] anekam upacāraṣ cŏlli nammuṭaiya mucukuntarācāvukku kŏṭukkac cammitile…suṭṭiccu [kkŏṭukka]… atarku vicuvakarmma [suṭṭi] ccut tarukuṟeṉ ĕṉṟu

vicuvakarmmā tiyākarācaraip pole āṟuviṭaṅka mū[rt]ti suṭṭiccu teventiraṉ kaiyile kŏtukkuṟatu i viṭam

PANEL

46

To the left: vicuvakarmmā {ti} suṭṭiccu kŏṭukka teventiraṉ vāṅki mucukuntaṉ kaiyil kŏṭuccu atarku mucukuntaṉ ivarkaḷ tiyākarācar allav ĕṉṟu mucukuntaṉ cŏnnatu i viṭam…

yitarku….pattiyile tiyākarācarai teventiraṉ kŏṭukka mucukuntaṉ…vāṅkuṟatu

Upper middle: vicuvakarmmā {ti} [su]ṭṭiccuk kŏṭutta mūrttiyai āṟu mūrttiyum al…teventiraṉ tiyākarācarait tāṉ ĕḻunt'aruḷap paṇṇi kŏṭukkum potu tiyākarācarai mucukuntaṉ kaṇṭu muṉ cuvāmi cŏṉṉa…kaṇṭu anekañ cantoṣattai yaṭaintu manaskarittu [ttiyākarācarai] mucukuntaṉ vāṅkuṟatu i viṭam

Lower left: mucukuntaṉ vicuvakarmmāvai aḻaippittu…poyi pūmaṇṭalam ĕṅkum…paṭṭa pūmiyāka pāttu…

---

47 tiyākarācare tuṇai / mucukunta cakkaravartti cŏṉṉa pirakāram vicuvakarmmā pūlokattukku vantu…bhūmi iṅkĕllām…ṉiṟuttu pāttu…viśeṣam illāta paṭiyiṉāle tiruvārūrile vantu… parācattiyum tĕricittu aneka[ṣ can]toṣattai aṭaintu pūmaṇṭalaṅkaḷ ĕllām ŏru taṭṭum vayittu…mai ŏru taṭṭum vayittu…pārkkum aḷavil tiruvārūr anekam atikamāy irunta paṭiyiṉāl atika cantoṣattai yaṭaintu….aṉekam māṭakūṭappirakāraṅkaḷ ĕllām tisuttu…tiruvārūrāy

itarku vaṭakku vicuvakarmmā tevalokattukkup poṟatu i viṭam

Top left window: vaṉmīkecura

---

50 tiyākarācacuvāmi teva[lokattai] viṭṭu pūlokattukku mucukuntaṉ…

52

On painted pillar: kŏṭikkampam

Below: teventiraṉ pūcai…ĕḻunt'aruḷi vīti…tevâtikaḷum…anekam upacāram paṇṇat takkatāka tiyākarācarukku…

PANEL 55 Far left: vaṭakku inta maṭṭum piḷḷaiyār tiruviḻā
itarku vaṭakku nātakacālainaṭaṉam paṇṇukuṟatu i viṭam

Center: tiyākarācar…cuppiramaṇiya tĕṭciṇa[mūrtti?]

---

56 Left to right: pairavan tiruviḻā/ mutaliya mūvar tiruviḻā/ māṇikkavācar/ cammanta (=campanta?) mūrtti/ cuntaramūrtti/ appar/ ṉantikecuraṉ

… kŏttu parikalattukkum kāṭci kŏṭuttutu yi viṭam
yitarku tĕrku canti[ra]cekar…

58 tiyākarācare tuṇai / teventiraṉ mutalākiya muppattu mukkoṭi tevar[ka]ḷukkum ṉārpatt ĕṇṇāyiram ṛṣicurarkaḷukkum mutaliya mūvarukkum mucukuntaṉ mutalākiya aṉpattāru tecattu rācākkaḷukkum rurakottu? parikalattukkum yiṉṉilattil canaṅkaḷukkum kāṭci kŏṭuttutu yi viṭam /

kāṭci kŏṭuttavar tiruviḻā /
tampirāṉ kaṭṭalai capparam /
kuru-pātame tuṇai

Left to right: meḷavartiyakāṟar/ naṭṭuvar muṭṭukā[rar]/ naṭai-nāṭaka-cālai naṭaṉam paṇṇukuṟatu yi viṭam /
yitarku tĕrku vacantaṉ

vikkinecurar/ cuppiramaṇiya cuvāmiyār/ pūta-niruttam? / kayikāṭṭu-muṟaikāri/
astiratevar?/ cantiracekar cuvāmiyārukku aneka…[upa]cārattuṭane mucukuntaṉ tiruviḻā naṭakkuṟatu i viṭam
59 yitarku tĕrku vacan[ta]cittravelai ciṅkâkataṉam….

Note missing vertical divider. *pūta-niruttam* = "dancing with one leg raised and bent" (MTL). *kai-kāṭṭu-muṟai = abhinaya*?

Far right: tiyākarācare tuṇai. tu[va?]cârokaṇam mutal…ṇā nāḷ pūraṭṭāti naṣṣettirattile…kaṭṭikŏṇṭu vītippiratĕṭ[ciṇam?] varukkuṟatu yi viṭam
yitarku tĕrku vacantam

PANEL 60

māṉentiyāpiḷḷaiyavarkaḷ maṇṭapattukku cantiracekaracuvāmiyār ĕḻunt'aruḷi tirukkaṇcāttukk' aṇṭ'aruḷukuṟatu yi viṭam
yitarku tĕrku cāmantaṉār muka....tiyākarācare tuṇai tevi-cakāyam

This inscription occurs, in identical form, twice beneath the panel. *tirukkaṇcāttu*: "to carry a deity to a halting place in a procession" (MTL).

61

Left to right: ceppĕrumā[ḷ?].../ rāyacāmantaṉār vācalppiratāṉi cittiravelai ciṅkâtaṉam

---

62

Left to right: ...kurupātam/ pĕriya maṭattup paṇṭāram avarkaḷ maṭam/ kaṇakku pĕrumānayanāppiḷḷaiyavarkaḷ/ pĕriyamaṭattiyākarācayyaṉ/ tūruvācamakariṣiyāṉa pĕriyamaṭattuppaṇṭāram

---

63

varukura ciṅkāra...lokattile uḷḷa anekañ cantoṣa...cevikkuṟatu

---

64

Far left: yitarku tĕrku vacantamaṇṭapam naṭṭunāyakamār vacantaṉukku varukuṟatu
yitarku tĕrku maṇṭapam

Middle: ...āṇa viḷaiyā[ṭal]...

Appendix

Conservation of Mural Paintings in Tyagarajaswamy Temple, Tiruvarur, Tamilnadu: A Case Study

Madhu Rani K.P.
ICKPAC, Bangalore

Introduction

In Tamilnadu (Southern India), a state which has a profusion of magnificent old temples, particularly Shiva temples, Sri Tyagarajaswamy Temple at Tiruvarur in Nagapattinam District, about 60 km from Thanjavur, is one of the seven most important Shivasthalas, that is, shrines dedicated to Lord Shiva. It belongs to the early Chola period, the original shrine having been built in the ninth century AD (on inscriptional evidence, this temple antedates the Brihadisvara Temple in Thanjavur, which belongs to the early 11th C. AD). Additions and expansions have taken place in the subsequent Vijayanagara and Nayaka periods. This temple also has the biggest temple chariot in the country (even bigger than the one at Puri Jagannath). There is a huge temple tank, called Kamalalaya, in front of the temple.

Yet another distinguishing feature of this temple are the beautiful mural paintings on the ceiling of the Devasiriya Mantapam (also known as the thousand-pillared hall), situated in the south-east corner of the temple. The main deity is kept in this Mantapa on certain festive occasions, and all rituals are conducted in it.

Birds eye view of the Temple complex. The Devasiriya Mantapa is encircled in white

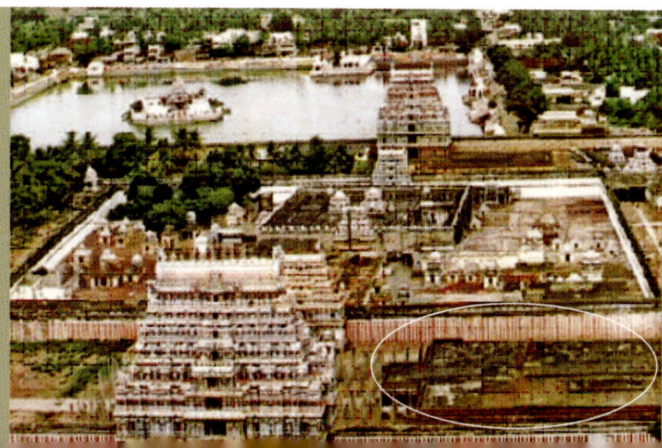

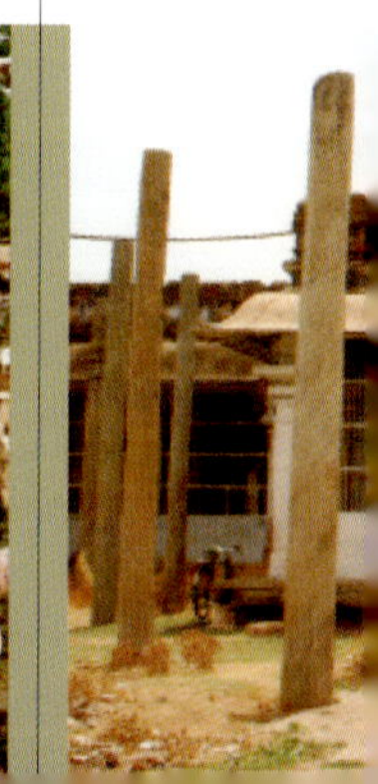

On stylistic grounds, the paintings appear to belong to the late Nayaka period, the figures bearing a strong resemblance to those of the Ramalingavilasam Palace paintings of Ramanathapuram, which were done in the early eighteenth century. There is a school of thought that these paintings were produced under the patronage of the Maratha rulers of Thanjavur and, if this were so, even then the earlier Nayaka influence seems to be strong, since these paintings are quite different from the Maratha-period paintings in other temples.

The paintings depict the Sthalapurana, that is, the local legend of the mythical monkey-faced king, Mucukunda, who was a great devotee of Lord Shiva and was able to bring the image of Tyagarajasamy from the abode of Indra.

Tamilnadu is particularly rich in mural paintings, which constitute an important part of the cultural heritage of this country. The need to preserve them properly is self-evident, and the responsibility for this rests on all of us. It needs to be specially mentioned here that the project of conserving and restoring the valuable murals in this temple has been possible only due to the initiative and relentless efforts of a single individual, Sri Ranvir Shah, an industrialist of Chennai, who has also kindly come forward to provide the necessary funding for the project. This is a striking example of private participation in a public cause, which needs to be not only appreciated but emulated. (The donor had actually to struggle for more than seven years to overcome bureaucratic hurdles and obtain sanction from the Hindu Religious & Charitable Endowments (HR&CE) and Dept of Govt. Tamil Nadu for the conservation project.)

Composition of the murals

The paintings appear to have been done on lime plaster applied to the stone surface of the ceiling, which consists of a series of granite slabs placed in close juxtaposition. The technique is tempera, with a water-soluble binding medium like gum or glue. One notable feature is that the ground viz lime plaster is quite thin, of the order of only 4 or 5 mm, in many places. It is the normal practice to first apply a rough lime plaster of some thickness, over which is applied a fine, thin plaster, consisting predominantly of lime (called intonaco), on which the painting is carried out. But here the rough plaster seems to have been dispensed with, and the intonaco has been directly applied on the rock surface.

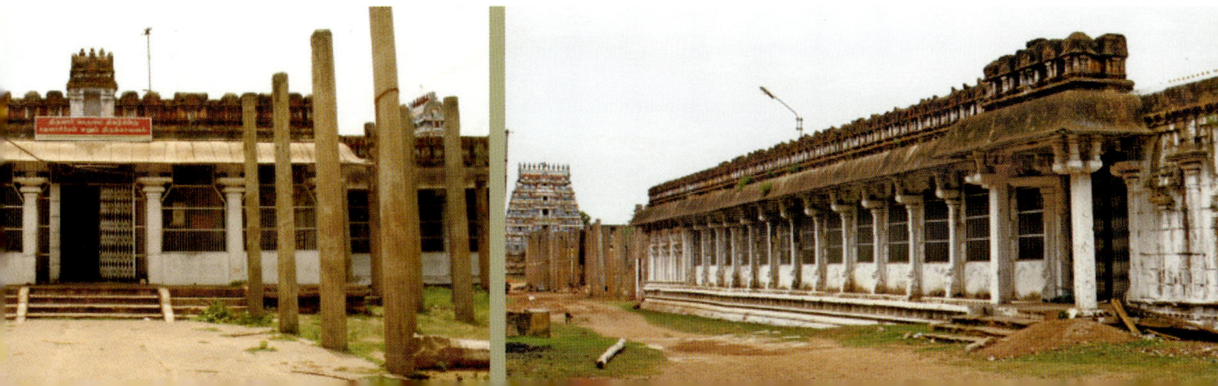

Outer views of the Devasiriya Mantapa

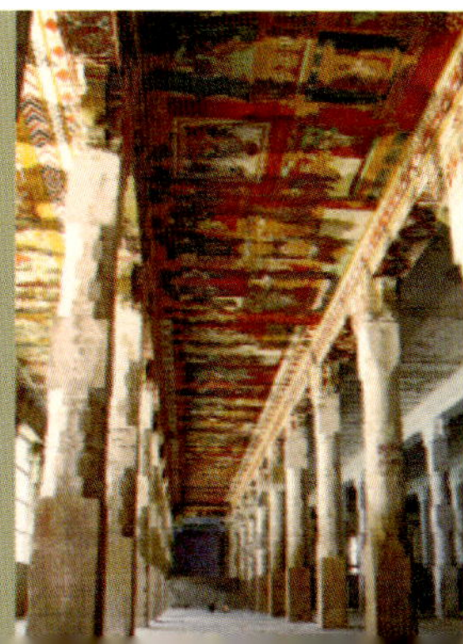

A view of the paintings on the ceiling of the Mantapa

Composition of the painting

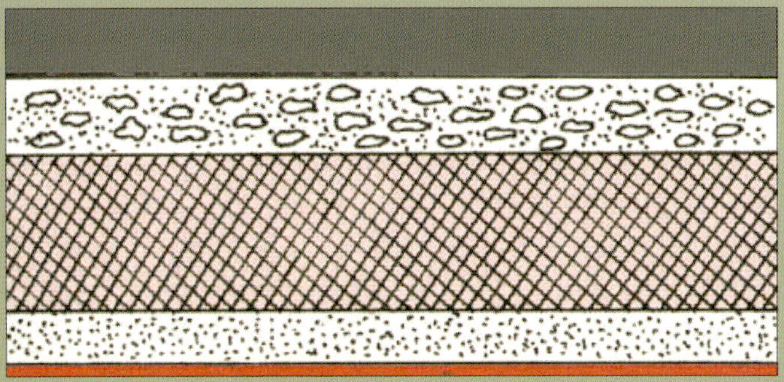

Analytical data by ICI, Lucknow

of Shri Tyagarajasamy Swamy Temple, Tiruvarur

Pigment Analysis

Sample No.	Colour	Micro Chemical Analysis	Identification
1.	Red	Fe +3, Al+3	Red Ochre
2.	Yellow	Fe +3	Yellow Ochre
3.	Green	Cu +2	Malachite
4.	White	Ca+2, CO3 -2, negative test with rhodizonate and NaOH Solution	Calcium Carbonate
5.	Black	C	Lamp Black

Result

Red is identified as red ochre
Yellow is identified as yellow ochre
Green is identified as Malachite
White is identified as Calcium Carbonate (Chalk)
Black is identified as Lamp black

Analysis of lime plaster

by Government of Karnataka Dept. of Mines and Geology Chemical Laboratory, done on 14th October 2008, Bangalore

Certificate of Analysis

S. N.	SAMPLE	SiO2%	CaO%	MgO%	LOI%
1.	Sa.No.1 LIME PLASTER Thiyagarajaswamy Swamy Temple, Tiruvarur, Tamil Nadu	1.64	53.76 (CaCO3)= 95.69%	0.89 (MgCO3)= 1.87%	43.05
2.	Sa.No.2 LIME PLASTER Thiyagarajaswamy Swamy Temple, Tiruvarur, Tamil Nadu	52.66	23.74 (CaCO3)= 42.26%	0.97 (MgCO3)= 2.04%	19.85
3.	Sa.No.3 LIME PLASTER Thiyagarajaswamy Swamy Temple, Tiruvarur, Tamil Nadu	1.56	53.98 (CaCO3)= 96.08%	0.81 (MgCO3)= 1.70%	43.15

Samples 1 and 3 are of the painted plaster from the ceiling. The analytical report also supports our view that fine plaster has been directly applied on the rock. Plaster Sample 2 is of the rough plaster from the beams. The high loss on ignition indicates the presence of organic matter, which could have been added to the plaster to lend it additional strength and flexibility.

An interesting find at the temple that we have made is locating the traditional lime mill that was used to prepare the lime plaster used in the Mantapa. (We had some plaster examined from this spot and it produced the same results)

State of preservation of the paintings

The main source of damage to the paintings has been moisture infiltration (seepage of rain water) from the roof. The water has entered through the gaps between the stone slabs of the ceiling and has partially washed off the colours in large areas of the paint surface. As a result, there is now a pattern of alternate light and dark coloured patches (almost throughout what is left of the paintings).

Loss of entire panels, along with the lime ground, has also occurred, although on a larger scale near the staircase toward the rear. Probably due to moisture, the painted plaster has bulged and become partly detached from the stone surface in several places.

On the southern side, due to the direct impact of rain water, there is slight physical erosion of the paint surface in the upper portions of the paintings near the beams; and also due to continued dampness, growth of micro-organisms like moss, fungi and algae has taken place.

The other problems were general deposition of dust and dirt all over the paint surface, presence of plaster splashes, fecal deposits (bat excreta), insect nests, cobwebs in abundance, flaking of paint surface, cupping of colours with ground, earlier plaster (cement) repairs. There are several patches of soot deposits. On the south west corner of the Mantapa, there was a room (used as a storage space), the paintings on its ceilings being an extension of the paintings on the ceiling of the hall, and these have large patches of soot deposits. (The walls of the room have now been dismantled and its ceiling paintings are now a part of the other paintings of the Devasiriya Mantapa).

Bee hives had been built on the paint surface in the past, and therefore there are waxy deposits in these places.

There are paintings on the wall at the eastern end of the Mantapa which are in fragmentary condition. These are covered with thick deposits of dust as well as a number of scratch marks and graffiti. The lower half of this wall has been whitewashed (when we

Dissolution of paint layer and growth of fungus and Algae due to infiltration (water seepage)

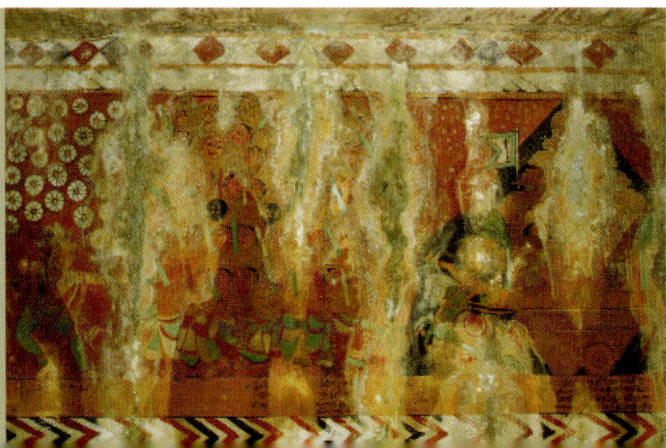

Detachment of the painted plaster from the stone support

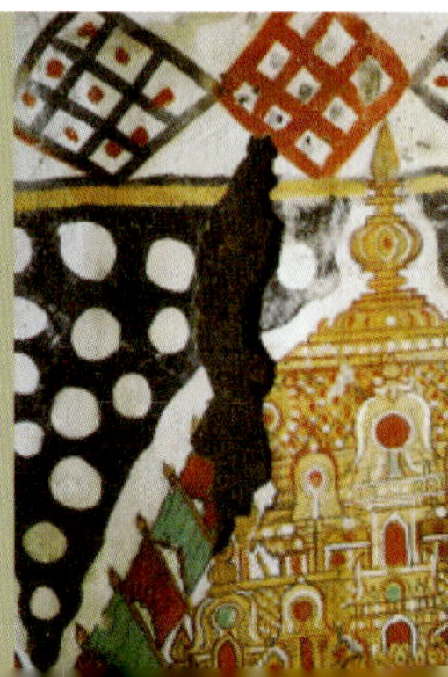

Paintings with evidence of heavy growth of moss, fungi and algae due to infiltration

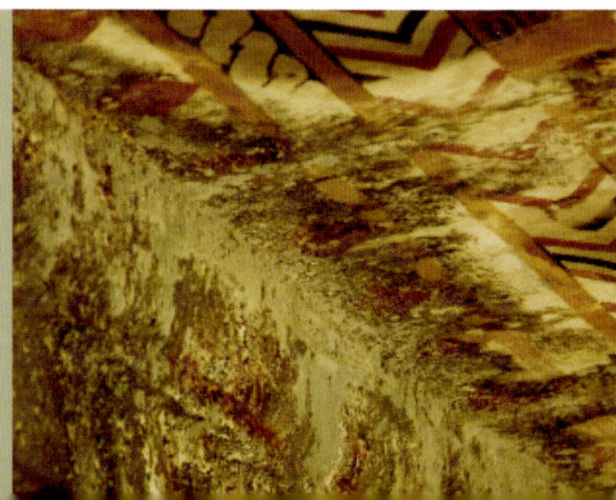

carefully removed a portion of the lime mechanically to test if any original paintings remain under the wash, we just found many layers of lime; the second layer had some red ochre design patterns, but the original paint surface was almost gone with only fragments of red and yellow colour remaining here and there).

Conservation work

Before undertaking the work of conserving the paintings, it was essential to totally stop all ingress of rain water from the ceiling. The roof had to be repaired and also given an effective water-proofing treatment. This civil work was also carried out by the temple authorities with the help of Mr Ranvir Shah (there is still some seepage of rain water which we noticed during this monsoon, which we have requested to be rectified at the earliest).

The next important step was to remove all the debris piled up in the Mantapa under the paintings and in the temporary room, as well as to remove the walls of the room, to have the whole place cleaned, and to cordon off the area around the paintings. Every step was difficult, as the people responsible there were so slow. Once labour was provided to bring down the wall, we took the initiative of removing the walls ourselves, particularly the topmost 1-foot portion of the wall from the roof with the paintings to check damage to the paintings, as the wall was built on them. So we worked on the wall inch by inch, then loosened the bricks one by one and removed them. After we removed about one foot, the workers removed the rest of the walls. It was heartening to see the paintings – a continuation of the panels – intact.

Next was to clean the hall with the help of local volunteers to remove the debris piled up on the floor for many years. (NSS volunteers of a local college came in to help with the effort).

Documentation

Before we commenced the actual treatment, a complete graphic and photo documentation of the whole area with all the problems was carried out.

Paintings affected by soot deposits

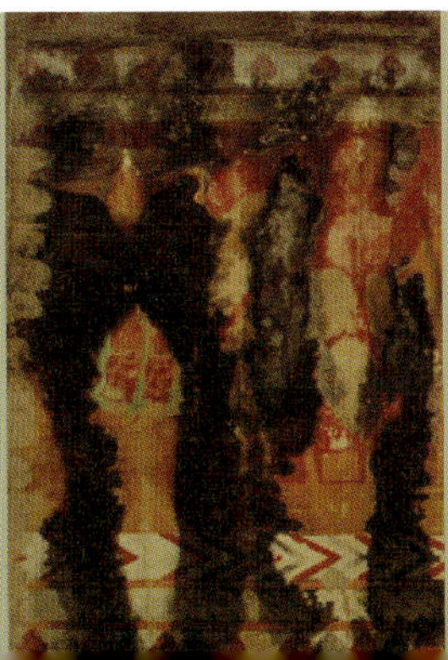

Cleaning of fungus, before and after

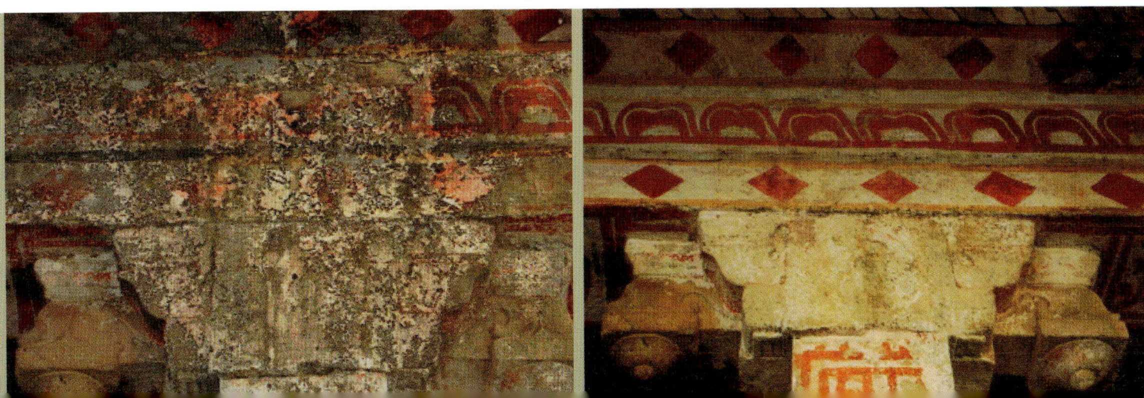

Cleaning

General Cleaning: All loose dust and cobwebs was brushed off with the help of soft brushes. The adhering accretion of dirt was removed with the help of solvents like Rectified Spirit and Isopropyl Alcohol. Cotton swabs with the solvent were carefully rolled over the paint surface to avoid any sort of friction. This was necessary in view of the highly friable nature of the paint surface. Insect nests were taken off mechanically. The plaster splashes were softened and then removed mechanically.

The moss and algal growths on the upper portions on the southern side were first carefully removed by mechanical means as much as possible. The remaining portions were removed by using Ammoniacal Spirit (Rectified Spirit to which has been added a few drops of Liquor Ammonia).

The removal of soot deposits was a little more time-consuming. The sooty patches on the rock surface, where the paintings had fallen off, were removed comparatively easily by using an aqueous solution. A 5% solution of a mixture of Ammonium bicarbonate and Sodium bicarbonate was applied on tissue paper placed on the required spot and allowed to react for about 20 minutes. When the tissue paper was removed, it was found to have absorbed the dissolved soot. Sometimes two or three such applications were necessary for the complete removal of the soot.

For the removal of soot deposits from the paint surface, a safe and tested solvent, Triethanolamine, was used (as it is an effective as well as safe solvent for this purpose). A 5% solution of the Amine in Ethanol was applied on tissue paper of suitable size placed on the soot-covered paint surface and allowed to remain in contact for some time. The tissue paper was then removed, and the partially dissolved and softened soot was removed from the paint surface by rolling cotton swabs dipped in Rectified Spirit. This procedure was repeated two or three times, but in some areas the soot still remains. This cleaning procedure is still going on. (In some areas the soot removal is proving very difficult. Any suggestions for alternate techniques would be very welcome).

Removal of soot deposits, before and after

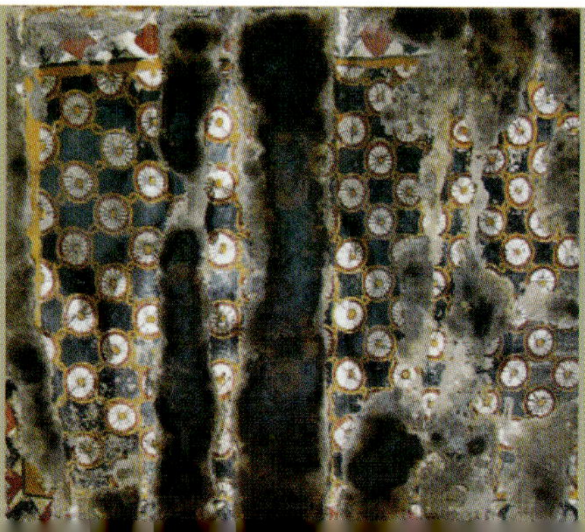

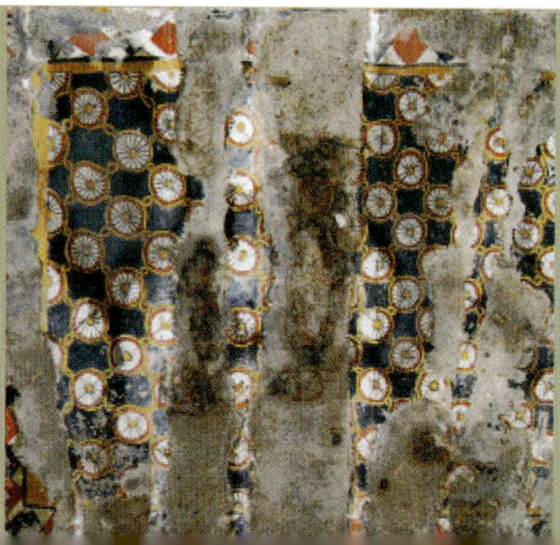

There were lime encrustations in several places, carried down by rain water from the roof and covering the paint surface. These were first removed by mechanical means with very careful use of scalpels. The final, very thin, adherent coat of lime was removed with the help of a 5% solution of Formic Acid, allowed to remain in contact with the surface for the minimum possible time.

Consolidation

In the conservation of the paintings, an important step was the consolidation and strengthening of the painted plaster in order to ensure that no further loss of even a small bit of the paintings will occur in the future. Since the lime plaster here is very thin and its adhesion with the stone support had been considerably weakened, in places the merest touch was enough to detach it completely. Therefore the consolidation work had to be done with the greatest possible care and skill.

Wherever there was peeling of only the paint layer, it was fixed back with the help of Paraloid B-72 solution (3 to 10%). We also used Polyvinyl alcohol solution, as it worked better on the painted wall at the rear end (where only traces of pigments remained).

Refixing of the painted plaster

It was a big challenge to fix back large portions of the detached painted plaster to the stone support firmly.

For this refixing process, two crucial steps had first to be decided on, to ensure the success for the procedure:

1. Choice of the correct adhesive to achieve proper bonding between the lime plaster and the stone support. (As in conservation it is always a sound principle to choose materials as similar to the original materials of the object as possible for any conservation treatment, to ensure proper bonding and to achieve optimum results)

2. The means of achieving effective reattachment of the lime plaster to the stone support after introducing the adhesive between the two.

Specially modeled spring arrangement to generate required pressure to ensure reattachment of the detached painted plaster (after the injection of the adhesive)

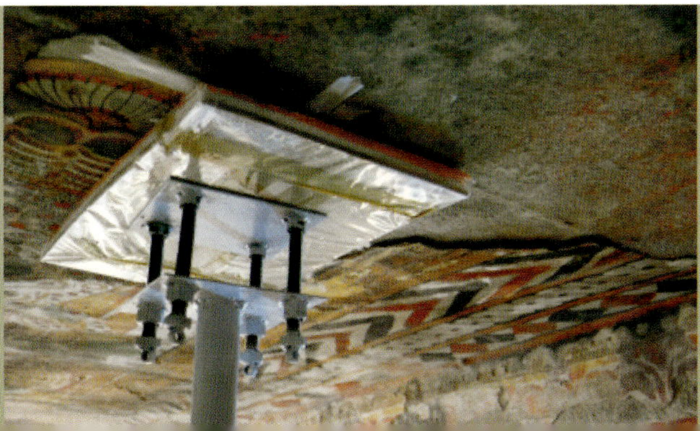

Filling and reintegration of lacunae, before and after

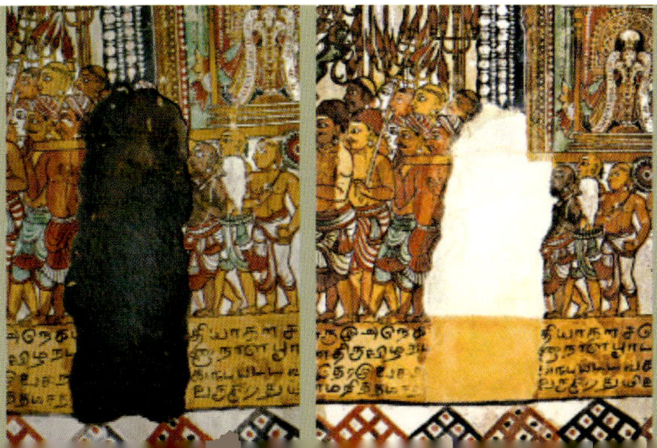

In the present case, we decided upon a paste of lime caseinate slurry (9 parts of shell lime + 1 part of casein + a very small quantity of polyvinyl acetate emulsion) as the adhesive to be used after many tests and trials.

For fixing back the bulging portions of the painting, first the free edges were hinged by paper tape to the surrounding stronger areas. Then the adhesive of thin paste of lime caseinate slurry was injected through a small hole into the space between the plaster and the stone surface and gently pressed so as to avoid any possible detachment. After the adhesive was introduced and when it was partly set was the correct time to apply pressure from below with the help of jacks (specially modeled) so that the board with the cushioning pushed the plaster back to ensure firm reattachment.

The edges were then filleted with specially prepared lime plaster (ratio – 3 parts of lime and 2 parts of sand). The many cracks and lacunae in the side beams (with thick lime plaster) are being filled with the same specially prepared lime plaster.

Filling and Reintegration

The missing areas and small gaps within the body of the paint surface (that had occurred due to loss of the painted plaster) have been filled with lime plaster and after drying, tinted with suitable high quality powder colours so as to be reintegrated with the paint surface. If the gap was large, only the free edges were fixed with the help of lime plaster (filleting has been done), as mentioned earlier.

The major area of concern and debate were:

1. Do the large gaps of loss in the plaster have to be filled in completely with newly prepared plaster? If yes, then should the area be reintegrated?

2. The large areas where colour has been lost due to infiltration, as a result of which there is now a distinct pattern of alternate light and dark coloured patches – what does one do?

Reintegration, before and after

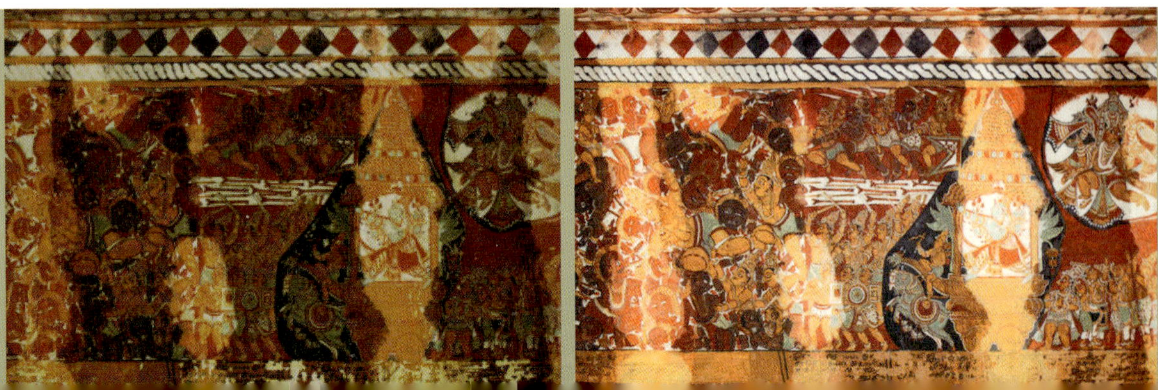

(Together with the donor we have taken a stance that no missing portions of the paintings are going to be recreated, but as it is a living temple the temple authorities seem to think otherwise)

3. Is it permissible to re-create the damaged areas, where repetitive floral or geometric designs on the beams would give a sense of continuity and would be visually more pleasing?

Or should we adopt a middle ground?

All the people involved were consulted and finally a decision was taken that only the border areas (repetitive patterns), which were redone at a later period, will be recreated where necessary.

Preservation

We have decided upon giving an application of a coating of 2% solution of Paraloid B72 on the paint surface as a preservative coating.

A panel
before and after restoration

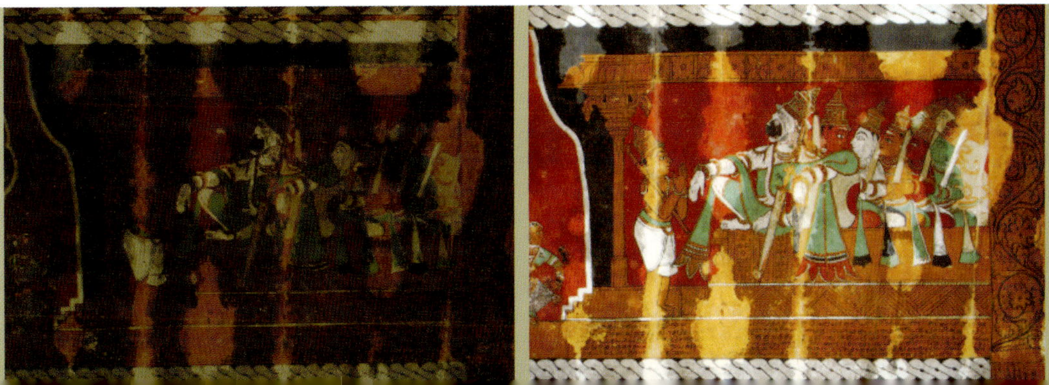

Bibliography

• Examination and conservation of wall paintings – a manual, Dr. O.P. Agrawal and Rashmi Pathak, Sundeep Prakashan, 2001

• Biodeterioration of Cultural Property, edited O.P. Agrawal and Shashi Dhawan, International Council of Biodeterioration of Cultural Property

• Artists' Pigments: A handbook of their History and Characteristics, Robert Feller, 1986

• Conservation of Wall Paintings in India – Achievements and Problems, O.P. Agrawal, INTACH Indian Conservation Institute, 1995

• Structural Conservation of Monuments in South India, K. Lakshmana Murthy, Bharatiya Kala Prakashan, 1997

• The Conservation of Cultural Property – with special reference to tropical conditions, UNESCO, 1968

• Cleaning, Retouching and Coatings, Preprints of the Contributions to the Brussels Congress, 3-7 September 1990, International Institute for Conservation of Historic and Artistic Works, 1990

• Lime putties and mortars: insights into fundamental properties, Eric Hansen, Carlos Rodriguez Navarro and Koenraad Van Balen in Studies in Conservation, Vol. No.53 (1), 2008

Acknowledgements

We are grateful to Sri Subbaraman Sir, Former Director, ICKPAC, for his encouragement, guidance and constant support throughout the project.

We also wish to express our gratitude to Dr. O. P. Agrawal, Director General ICCI for all his invaluable guidance.

Special thanks to Sri. Ramsagar Prasad, Photographer ICCI Lucknow for his contribution.

We wish to thank the dedicated administrative staff at ICKPAC, Bangalore, and ICCI, Lucknow. Our thanks are particularly due to Mr. Bala from Prakriti Foundation.

We would also like to extend our gratitude to the Analytical Dept, ICCI Lucknow and the Dept. of Geology, Karnataka for helping with scientific testing of samples.

Mr. Dandapani, artist, Tiruvarur, provided invaluable help as a local guardian.

Our humble gratitude to all the persons who worked along with us, as no conservation project or endeavour is complete without teamwork.

Our team: 2008 to 2010

Ms. Madhurani K.P., Ms. Mrinalini Mani, Ms. Saujna Preetham, Ms. Shruti Asoka, Mr. Sharanu M. Barangi, Mr. M. N. Patil, Mr. Raju, Mr. Ashok Kumar S., Mr. Mohan, Mr. Bhanu Prakash T.V., Mr. Vishwa Narayan Shah, Mr. Bishnu Prakash, Ms. Arulmugi, Ms. Sophia, Mr. Chandra Bose and Mr. Muthu Kumar.